LATIN AMERICAN CULTURAL CRITICISM

LATIN AMERICAN CULTURAL CRITICISM
Re-Interpreting a Continent

Patricia D'Allemand

The Edwin Mellen Press
Lewiston•Queenston•Lampeter

Library of Congress Cataloging-in-Publication Data

D'Allemand, Patricia.
Latin American cultural criticism : re-interpreting a continent / Patricia D'Allemand.
    p. cm.
Includes bibliographical references and index.
ISBN 0-7734-7811-6
1. Spanish American literature--History and criticism. 2. Criticism--Latin America. 3. Latin America--Intellectual life--20th century. I. Title.

PQ7081 .D233 2000
801'.95'098--dc21
                                        00-021154

This is volume 7 in the continuing series
Studies in Latin American Literature & Culture
Volume 7 ISBN 0-7734-7811-6

A CIP catalog record for this book is available from the British Library.

Front Cover Illustration: José Gamarra's painting *Cinco siglos de tormenta* (*Five Centuries of Storm*, 1983. Oil on canvas 150 x 150 cms.) was reproduced with the kind permission of the artist. The photograph was courtesy of Galerie Albert Loeb, Paris.

Copyright © 2000   Patricia D'Allemand

All rights reserved. For information contact

              The Edwin Mellen Press   The Edwin Mellen Press
                    Box 450   Box 67
              Lewiston, New York   Queenston, Ontario
              USA 14092-0450   CANADA L0S 1L0

                        The Edwin Mellen Press, Ltd.
                        Lampeter, Ceredigion, Wales
                        UNITED KINGDOM SA48 8LT

                     Printed in the United States of America

CONTENTS

Acknowledgments	v
Prologue	vii
Introduction	3
1 Jose Carlos Mariátegui: Beyond "El proceso de la literatura"	15
2 Angel Rama: Literature, Modernization and Resistance	49
From National Criticism to Continental Criticism	54
Towards an Autonomous Criticism: Angel Rama's Nationalist Discourses	64
3 Alejandro Losada: Towards a Social History of Latin American Literatures	77
Losada's Conceptual System: Some Definitions	105
Social Praxis	105
Literary System	107
Losada's *Sujeto Productor*	110
Mode of Literary/Cultural Production	111
Literary Forms	115
Horizon of Existence	116
Aesthetic/Cultural Paradigm	117
Periodization	118
Social Space	120
4 Antonio Cornejo Polar: On Cultural and Literary Heterogeneity in Latin America	123
For a Historical and Cultural Reading of Latin American Literature	125
Towards a Redefinition of the Latin American Literary Corpus	136
The Category of Heterogeneity: An Approach to Cultural Plurality in Latin America	138
"New Latin American Narrative" in Antonio Cornejo Polar's Discourse	149
5 Beatriz Sarlo: Towards a Reading of Plurality	153
6 *Fin de siècle:* Assessment and Perspectives	167
Bibliography	171
Index	187

ACKNOWLEDGMENTS

I would like to express my gratitude for all the tremendous encouragement and stimulation which I have received from William Rowe throughout the preparation of this book. I also very much appreciate the many useful comments that I have received from John Kraniauskas, Carlos Pacheco, my colleagues at Queen Mary and Westfield College, University of London and numerous others. I am grateful, too, to Jody Gillet, Luis González Fernández and Keith Richards for their translating skills, and to Andrew M. Beresford for his formatting expertise. Finally, I must thank my editor, Bernard McGuirk, for his wise advice and my family for all their support and patience.

Earlier versions of various sections of this book have been published in *Bulletin of Latin American Research* 15: 3 (1996), *Thesaurus: Boletín del Instituto Caro y Cuervo* XLIX: 3 (1994), *Travesia. Journal of Latin American Cultural Studies* 3: 1–2 (1994), *Nuevo Texto Crítico* 16–17 (1995–96), *Journal of Hispanic Research* 3 (1994–95), *Estudios. Revista de Investigaciones Literarias* 2 (1993), *Neophilologus* (in press).

PROLOGUE

Ten or fifteen years ago it was not possible to say "Latin American literary criticism" and be heard seriously. It sounded like some marginal activity, a brief footnote, perhaps, to the history of Literary Criticism or else some quirky provincialism not useful for deciding how to read Latin American literature. At least, this was true in most circles, the important exceptions being members of AELSAL in Europe, or people who had worked with Antonio Cornejo Polar in Peru, Venezuela or the USA or with Beatriz Sarlo and Carlos Altamirano in Argentina. What were the reasons for this? Why this difficulty to accept that there might be a serious intellectual tradition in Latin America?

The question has several dimensions. What immediately springs to mind is the force of colonial prejudice: not just the history of it but that despite two or more decades of routine condemnations of Eurocentrism what still goes on might be the same business. Perhaps, as some have said in recent years, Latin-American Studies are a type of Orientalism. But that hypothesis doesn't get to the fact that Latin America has been producing its "own" differential readings of the West, in Machado de Assis, say, or in Mariátegui or Borges, to mention three vastly different interpretations. And this has been going on, to use that grotesquely neutral word, ever since "contact" in 1492.

More focused is the hypothesis that institutional power struggles are what tend to make Latin American intellectual traditions invisible. In this case, one is talking —in rough historical order— about stylistics, structuralism, post-structuralism, "French Theory", post-modernism and so on as forms taken by a struggle for interpretative power whose lines of force have by-passed the production of theories and methods in Latin America. One would have to see why this might be so. To invoke globalization is insufficient, since there is inside that proposition a weak analogy between different kinds of process —economic and intellectual, to give the end terms— and the explanation merely reproduces what it is supposed to explain. Recent correctives to this situation, such as cultural studies, subaltern studies and postcolonial theory, which are the main topics of current debate, risk having the same effect, whatever the aims they proclaim. Certainly, they, or rather their exponents, tend to use their canon of concepts in such a way that no-one would guess that similar types of thought and ways of working have already been in existence in Latin America for some time. That is, no-one would guess it until a Latin American scholar happens to point it out. And certainly, again, the phenomenon I refer to does have something to do with the will to set up an apparatus of interpretation which will last long enough for its representatives to become the central voices in the academy. And that is an epistemological weakness: concepts used in such a way that they become a screen which causes the necessities and traditions specific to Latin American societies to become less interesting. And that, in turn, determines the research agenda. The main difficulty, though, which is that the effect is largely invisible, remains. At which point it is perhaps useful to remind oneself of why the stakes are high: what is involved are not just models of reading but the prestige of the humanities.

Another way to sharpen the initial question is to consider the prestige of literature as an institution. When, in the 1970s, the publishing "boom" in the Latin American novel got under way, critical languages and procedures were elaborated on that basis and critics' voices got heard, but to the detriment of any serious consideration of the relationship between literature and knowledge, that is, specifically, of its relationship with the many forms of knowledge, with their history and transmission, to be found in the sub-continent. Interestingly, two questions converge here: what got left out of that particular marriage between literary criticism and the market and what was excluded by that Latin American criticism which turned away from local forms of knowledge. The answer to both could be given quickly in the phrase popular culture, but with the serious reservation that "popular" is not a value (that's populism) but a way of talking about the cultural field as a whole, and that not as a pre-given framework, but as a process of discovery —as happens, say, though on a smaller scale, in anthropological field-work.

That there is no universal method or language, no collection of transferable concepts, is a proposition which runs head-on into two types of resistance. On the one hand there's the apparently naïve objection that "we can't read like Latin Americans". The appeal to common sense rather covers over the assumptions implicit inside it: that readers are not formed and that reading does not have a historicity. And to go along with that is to leave behind any idea that the function of criticisms might be to change the way one reads. The other type of resistance is intellectual and epistemological. It sustains, or acts as if it were true that there is still a sufficient degree of universality in certain concepts such that a theory can be justified by its applicability and that applicability is a question of being expert enough in how to use it. That kind of position is incompatible with taking seriously the possibility of a Latin American episteme or with the principle that —to use Deleuze and Guattari's statement in *What is Philosophy* (1994)— "Universals explain nothing but must themselves be explained."

Again, the difficulty is that it's not enough to draw attention to what people are doing, it's also a question of doing something different. That is where Patricia D'Allemand's book is an important intervention. She takes us through the work of five of the key practitioners of Latin American criticism and shows us what can be done with it. Thus her concern to return these works "to [...] their multiplicity of meanings and to the wealth of their potential." Which means reading them as belonging to a tradition and as producing knowledge. The test of a tradition is its aliveness in the present, its capacity to speak vitally to present necessities or to reveal necessities otherwise not seen; anything else is pedantry. D'Allemand's study does display that vitality, crucially, for example, in showing how these critics take us into "the complexity of the cultural sphere and the plurality of [...] the corpus of the region's literature." That is, as she shows, that Latin American literary criticism is a cultural criticism —*avant la lettre*—. Thus with Mariátegui, for example, who wrote between 1920 and 1930, there is a proposal to study the interrelation of artistic and social imagination and to interpret literature as a multiple action involving the social, the political, the religious, the aesthetic. Out of that multiplicity comes, precisely, the capacity to enter the density of the local —which is a useful counteraction to current new universalist approaches. Mariátegui's work is nourished by a very serious analysis of the question of socialism and the irrational, a problem that arose very acutely in Peru, given that the majority of the population lived in non-modern societies. But his attitude is not archaeological. He places the arts right there in the invention of futurity, which is also precisely where tradition is: "The real tradition is invisible, it is there ethereally in the work of creating a new order." (La verdadera tradición está invisible, etéreamente en el trabajo de creación de un orden nuevo.) What is our invisible tradition?

D'Allemand gives us both clear exposition and necessary critique. She does not avoid risk, as when pointing out the narrowing effects of Angel Rama's nationalism or of his conception of the city. And she wisely draws attention to the usefulness of Beatriz Sarlo's work in driving a wedge between literature and politics in order to prevent the reduction of one to the other and in offering "a redefinition [...] of the very concept of politics and of the place of political discourse within the public sphere." As Sarlo writes, "I refuse to understand Argentinean culture as a homogenizing enterprise carried out in the name of national unity." (Me resisto a pensar la cultura argentina como una empresa de homogenización realizada en nombre de la identidad nacional.) With Alejandro Losada, a critic little read nowadays, D'Allemand carries out an important rescue action, showing how Losada proposes a coherent set of concepts in order to bring into focus the relationship between specific Latin American literatures and specific societies and sub-societies in specific temporal periods. Thus Losada's method permits a useful way of checking the premises with which one works and whether they are adequate to the material under study. He draws attention, for example, to the difference of regions and to the fact that these do not coincide with national frontiers. Crucially, he developed ways of locating literature within the larger cultural field (particularly in the anthropological sense), which is, among other things, to open up literary studies to less prestigious genres, such as chronicles, *testimonios* and *folletines*.

D'Allemand's handling of the work of Antonio Cornejo Polar is particularly useful in that as yet no systematic account of it has been carried out. She draws attention to his vital intervention against the prevailing reading of regional novels which has ghettoized them by turning the market values of the "Boom" into terms of pseudo-analysis. Cornejo went on to call for a redefinition of the Latin American literary corpus. Throughout his work he used and developed Mariátegui's concept of heterogeneity as a way of understanding the differential modernity of Latin America and breaking with European conceptual programmes. The epistemological fruitfulness of that concept has still fully to be worked out. What is clear enough though is that D'Allemand's study is a vital handbook for those who want to know the history of where Latin American cultural criticism is now. If you want to take decisions you have to know the history of the field you're dealing with, otherwise you may blindly be following an alien set of necessities. How much current Anglo-american work does just that?

William Rowe, London, Summer 1998

LATIN AMERICAN CULTURAL CRITICISM

INTRODUCTION

It has often been observed that Latin America is devoid of critical self-analysis, that it does not have "un pensamiento crítico propio [capaz de] fundar [o] configurar" the literature of the region, or of articulating it to wider historical or social processes. Nevertheless, as Antonio Cornejo Polar reminds us, this is a

> vacío que es algo así como una ilusión óptica: parece ser que no hay crítica porque no hemos leído los textos pertinentes con ánimos de incorporarlos en una tradición (con sus continuidades, rupturas y disidencias) que no es ni más ni menos propia que la literatura producida en nuestra América. (Cornejo Polar 1992, ix)

This kind of blindness can be explained, at least in part, as a result of the tendency amongst Latin Americanists towards the privileging of theories that emanate from metropolitan academic centers at the expense of those that are advanced from more modest and less prestigious Latin American institutions. As a general rule, it is the former that establish the research agendas and launch and circulate debates, which are then avidly accepted by the latter. The inertia of colonial habits of thought, which we are unable to shake off, still weighs heavily and has led to the undervaluing of Latin America's potential as producer of knowledge, and to the silencing of projects that emerge in the region.[1]

The suggestion here is not that Latin American critics are not read at all. Some are read more than others, and, amongst those that are read, very often it is particular parts which are read (or at least quoted) a great deal more than others. Meanwhile, the rest remains in obscurity. The genesis of this process of selection must be addressed, as well as the criteria upon which this selection is made. To what extent, one should ask, does this selection meet the specific needs of the agendas and debates that emerge from metropolitan academe? It should also be questioned to what degree this selection, which subordinates critical voices to these needs, not only impoverishes our reading of them, but also erases their agendas, depriving them of their capacity to pose their own questions and to shape debates.[2]

---

[1] This complaint informs, to a large extent, the reassessment of the critical and meta-critical works of Roberto Fernández Retamar undertaken by Walter Mignolo from the debates concerning the application of Post Colonial Studies to the Latin American milieu (1991, 1996).

[2] This preocupation is to a large extent present in both Román de La Campa's examination of the category of transculturation (1994) and Neil Larsen's discussion of Mariátegui in relation to Post-Colonial Studies (1996).

To cite a few examples, there is much more to be found in the works of Rama and Cornejo Polar than the notions concerning transculturation and heterogeneity, just as there is a great deal more in Mariátegui's critical thought than his reading of Peruvian literature in his "El proceso de la literatura" (1986).

What is needed is a thorough exploration of Latin American criticism and a reading of the works in their own terms, looking beyond the segments highlighted by this somewhat arbitrary selection. Such an approach would avoid the temptation to assimilate them into those dominant tendencies with which they may have affinities (a temptation, in fact, to legitimize them by this strategy). The price paid is, in any case, a high one: the de-historicizing of their discourse and the loss of meaning. It is not a matter, either, of denying the possible existence of affinities between the objectives of the critical thought of the left or of cultural criticism in Latin America, for example, and, let us say, the most radical trends within Post Colonial Studies or Cultural Studies. Finally, neither is it a matter of rejecting the possibility, or even the usefulness, of building bridges between the former and the latter; rather, what is called for is a questioning of the procedures, and a drawing of attention to the risks that a particular strategy can involve.[3] The challenge is to reinsert these works into their contexts and to understand them within traditions of thought with their own specific characteristics, in order to return to them their multiplicity of meanings and the wealth of their potential. But my objective is not only a reconstruction of archeological value, but an attempt to shed light on the validity of the projects proposed by these works and to restore to them the capability to intervene in current debates on Latin American culture.

Going back to the initial quotation, the void referred to, as Cornejo perceptively points out, is not a void in critical practice, but in reflections upon critical practice (1992, ix). This is due to the fact that we do not possess a comprehensive history of the development of Latin American criticism, but only sketches of some lines of work: Portuondo (1972, 1975), Fernández Retamar (1975), Sosnowski (1987), Mariaca Iturri (1992). Neither do we have a sufficient number of studies of theoretical works or of specific criticism (the same authors), nor of the theoretical or methodological problems which critical discipline has encountered along the way, nor of the paths it has opened up in order to resolve them: Cornejo (1982), Raúl Bueno (1991), Carlos Rincón (1973, 1978).

---

[3] A close questioning of a strategy that attempts to assimilate Mariátegui into postcolonial thought forms the basis of Neil Larsen's article, cited above.

The present study occupies precisely that space concerned with the reflections upon a particular critical practice —cultural criticism, which has already traced a long trajectory in Latin America. At the risk of stating the obvious, it should be emphasized that speaking of Latin American cultural criticism means speaking of a historically specific critical practice, the profile of which I seek to outline, at least partially, in this book. The specific nature of the various directions taken by Latin American cultural criticism tends to become diluted when it is grouped under the banner of "Estudios culturales", now a much used term.[4] In a recent book, William Rowe sounds an appropriate warning about the current tendency to assimilate in an undiscerning manner the terms "Estudios culturales" and "Cultural Studies". Rowe questions the validity of these types of assimilation which overlook the historical differences between the British tradition of Cultural Studies and other traditions of cultural analysis both *in* Latin America and *about* Latin America (1996).[5]

The projects examined in this study constitute part of a critical process that, through various avenues of approach, seeks to account for the particular features of literatures produced in societies which, from their origins, have been tied in conditions of dependency to centers of external domination. They constitute a criticism which shares a concern for the understanding of the literary phenomenon in its historical and socio-cultural articulations, a criticism which puts forward reinterpretations of Latin America and its literary production which emphasize the complexity of the cultural sphere and the plurality of the projects that make up the corpus of the region's literature, while at the same time taking care to distance itself from any universalizing or homogenizing visions of either that same literary production or of the region as a whole.

The book focuses on some of the most important landmarks in the development of Latin American cultural criticism: the writings of José Carlos Mariátegui, Angel Rama, Alejandro Losada, Antonio Cornejo Polar and Beatriz Sarlo. Of course, Latin American cultural criticism is not limited to the works of these authors, though they undoubtedly offer the most fruitful re-readings of Spanish-American literatures. This study is not concerned with writing a comprehensive history of Latin American cultural criticism;[6] rather, its purpose is the scrutiny of key moments in its

---

[4] See, for example, Moraña (1995).

[5] For a differentiation between British and U.S. "Cultural Studies", see John Beverley with Goffredo Diana and Vicente Lecuna (1996).

[6] A comprehensive history of the continent's cultural criticism —a task of some urgency— should, without doubt, consider Brazilian cultural criticism, including the contributions of authors of the stature of Antonio Cândido and Roberto Schwarz.

development while presenting an outline of the context within which it has been formulated and suggesting a perspective from which to read it, with a view to breathing new life into the productivity of its texts.

If the critics studied in this book are separated, one from another, by the different intellectual traditions and historical circumstances within which they operate, as well as by the various perspectives from which they approach their subject matter, they are brought together, though, by their rejection of hierarchical aesthetic conceptions which either undervalue or ignore the contribution of popular culture to the specific features of the continent's literatures of the region. This study sets out to reconstruct the proposals of the authors listed above, to assess their achievements and examine problematic aspects engendered by a discipline shaped by its quest for intellectual autonomy.

One of the main axes upon which this book is structured is the scrutiny of the ways in which political and aesthetic discourses interact in the works of each of the authors under discussion; of equal importance are the positions taken by each author in relation to the said interaction of those discourses. This is, perhaps, not altogether surprising in Latin America, since the region's cultural history has, from the very beginning, seen an interweaving of politics and culture mutually informing each other —with a variety of outcomes. The debate concerning "lo nacional"— or, more precisely, the production of national, regional and continental identities— which informs the critical proposals examined in the present study, is placed within the space where the cultural and political spheres meet. This debate plays a central role (and, to a certain extent, an inescapable central role if scrutinized through the lens of history) in the development of the region's cultural criticism. In fact, it is possible to argue that, in spite of widespread predictions, the current processes of globalization have not managed to render it anachronistic.[7] The diverse ways in which each of the authors relates to the debate are discussed, together with the multiple reasons for its persistence and its various formulations, as well as its problematic effects on the projects dealt with in this book.

All these projects are grounded in the conviction that the processes of aesthetic and cultural production and reception are historical in nature. This approach distances Latin American cultural criticism from any immanentist critical framework and renounces universalist interpretive models which obstruct the perception of difference. Latin American cultural criticism is concerned with highlighting the peculiarities of the

---

[7] Hugo Achugar convincingly defends this argument (1996).

region's literatures and societies, and their differences from those of the metropoli. At the same time, it calls into question the legitimacy of homogenizing discourses which support universalist models.

Any examination of a criticism which vindicates the historical and cultural specificity of the society in which it is articulated obviously refers us to the thinking of José Carlos Mariátegui. The continued relevance of his work is guaranteed by the persistence of an unresolved problem, namely, the conflictive relationship between the various projects of modernization embarked upon by Latin American societies and these societies' respective national cultural traditions. Since the 1970s, this problem has once more become a key issue for Latin American social sciences. It is generally acknowledged, within the field, that the basis for the dismantling of universalist and Eurocentric perspectives and the development of an autonomous body of theory on Latin American social and cultural processes are to be found in the discourse of Mariátegui's generation.[8] In this sense, Mariátegui's proposals, which are examined in the first chapter of this study, are a vital point of reference for the various attempts made during the 1970s to formulate an autonomous Latin American criticism which are considered in chapters two, three and four.

However, Mariátegui's aesthetic reflections represent more than a simple blueprint for the construction of an autonomous Latin American criticism. They merit a re-reading which acknowledges his capacity to intervene in the contemporary cultural debate — an intervention which goes beyond the "Proceso de la literatura peruana" (1986) and whose density, which has come to be neglected in the discipline, should be recognized anew. Although Mariátegui's political discourse has been widely discussed, the same cannot be said of his writings on art and literature. This is equally true of his subtle treatment of the relationship between artistic imagination and social imagination, and between aesthetics and politics, which neither subjects the logic of the former to that of the latter, nor allows form to be swamped by ideological content. His handling of the relationship between aesthetics and cultural nationalism is also important, as are his thoughts on the cosmopolitan and the national aspects of the shaping of Peruvian culture, which are relevant, in turn, to Latin American culture in general. Latin American criticism still has much to gain from the proposals of Mariátegui.

---

[8] The Dominican Pedro Henriquez Ureña is another key figure of that generation. Angel Rama credits him with pioneering the introduction of an anthropological perspective which supported his endeavour to account for the specificity of Spanish American literatures in his *Seis ensayos en busca de nuestra expresión* (1987, 17–18).

In recent decades the Latin American intellectual sphere has been engaged in reinterpretations of the region's history and culture, distancing itself from universalist perspectives which had become hegemonic within the field of Latin American social sciences.[9] This reaction against the Eurocentrism of such perspectives is exemplified by criticism which has questioned its long-standing submissiveness to aesthetic theories built around the development of European metropolitan literatures.[10] The supposed universal validity of these theories and their mechanical application to the literary process in Latin America have also been called into question. Moreover, emphasis has been placed on the fact that criticism, inevitably a social discourse, has fulfilled concrete social functions in Europe, and that these are clearly not transferable. Neither, indeed, are the categories which constitute the conceptual systems of literary theory; critical categories are derived from concrete literary praxis, and the most important Latin American critics of recent years have made a collective commitment to their formulation.

This concern with giving an autonomous voice and perspective to Latin American criticism, allowing a full examination of the inherent features of the region's literatures, is explained by Angel Rama in the following excerpt from his article "Sistema literario y sistema social en Hispanoamérica". Rama was a precursor of this nationalizing impulse within Latin American criticism:

> La sociedad latinoamericana comporta una estratificación y una dinámica enteramente distintas de las sociedades europeas de los últimos ciento cincuenta años y no le son aplicables sin graves deformaciones los esquemas teóricos que interpretan a las últimas. Además, la literatura hispanoamericana, como su sociedad, presupone siempre la existencia previa de la europea, mientras que ésta se ha desarrollado, al margen de las normales influencias, sobre carriles propios, expandiéndose por el universo respondiendo a sus necesidades intrínsecas y no a las de las zonas que fue encontrando en su camino. (1974, 87–88)

This appeal to universalist hypotheses leads to a denial of the particularities of Latin American cultural and literary development, the specific features of which ultimately become, at best, diluted by contact with the

---

[9] An example of this is Pedro Morandé (1987), who analyses the limitations within Latinamerican sociology in recent decades caused by its reliance on "universal" models and categories and the lack of attention to culture which obstructed the establishment of an autonomous intellectual space for the discipline.

[10] Raul Bueno (1991) assesses the state of development of the discipline at the time of the emergence of the projects of autonomous criticism.

supposedly universalist model. At worst, such features are silenced, especially when they have little or nothing to do with Western traditions and have stronger links with the other main cultural formations —primarily of indigenous or African origin— which have helped to form the present cultural profile of the region misleadingly called Latin America.

Furthermore, the establishment of the European historico-cultural project as universal paradigm necessarily entails its institution as an exclusive model and as a yardstick against which all other proposals will be measured. This sets up a hierarchical vision which condemns Latin American culture to be read as "repetition", as a "copy" which is on the whole "imperfect": a mere follower of European trends. Latin America is assigned the passive role of receiver and duplicator of discourses produced in the centers of power, as if the process of appropriation and rearticulation of these discourses had occurred within a historical and cultural vacuum. The act of reading is, in this way, de-historicized; moreover, this approach ignores the important fact that such an intertextual dynamic constitutes a new product with characteristics distinct from the "original", with a new function and new meanings conferred upon it by its own socio-cultural environment.

Various proposals within Latin American criticism have sought to respond to this problematic question during the last few decades. These are concerned, above all, with providing ways to approach the cultural output of the continent in its specificity, retrieving the contributions of popular and autochtonous cultures, their creativity and their counter-hegemonic potential —in short, their capacity to offer alternatives to dominant formulas.

At this stage, the objective is not to argue the legitimacy of an autonomous Latin American criticism, or to fight for its recognition within the academic sphere. This task was eloquently carried out in important works of the early 1970s. Worthy of note is the influential study by the Cuban Roberto Fernández Retamar, *Para una teoría de la literatura hispanoamericana y otras aproximaciones* (1975).[11] Latin American criti-

---

[11] This Cuban critic, who was to enjoy enormous prestige amongst the region's Left wing intellectuals, conceives of his work as a contribution towards the decolonization of Latin American literary criticism. His proposals, which form a part of the process of institutionalization of the Cuban Revolution, has close ties with both the cultural policies that emerge from the Revolution, and the nationalist anti-imperialist tradition of the Cuban revolutionary process. For a contextualization and a synthesis of Fernández Retamar's study, see Hugo Achugar (1977). For critical commentary and an evaluation of the significance for the region's criticism of this work, see Guillermo

cism is already an established fact, and can draw upon not only an important body of methodology and theory, but also upon a series of re-readings of the region's literary history, a series begun by Alejandro Losada[12] and Ana Pizarro.[13] Projects such as these have involved contributions from the most important Latin American critics. The concern here is with weighing up the achievements and perspectives of this development, and with examining its limitations with a view to finding alternatives. Amongst these limitations are, specifically, the nationalist dimension which runs through it, and its emphasis on the political engagement of the intellectual producer. Both are the object of a virulent and destructive challenge coming, this time, from neoliberalism;[14] the projects of autonomous criticism must answer this challenge, taking on board the problems of theory and methodology which the aforementioned conceptual axes have produced.

This quest for self-definition in Latin American culture and literature has its background in the wave of revolutionary activity unleashed by events in Cuba, which would shake the continent throughout the 1960s and early 1970s and influence the intensification of the cold war in the Americas. The North American aggression against Cuba and the clear intention of the United States to prevent this political experiment from spreading to other countries in the region (as evinced by its open support for counter-revolutionary forces throughout the continent) acted as an incentive to anti-imperialist discourses which gained momentum during those years, and which warned against the United States' economic and cultural penetration in Latin America. The nationalist and Latin Americanist projects reactivated and reformulated at that time are articulated to this juncture, and occupy a dominant position within the Left wing of the intellectual field of the period. While the present study places emphasis on that immediate juncture, it should not be forgotten that the

---

Mariaca Iturri (1992). And for an attempt to articulate Fernández Retamar's discourse to the cultural debates of the 1990s, see Mignolo (1991, 1996).

[12] Alejandro Losada (1991, 1996) founded and coordinated a collective project to establish a Social History of Latin American Literature when he was based at the University of Berlin, and later with the AELSAL group (Association for the Study of Latin American Literatures and Societies). AELSAL continued developing this project after the Argentinan critic's death.

[13] See Ana Pizarro (1985, 1987) for the project initially directed by Angel Rama and Antonio Candido and later coordinated by Pizarro.

[14] On neoliberalist objections to nationalism of the left and to the latter's notion of "commitment" in the work of the intellectual, see William Rowe (1991).

nationalist and anti-imperialist vocation of the Left, and of Latin American progressive thought, dates back to the nineteenth century. As Jorge Castañeda points out, their project of social transformation for Latin America has, historically, gone hand in hand with one of national, even continental, emancipation, where the principal obstacle to change and the greatest threat to national sovereignty have come from the United States.[15]

This siege-like atmosphere meant that developments such as the defense of the region's cultural identity and the autonomy of its intellectual production became a common cause. Latin American integration is perceived as a strategy of resistance to imperialism. While efforts were made to establish intercommunication through journals, conferences etc., the Americanist utopias of Bolívar and Martí were revived. Effectively, the "second independence" postulated by the Cuban poet and essayist was to become a symbol of resistance for the Latin American left. Paradoxically, the military dictatorships which brutally ended this period of revolutionary mobilization and Latin Americanization of the continent would also make their contribution to the same process through the massive exodus which they provoked, and the consequent contact made by Southern Cone intellectuals with the realities of the countries in which they sought refuge.

One of the objectives of this study is an examination of the ways in which the defense of continental identity has been taken up, in recent years, by Latin American intellectuals. In one way or another, the contributions of Angel Rama, Alejandro Losada and Antonio Cornejo Polar to the development of an autonomous Latin American literary criticism share this historical experience, and attempt to respond to the need to formulate a conceptual framework which would provide the discipline with sufficient autonomy to define and discuss its subject matter.

In addition to these nationalist, Latin Americanist and anti-imperialist positions, there are other characteristic features of Latin American criticism. These may be summed up as follows: a questioning of the traditional concept of the intellectual and his/her relationship to society; a revival of the idea of "committed" art; a re-examination of the problem of distance between political and artistic avant-gardes, which, in most cases, leads to the subordination of the aesthetic sphere to those of ideology and politics. To complete this schematic outline of some of the principal cultural issues under debate at that time, we must emphasize the importance of Dependency Theory. The analytical perspectives which this theory

---

[15] For an examination of the reasons behind the association between nationalism and social transformation, see Jorge Castañeda (1994).

brought into vogue within the social sciences to account for the relationship between the central and peripheral zones of the international capitalist system, were uncritically transposed into the debate over the circulation of discourses between Latin America and the metropoli. Such an association between social and cultural-aesthetic processes not only had the effect of diluting their differences, but also imposed the principles of the former onto those of the latter. In the chapters dedicated to Rama, Losada and Cornejo, we will discuss how these issues are handled and the questions they raise with regard to each of these writers' work.

Angel Rama is regarded as having pioneered the innovation which took place within contemporary literary criticism in Latin America, and is seen as the instigator of the Latin Americanization of the field. The Uruguayan critic is responsible for the first challenges to "national" readings of the literature of the continent, and the first attempts to construct an autonomous critical discourse, independent of the metropolitan discourses hegemonic in Latin America until that time. The focus of our analysis is his work on narrative transculturation which highlights the vitality, creativity and capacity for resistance of the rural popular cultures which are the source of such narrative.

Both the Argentinean Alejandro Losada and the Peruvian Antonio Cornejo Polar pursue the task of establishing a criticism which could account for the specific features of Latin American literature as distinct from that of Europe or North America. Both men share Rama's interest in the redefinition of the Latin American literary corpus, the retrieval of popular cultures, and the removal of the discipline from the realms of the elite. Losada's work represents one of the most important efforts to provide Latin American criticism with a scientific foundation and a conceptual system upon which to base his project —a collaborative social history of Latin American literature. In the chapter dedicated to Losada, we trace the evolution of his theoretical system and list, summarize and discuss the successive definitions of the essential categories within that system.

Cornejo Polar's work draws on the rich tradition of socio-cultural debate which has taken place in Peru since the 1920s. Cornejo acknowledges his debt to the thought of José Carlos Mariátegui, especially in Cornejo's discourse on "heterogeneous literatures" — those shaped by the conflictive intersection of cultures resulting from the effects of the Conquest on Latin American societies. Cornejo's theoretical point of departure in handling these literatures is a reappraisal of *indigenista* narrative and a clarification of this literature's socio-cultural composition. This allows for a re-reading of Peruvian and Latin American literary processes from their traumatic origins, dealing with their plurality of projects, the multiplicity of their socio-cultural articulations and the vindication of their heterodox proposals and innovative character.

Chapter five is dedicated to the Argentinean Beatriz Sarlo, whose critical work offers as important a contribution to the proposals of 1970s nationalist criticism as that of Mariátegui, despite the fact that the two writers' discourses are articulated to different periods and geographical areas. Strictly speaking, Sarlo's work lies outside the central project of Latin American criticism: it arises from a debate which occurs within the Argentinean left during the 1980s concerning the problems posed for criticism in the country by cultural nationalism —problems such as the breakdown of divisions between art, politics and ideology. In short, this is a series of perspectives which the Argentine left shares with the rest of Latin America during the 1970s and which are, to some extent, present, as we have already indicated, in the projects of Latin American criticism to be examined in this study. The future development of Latin American criticism depends, to a large extent, on its ability to negotiate the new paths for cultural debate in Latin America opened by Beatriz Sarlo.

The final chapter offers an assessment of the projects examined, rethinking their place within the context of current debates on the region's literature and culture, and suggesting possibilities for the development of the discipline.

CHAPTER 1
JOSE CARLOS MARIATEGUI: BEYOND "EL PROCESO DE LA LITERATURA"

There is an abundance of commentary on Mariátegui's work, yet relatively little attention has been paid to his aesthetic and cultural reflections.[1] These require a re-reading not merely because they are an obvious antecedent to Latin American criticism's return, in the 1970s, to the focus on the historical and cultural specificity of the continent, but also because of their capacity to intervene in a debate which remains open. Such a re-reading of Mariátegui, then, is not simply a matter of "archeological" interest; nor should it only be an attempt to reconstruct a tradition with a view to legitimizing the project of an autonomous Latin American criticism —that project in fact being the subject matter of the following three chapters of this study. Rather, Mariátegui's criticism deserves a reading which recognizes its density and multiplicity of dimensions, characteristics which his critics have generally overlooked.

The emphasis of Mariátegui's critics has largely centered on the discussion of his political discourse and its analysis in connection to Marxist thought. The significance of his contribution to Latin American cultural criticism is repeatedly relegated to a secondary position. The tendency among his critics to divorce politics from culture in his writings, and to favor one above the other, produces an incomplete picture of both his vision and the meaning of his project. For Mariátegui, these two spheres, far from existing independently, intersect and mutually inform each other, as we can deduce from his interpretation of the transforming capacity of surrealism for example. Furthermore, this illustrates the importance of art and culture within his conception of revolution; in general, this importance is acknowledged by critics only with reference to *indigenismo*, thus omitting or greatly understating his interest in the various proposals of the avant-garde, along with the other manifestations of what they saw as his "idealist facet". Mariátegui does not set up an opposition between *indigenismo* and the avant-garde, and he does not opt for one at the expense of the other; for him, both paths are valid in the process of innovation of Peruvian culture. With a few exceptions, such as

---

[1] Abril (1980), Cornejo Polar (1980c), Dessau (1971), Flores Galindo (1980), Garrels (1976), Larsen (1996), Melis (1971, 1973, 1976, 1980, 1981), Moraña (1984), Moretic (1970), Posada (1968, 1980).

Antonio Melis and Alberto Flores Galindo, Mariátegui's critics have not been disposed to engage in a positive reading of the unorthodox aspects of his writings, which have thereby been ignored or discounted as "irrational" or "idealist" deviations within his Marxism. This reticence on the part of Mariátegui's critics to approach what in fact constitutes one of the creative aspects of the Peruvian's Marxism, has led to an incomplete reading of his proposals which in some ways distorts them. That reticence is partly explained by the difficulties which have traditionally accompanied Marxist thought when accounting for the creative phenomenon, and, on a more general level, is a consequence of the dominance of the scientifist tendency within Latin American social sciences until a few years ago.[2]

As far as his aesthetics is concerned, the Mariátegui retrieved by the literary discipline is the Mariátegui of the seventh of his *Siete ensayos de interpretación de la realidad peruana*, an essay which covers just one aspect of his multiple quests within the process of intellectual creation of Latin America. This narrow treatment of Mariátegui's work is evident even in connection with one of his best critics, Antonio Cornejo Polar, whose work can be largely understood as a development of central aspects of the said essay (see the chapter of this study dedicated to Cornejo). This selective treatment of Mariátegui's critical project can be understood, to a certain extent, in terms of the nationalist and anti-imperialist positions hegemonic within intellectual production of the Latin American left from the 1960s onwards. Within criticism, these positions have led to a privileging of literatures articulated to local traditional cultures, in opposition to and in preference to urban literatures which are a part of the internationalized circuits of culture. This bi-polarization of Latin American literature is actually a perspective more typical of contemporary criticism than of Mariátegui's proposals.

In synthesis, although the image of Mariátegui's discourse offered by critics may be valid, it is certainly incomplete; a good part of his reflections on questions of art and culture are not included. Such reflections do not merely constitute an appendix to his political discourse. On the contrary, contemporary continental criticism can find alternative ways of dealing with some of its central problems by referring to both Mariátegui's approach to the articulation of the two spheres without subordination of one to the other, and his treatment -derived from this approach— of the languages and formal experimentation of the avant-garde. Further-

---

[2] Jean Franco refers to this issue and the difficulties of finding a new critical language in her commentary on García Canclini's book, *Culturas híbridas: estrategias para entrar y salir de la modernidad* (1992).

more, an examination of the plurality of aesthetic projects which Mariátegui is able to handle is as useful for the current cultural debate as is an analysis of the ways in which his understanding of the national question brings him to vindicate Andean tradition and to retrieve it for modern Peruvian culture, without falling into sectarian or programmatic attitudes. The revolutionary and transforming potential of art is not the preserve of spaces articulated to traditional cultures; the innovation of Peruvian literature allows for a multiplicity of quests which does not exclude that of languages which are produced in the cities and become part of the internationalized circuits of culture. Finally, it would also be a great loss to the discipline to undervalue the importance of the very nature of Mariátegui's approach to literature, an approach which keeps him from falling into either a-prioristic ideological positions or readings centered on the content of works of art to the exclusion of formal aspects. Mariátegui's enthusiasm for Martín Adán's work, for example, demonstrates his integral conception of art and his awareness that form, and not just ideological content, is an object of criticism. This aspect of his aesthetic discourse has been either neglected or, more often, undervalued as part of his "idealist" or "irrational" outlook. The orthodoxy which has colored the reading of his work has prevented a balanced evaluation of the more creative dimensions of his proposal, since they have been discarded for their very heterodoxy. The fact is that, without breaking with a Marxist and historical perspective, Mariátegui sets out to study the problems of form specific to literary activity —problems which at that time, incidentally, also constituted the subject matter of the Russian formalists' theorization. Today the discipline has yet to credit him for a conception of art which emphasizes its anticipatory, prefigurative and subversive capacity, taking it beyond mere reflection or representation. Latin American criticism is also indebted to him for his project of articulation of the literary, the historical and the ideological, a project which neither falls into ahistorical aestheticism, nor reduces critical reasoning to a reading of an ideological order in which formal processes are swamped by content. The objective of this chapter is to examine the Mariátegui who has been silenced until now.

Mariátegui's literary criticism is an important part of his nationalist revolutionary project. The debate on culture and artistic activity constitutes a central axis of his discourse and is an integral component of his project of general transformation of Peruvian society, as is so eloquently illustrated by the politico-cultural work undertaken by his journal *Amauta*.[3]

---

[3] For Mariátegui, the struggle for socialism constituted a long-term project which involved not only the political development of the masses, but also patient work within

Although Mariátegui would never undertake the systematic development of an aesthetic theory, he expresses his interest in the art and culture of his time in numerous articles. It is possible to deduce his theoretical perspectives from them —many of which are directly relevant to current cultural debate and criticism in Latin America. Latin American thought is indebted to Mariátegui for appropriating Marxism from a national perspective and adapting it to the data offered by Peruvian reality, thus challenging its universalist proposals and converting it into an instrument to reveal the specificities not just of Peru, but of the various socio-cultural formations of Latin America.

We are particularly, although not exclusively, interested in determining the articulations between Mariátegui's polemical notion of "myth", his conception of popular-national culture and his critical discourse, with the aim of elucidating the aesthetic status of the said notion of "myth".

Mariátegui's process of appropriation of the Marxist perspective is complemented by wider reflections on the problematic of art and culture, both within bourgeois societies and in the post-revolutionary Soviet context.[4] In the post-war Europe in which he lived, Mariátegui witnessed the convulsions the war caused within the intellectual field in terms of the breakdown of some hitherto unquestioned fundamental ideological certainties of bourgeois society, such as the inevitability of progress. Now he saw the rise of pacifist discourses and of critiques of bourgeois order, and the alignment of a good part of the intellectual avant-garde with revolution and social change.[5] Mariátegui followed the developments of the European avant-garde movements with particular interest, noting their aesthetic formulations and the views they put forward regarding the relationships between the political and social spheres —in short, their proposals in terms of cultural politics and of the general organization of culture. During this initial period, however, both his literary criticism and his political essays are framed by an internationalist perspective,[6] from which Mariátegui

---

the cultural sphere. His conception of the journal *Amauta* should be seen within this framework. He founded it in 1926 with the double purpose of serving as an organ of expression for the various progressive forces within Peruvian society in the 1920s and of stimulating a process of innovation which he intended eventually to lead in order that it might oppose the dominant culture en bloc.

[4] See mainly his critical articles in (1959, 1964b, 1970b).

[5] See, for example, "El grupo Clarté" or "Henri Barbusse"(1964b) and "La emoción de nuestro tiempo" (1970b).

[6] The following articles, among others, testify to this position: "Aspectos viejos y nuevos del futurismo" (1959) or "Nacionalismo e internacionalismo" (1970b).

introduces the series of themes and problems mentioned above. In his later nationalist period —which does not imply a total eradication of an international dimension in his analysis— the said issues are largely rearticulated to his reflections on art and culture in the context of his project for social transformation in Peru.

Mariátegui's discourse on the relationship between the intellectual and revolution, on the articulation between the political avant-garde and the aesthetic avant-garde, occupies a privileged place in his critical writings. In his writings on the politico-cultural work of Henri Barbusse and his journal *Clarté*, he expresses his interest in the commitment of the writer and the intellectual to politics, and the need to unite the two avant-gardes into one force. It is not difficult to find points of contact between the objectives which he was later to conceive for his own journal, *Amauta*, and the synthesis he makes of the meaning of Barbusse's journal in France in the 1920s:

> Significa un esfuerzo de la inteligencia por entregarse a la revolución y un esfuerzo de la revolución por apoderarse de la inteligencia. La idea revolucionaria tiene que desalojar a la idea conservadora no sólo de las instituciones sino también de la mentalidad y del espíritu de la humanidad. Al mismo tiempo que la conquista del poder, la Revolución acomete la conquista del pensamiento. (1964b, 156)

Although criticism has clearly established this as one of his fundamental preoccupations, perhaps it has failed to examine sufficiently other equally important aspects of his thought: the relationship between the spheres of art and politics; between the fields of aesthetic production and ideology; between the artist's work and the artist's political militancy; in short, what he understands by "revolutionary" in art as opposed to his understanding of "revolutionary" at a social and political level. In Latin America, this discussion would arise again in the 1960s and come to constitute a problematic issue for the projects of autonomous criticism which would gain momentum in the following decade. This lends added importance to the analysis of the quests of a similar nature undertaken by Mariátegui.

Mariátegui does not conceive of art as totally independent from politics, because for him politics is, in fact, "la trama misma de la historia" (1959, 3-4). Although it is true that for Mariátegui the "mito de la Inteligencia pura" —the supposed autonomy of the intellectual in the face of political ideologies— is no more than the acceptance of the status quo, it is also true that he does not consider it possible to assimilate the work of the intellectual or artist and political discourses without some mediation (1969a, 121). In the article mentioned above, "Aspectos viejos y nuevos del futurismo", Mariátegui states that no great artist can be apolitical:

> El artista que no siente las agitaciones, las inquietudes, las ansias de su pueblo y de su época, es un artista de sensibilidad mediocre, de comprensión anémica. ¡Que el diablo confunda a los artistas benedictinos, enfermos de megalomanía aristocrática, que se clausuran en una decadente torre de marfil! (1959, 58)

This does not mean that intellectual work is subordinated to political discourse. Referring to criticism, Mariátegui emphasizes the "indivisibility" of the "spirit" of man and the consequent "coherence" between his intellectual work and his political thinking. But he is keen to add that this cannot imply,

> ... que considere el fenómeno literario o artístico desde puntos de vista extraestéticos, sino que mi concepción se unimisma, en la intimidad de mi conciencia, con mis concepciones morales, políticas y religiosas, y que, sin dejar de ser concepción estrictamente estética, no puede operar independiente o diversamente. (1985, 231)

But, on the other hand, he writes that politics cannot be dictated to by art either: "... La ideología política de un artista no puede salir de las asambleas de estetas. Tiene que ser una ideología plena de vida, de emoción y de verdad. No una concepción artificial, literaria y falsa..." (1959, 58).

In his analysis of the surrealist aesthetic and the ideological postulations of the movement, his position on the limits between the fields of art and politics and their specificities are even clearer. For Mariátegui, surrealism (the term in usage at the time being super-realism) to a certain extent constitutes a paradigm of the innovative and revolutionary potential within avant-garde art. It must be emphasized, however, that for Mariátegui the notion of surrealism extends beyond the original French school, to encompass all artistic expression which made a radical break from the realist grounding of bourgeois aesthetics and set out on the search for, "...[la] realidad por los caminos de la fantasía". But this also involves a historical conception:

> ...la ficción no es libre. Más que descubrirnos lo maravilloso, parece destinada a revelarnos lo real. La fantasía cuando no nos acerca a la realidad, nos sirve bien poco...La fantasía no tiene valor sino cuando crea algo real... (23)

Mariátegui finds the historical meaning of surrealism in its capacity to take its aesthetic and political goals to the extreme, as can be deduced from his view of the other currents of the avant-garde, which "...[se habrían] limitado a la afirmación de algunos postulados estéticos, a la experimentación de algunos principios artísticos" (46). Mariátegui sees that surrealism possesses a transforming potential in the confluence of its aesthetic and political objectives and the coherence between them:

> La insurrección suprarrealista entra en una fase que prueba que este movimiento no es un simple fenómeno literario, sino un complejo fenómeno *espiritual* [read cultural]. No una moda artística sino una protesta del espíritu. Los suprarrealistas pasan del campo artístico al campo político. Denuncian y condenan no sólo las transacciones del arte con el decadente pensamiento burgués. Denuncian y condenan, en bloque, la civilización capitalista. (42; my emphasis)

But it must be stressed that the convergence of projects does not imply assimilation. In fact, Mariátegui carries out two parallel readings of history and the surrealists' revolutionary quests, making use of two differentiated languages: one language is used to speak about their political goals, and another to discuss their aesthetic goals; culture constitutes the articulating space of both spheres. Contrasting the behavior of the surrealist movement with that of the Italian futurists, Mariátegui underlines the fact that,

> [en lugar] de lanzar un programa de política suprarrealista, acepta y suscribe el programa de la revolución concreta presente ... *Reconoce validez en el terreno social, político, económico, únicamente al movimiento marxista. No se le ocurre someter la política a las reglas y gustos del arte* ... en los dominios de la política y la economía juzga pueril y absurdo intentar una especulación original basada en los datos del arte. *Los suprarrealistas no ejercen su derecho al disparate, al subjetivismo absoluto, sino en el arte* ... (42; my emphasis)

So, in Mariátegui's discourse, this "derecho al disparate" and "al subjetivismo absoluto" has nothing to do with the idea of "art for art's sake". Moreover, the notion of "disparate", with its antirationalist function, was to play an important role in Mariátegui's criticism precisely in terms of the avant-garde's historical and subversive character regarding the forms, values and conceptions of the world dominant in bourgeois aesthetics. Mariátegui hastens to point out that,

> ... nada rehusan tanto los suprarrealistas como confinarse voluntariamente en la pura especulación artística. *Autonomía del arte, sí: pero, no clausura del arte.* Nada les es más extraño que la fórmula del arte por el arte. (47–48; my emphasis)

Art cannot function as a vehicle for escaping from reality. What interests Mariátegui about the surrealists is the subsequent relationship between the artist and the man, although this does not lead him to allow the logic that governs the political action of the man to swallow the logic that governs the practice of the aesthete. If the surrealist's project of subverting bourgeois culture is realized in their art through recourse to "disparate", in their life their course of action is different, as described so graphically and humorously by Mariátegui:

> El artista que, en un momento dado, no cumple con el deber de arrojar al Sena a un *Flic* de M. Tardieu, o de interrumpir con una interjección un discurso de Briand, es un pobre diablo. (48; emphasis in the original)

Some clarifications of the Mariateguian conception of the processes of artistic innovation in the twentieth century are called for here before continuing with a reconstruction of the role played by "disparate", by the use of fantasy and imagination, and by his theory of myth within his aesthetic perspectives. Firstly, our repeated mention of the avant-garde here could mistakenly suggest the idea that, for Mariátegui, all avant-garde currents have the same innovative character within the Western cultural field. On the contrary, Mariátegui distinguishes between the numerous avant-garde tendencies, and the various potentials of their respective projects.

Although avant-garde art in general is articulated to a period of "transition and crisis", for Mariátegui it cannot be described as a uniform block, much less as a single quest in a new world: within avant-garde art, adds Mariátegui, "...elementos de revolución [y]...elementos de decadencia..." coexist. Authentic quests for an "espíritu nuevo" are confused with ficticious ones which take refuge in conformist conceptions and "teorías derrotistas sobre la modernidad" (30–31). Both coexistence and conflict between these elements take place in the artists' consciousness, even if they are unaware of this.

> La conciencia del artista es el circo agonal de una lucha entre los dos espíritus. La comprensión de esta lucha, a veces, casi siempre, escapa al propio artista. Pero finalmente uno de los dos espíritus prevalece. El otro queda estrangulado en la arena. (18–19)

Mariátegui believes in a mediated relationship between art and ideology; this underlies his critical discourse. His analysis of Martín Adán's dismantling of the sonnet is an illustration of this perspective. Adán's work, in spite of its own author, was to have more radical scope than that of surrealism itself, which had simply contented itself "...con declarar la abolición del soneto en poemas cubistas, dadaistas o expresionistas". Martín Adán, instead, subverts it from within, producing the anti-sonnet. This interpretation of Martín Adán sheds light on Mariátegui's view of the importance of form. Adán's subversive power lies not so much in the content of his poems as in his treatment of form:

> Martín Adán realiza el anti-soneto. Lo realiza, quizá a pesar suyo, movido por su gusto católico y su don tomista de reconciliar el dogma nuevo con el orden clásico. Un capcioso propósito reaccionario lo conduce a un

resultado revolucionario. Lo que nos da, sin saberlo, no es el soneto, sino el anti-soneto. No bastaba atacar al soneto de fuera como los vanguardistas: había que meterse dentro de él, como Martín Adán, para comerse su entraña hasta vaciarlo...Golpead ahora con los nudillos en el soneto cual si fuera un mueble del Renacimiento; está perfectamente hueco; es cáscara pura. Barroco, culterano, gongorino, Martín Adán salió en busca del soneto, para descubrir el anti-soneto, como Colón en vez de las Indias encontró en su viaje la América. (1970a, 156–157)

We have already indicated that one of the parameters which Mariátegui uses for this task of critical discernment involves an approach to the problem of form; however, we should clarify that, for him, technical innovation is in no way sufficient to formulate a challenge, or construct an alternative, to bourgeois aesthetics. A true alternative can only arise from a questioning of the values which form the "Absoluto burgués" and upon which bourgeois culture is constructed.[7] An example of artists on that false quest would be those initially associated with the surrealist project, who, finding themselves incapable of following it to its ultimate consequences, remained on the outside of the process of aesthetic innovation, and were finally to be absorbed and institutionalized by bourgeois society, or even fascism, as was the case with the Italian futurists.[8] In short, the gulf between technical —although he sometimes calls it "formal"— innovation and cultural innovation is clear to Mariátegui:

> No podemos aceptar como nuevo un arte que no nos trae sino una nueva técnica. Eso sería recrearse en el más falaz de los espejismos actuales. Ninguna estética puede rebajar el trabajo artístico a una cuestión de técnica. La técnica nueva debe corresponder a un espíritu nuevo también. Si no, lo único que cambia es el parámetro, el decorado. Y una revolución artística no se contenta de conquistas formales. (1959, 18)

The true rupture has to happen at the very heart of art and bourgeois culture; this is why Mariátegui is so interested in those proposals within the avant-garde which erode the rationalist foundation of bourgeois aesthetics. He initially notes this in connection with dadaism, a movement which, he says, "...arremete contra toda servidumbre del arte a la inteligencia ... [coincidiendo] ... con el tramonto del pensamiento racionalista" (69).

---

[7] It is worth noting here that Melis had already pointed out Mariátegui's interest in the avant-gardes' commitment to expose the crisis of the bourgeois world, and their role as bearers of revolutionary conviction in the article we have already cited, "La lucha en el frente cultural" (1981, 131).

[8] See "El grupo suprarrealista y Clarté" (1959, 43) and "Balance del suprarrealismo" (45, 46 & 48).

Years later, Mariátegui revises his perception of the scope of the movement, pointing out its limitations and judging it instead to be the precursor of surrealism. Without denying that the Dadaist movement was surrealism's point of departure, Mariátegui considers that surrealism surpasses it and pushes it towards an antirationalist undertaking which only then becomes truly radical (43).

This Mariateguian perspective is not confined to his aesthetic conception but is found within the frame of a broader critique of the domain of bourgeois Reason and permeates his whole discourse. In Antonio Melis' opinion, any reading of Mariátegui's project which does not take this issue into account runs the risk of being a distortion, or at best overlooks central aspects of his work. Melis begins by questioning the ideological definition of Mariátegui's Marxism proposed by his critics. This definition describes it as a discourse laden with irrationalist elements attributed to his attachment to authors such as Nietzsche, Bergson, Freud, Unamuno and especially Georges Sorel.[9] Melis believes that classifying Mariátegui as an idealist thinker involves overlooking certain historical junctures which influence his work as a political leader. These include his rejection of the Social-Democrats' subjection to bourgeois rationality, and his polemic with their reformism, as well as their evolutionist and positivist conception of Marxism (1976, 124). Melis' hypothesis on Mariátegui's critique of the ideological position of the Second International in terms of its continued links with bourgeois thinking can be examined in the following extract from Mariátegui's article, "La emoción de nuestro tiempo. Dos concepciones de la vida", in which he contrasts the politico-cultural atmosphere of the pre-war period with that of the years following the conflict:

> La filosofía evolucionista, historicista, racionalista, unía en los tiempos pre-bélicos, por encima de las fronteras políticas y sociales, a las dos clases antagónicas. El bienestar material, la potencia física de las urbes, habían engendrado un respeto supersticioso por la ideal de Progreso. La humanidad parecía haber hallado una vía definitiva. Conservadores y revolucionarios aceptaban prácticamente las consecuencias de la tesis evolucionista. Unos y otros coincidían en la misma adhesión a la idea del progreso y en la misma aversión a la violencia. (1970b, 13–14)

Furthermore, the appearance in the post-war period firstly of the Bolshevik phenomenon, and, subsequently, of the fascist response to it, had awakened a nostalgia among the "vieja burocracia socialista y sindical" and the "vieja guardia burguesa" for the peaceful coexistence of

---

[9] See mainly Paris (1981) and Paris in Aricó (1978) and in Podestà (1981).

the years before the war:

> Un mismo sentimiento de la vida vincula y acuerda espiritualmente a estos sectores de la burguesía y del proletariado, que trabajan, en comandita, por descalificar, al mismo tiempo, el método bolchevique y el método fascista. (16)

However, Mariátegui believes that, with the war, the bourgeoisie had lost their old dogmas, their "mitos heróicos", thereby falling into nihilism and scepticism. This crisis of bourgeois certainties was precisely what had opened up the space for the search for, and formulation of, new "myths" among the new generations, since without them history is left without any motor and man's life loses its historical meaning. This is how Mariátegui expresses his view of the crisis:

> ..la civilización burguesa sufre de la falta de un mito, de una fé, de una esperanza! Falta que es su expresión de su quiebra material. La experiencia racionalista ha tenido esta pardójica eficacia de conducir a la humanidad a la desconsolada convicción de que la Razón no puede darle ningún camino. El racionalismo no ha servido sino para desacreditar a la razón...La Razón ha extirpado del alma de la civilización burguesa los residuos de sus antiguos mitos. El hombre occidental ha colocado, durante algún tiempo, en el retablo de los dioses muertos, a la Razón y a la Ciencia. Pero ni la Razón ni la Ciencia pueden satisfacer toda la necesidad de infinito que hay en el hombre. La propia Razón se ha encargado de demostrar a los hombres que ella no les basta. Que únicamente el Mito posee la preciosa virtud de llenar su yo profundo. (1970b, 18–19)

It is worth noting Melis' justified insistence on articulating any interpretation of Mariátegui's theory on "myth" — a central component of his project — to his debate with social democracy in order to avoid dehistorisizing it, as most of his critics tend to do. In effect, they simply discard it as an irrationalist ideology or identify it as one of the "impure" aspects of Mariateguian Marxism (1980, 123). Instead these critics could have concerned themselves with the pluralism of his ideological formation and with the examination of the relationship between his "...bases marxistas y leninistas y [su] atención hacia otras líneas de pensamiento..." which could account for the "tactical" foundations of his discourse and his contributions to Marxism in terms of his critique of the economistic positions within it (1976, 126, 129–130). The atmosphere of intellectual rupture in Europe following the war provides the background to Mariátegui's retrieval of the Sorelian critique of parliamentary socialism, his denouncing of the "illusion of Progress", and, finally, his discourse on "myth" which he rearticulates and to which he gives a new function as a fundamental part of his counter-hegemonic project (1970b, 14). We will return to the significance of myth in Mariátegui's discourse as it is directly linked to his aesthetic proposals, and also to his notions of "disparate" and fantasy and their function within avant-garde art of subverting bourgeois values. Mariateguian myth serves as one of the fundamental axes of his critique of rationalist ideology.

But let us return to Melis' re-evaluation of Mariátegui's "irrationalism" in terms of a critique of the rationalism of bourgeois thought and an attempt to found a new concept of rationality; this is how the Italian author interprets this aspect of Mariátegui's project:

> En este culto dogmático de la razón, él percibe el peligro de una subordinación cultural a la burguesía de la fase de ascenso y triunfo. El pensador peruano, entonces trata de fundar un concepto distinto y autónomo de racionalidad...El límite profundo de la razón tradicional, expresada dentro del mivimiento obrero por la ideología social-demócrata, le parece ser su carácter de simple registro de lo existente. Mariátegui en cambio aboga por una razón creadora que esté a la altura de su deber fundamental de modificar la realidad. (1980, 133–34)

Mariátegui's proposal, upon which Melis makes no further comment, must be found in his discourse on myth. We will go on to examine this later.

However, we would like to point out here that Melis extends this important hypothesis on Mariateguian political thought to his aesthetic conception. That hypothesis also throws light on Mariátegui's critique of the aesthetic principles of realism. Melis states that the Peruvian's discourse on realism also shows evidence of, "...la intuición de que el dogma del realismo significa, de hecho, la relación de continuidad entre estado burgués y estado proletario" (133).[10] There certainly appears to be

---

[10] On the Mariateguian discourse on realism, see Melis (1973, 1981) and, Posada (1968). In contrast to Melis, Posada finds Mariateguian hypotheses on realism to be "insufficient", and frequently points out Mariátegui's "incapacity" to "understand theoretical problems". However, we would suggest that Posada's method suffers from an interpretation in terms of "influences" and from a continual attempt to assimilate Mariátegui to the classic texts of Marxist aesthetics, which, in turn, leads him to dehistoricize his discourse and to lose sight of the scope of Mariátegui's critical contribution. On the same theme see also Moretic (1970) who reads Mariátegui's discourse on realism from the point of view of Marxist aesthetics and then refers it to the current debate on realism. Finally, although Moraña (1984, 88–91) equivocally defines Mariátegui's proposal on bourgeois realism and the anti-rationalist methods of surrealism as "realism", she does offer a more useful analysis of the said proposal, stressing its creative function over a simply reproductive function.

a connection between Melis' observation about Mariátegui's conception of realism and his enthusiasm for surrealism's anti-rationalist methods and the avant-garde's recourse to "disparate", fantasy and imagination, and the break with the principle of verisimilitude. This can be deduced from, for example, his article "La realidad y la ficción" (1959, 22–25), or his writings on Martín Adán (1970a, 150–57).

Before continuing with a reconstruction of Mariátegui's theory on myth, it is worthwhile considering another interesting reappraisal of a central aspect of his discourse, namely, his views on the decadence of Western society. Like his "irrationalism", this is traditionally seen in a negative light. This theme in Mariátegui is generally discussed in terms of the reactionary "influence" of Spengler's discourse. Flores Galindo reinterprets it from a positive perspective, shedding light on the contribution —alien to the original meaning of Spengler's argument— to the development of an *indigenista* and nationalist consciousness, not just in Mariátegui's work, but in the whole of Peru. The reading of Spengler would have been an important factor in the Mariateguian proposal of an alternative historical project for Latin America, distinct from that of Europe. Flores synthesizes the "use" to which Spengler is put in Latin America in the following way:

> La Decadencia de Occidente... se convierte en un verdadero "best seller" en los paises de habla hispana...Pocos sabían que Spengler era un personaje conservador y nadie podía suponer que terminaría como ideólogo del nacional-socialismo. Pero estas referencias políticas no interesan, porque este texto reaccionario en Europa, tuvo efectos imprevisiblemente revolucionarios en América Latina, robusteciendo y afirmando a quienes hacían la crítica de lo europeo para reivindicar las raices propias de nuestra cultura. Sin *La Decadencia de Occidente*, no se hubiera escrito de la misma manera *Tempestad en los Andes*. (1980a, 43; emphasis in the original)

Our principal intention in highlighting this issue is to reinforce that which Melis draws to our attention: the methodological problem of Mariátegui's critics' interpretation of his "irrationality".[11] In fact, the type of treatment challenged by Melis tends to resort to readings of "influences", which do not take into account either the matrices or historical and cultural mediations which form part of any process of reception, appropriation and refunctionalization of discourses. Further, these readings overlook not only the operations involved in the selection of such discourses, but also the

---

[11] For an interesting contextualization of the "irrationalist" elements in both Sorel and Mariátegui's discourses, including an attempt to retrieve the historical dimension of the theory of myth in both authors, see Sylvers (1980, 19–77).

fact that, rather than clinging to the importance or significance of a discourse within its original intellectual field, it is more important to determine the different function it assumes once it has been rearticulated and readapted to a new context. This implies rethinking Mariátegui's appropriation of the Sorelian discourse on myth, with a view to retrieving its historical dimension and underlining the specificities of Mariátegui's cultural context.

We should here make some observations on certain historico-cultural conditionings of the processes of intertextuality present in Mariátegui's work. Firstly, within the attempt to relocate the Sorelian myth in Mariátegui's writings, it is worth noting Oscar Terán's comment on Mariátegui's *colonidista* experience, which, given its decadentist sensitivity, was to operate as one of the discursive matrices which would help to explain Mariátegui's inclination for the anti-"progress" and anti-intellectual ideology of Sorelism (1980, 24). Secondly, we must mention Estuardo Núñez's observation, cited by Alberto Flores, on the relationship between Mariátegui and surrealism, as it sheds light on yet another core issue in Mariátegui's discourse, which could also account for his interest in the Sorelian theory of myth. According to Estuardo Núñez, Mariátegui not only plays a fundamental role in the introduction of the surrealist movement in Peru, but he also finds,

> ...parentesco entre un movimiento que reivindicaba la imaginación y la espontaneidad creativa, con un continente alejado del racionalismo y la ilustración, donde el sentimiento importaba más que lo racional. (1980a, 43)

Thirdly, Melis emphasizes that Mariátegui's empathy with both Sorel and Bergson's voluntarist positions can be understood in the context of the historical circumstances which led him to reject the economicism of the Marxism of the Second International and to re-evaluate the "impulso ideal del movimiento obrero" over and above the passive acceptance of economic factors. Melis sums up the context which accounts for this central aspect of Mariátegui's discourse as follows:[12]

> Mariátegui se halla en presencia de un proletariado todavía débil y, en cambio, de un campesinado casi totalmente indio o mestizo. Su elección ya definida en Europa encuentra nuevas razones para afirmarse en la realidad peruana. La social democracia positivista ya ha hecho bancarrota en Europa y le parece una solución totalmente inadecuada para despertar

---

[12] For a reading in tune with Mariátegui's anti-economism see also Terán (1980b, 172–173).

las energías de las masas trabajadoras. Por eso, en primer lugar, valoriza las tendencias que más se alejan de este burdo economicismo. (1976, 130)

Furthermore, Mariátegui's critique of economicism and evolutionist attitudes is framed in the cultural atmosphere of his generation, which celebrates "el poder de la subjetividad y la acción creadora de la conciencia...[y] privilegiaba la 'voluntad heróica'...". José Aricó writes that, in consequence, Mariátegui's "idealist" perspective,

> ...está expresando así el reconocimiento del valor creativo de la iniciativa política y la importancia excepcional del poder de la subjetividad para transformar la sociedad, o para desplazar las relaciones de fuerza más allá de las determinaciones "económicas" o de los mecanismos automáticos de la crisis... (1980, 142)

As Oscar Terán points out, the notion of myth includes a cultural dimension which Mariátegui fuses with the economic dimension of his analysis of Peruvian society (1985, 88–89). Through this category of double contents, Mariátegui isolates the specificity of the agrarian problem of his country —the land has both economic and cultural value for the Indians. So this very double perspective of his counterhegemonic project is precisely what allows the articulation of socialism and indigenous cultural tradition:

> La fé en el resurgimiento indígena no proviene de un proceso de "occidentalización" material de la tierra quechua. No es la civilización, no es el alfabeto del blanco, lo que levanta al indio. Es el mito, la idea de la revolución socialista. La esperanza indígena es absolutamente revolucionaria... (1985, 35)

Finally, we would like to refer to Flores Galindo's comment on the character of Mariátegui's thought:

> El mariateguismo fue la obra de un periodista, un hombre en estrecho contacto con otros hombres, sumergido en la vida cotidiana, interesado más por el impacto de sus ideas, por la emoción que generaba en sus contemporáneos que por la certeza cartesiana de su pensamiento: de allí la tesis del marxismo como un mito —fuerza movilizadora, un elan, una agonía, un entusiasmo vital— de nuestro tiempo. (1980a, 59)

Flores Galindo disqualifies any orthodox reading of Mariáteguiís thought, because in Mariátegui there is no room for rationalist or doctrinal straitjackets. As William Rowe points out, the freedom of Mariáteguiís thought for the integration and transformation, in a productive manner, of ideas and experiences from diverse cultural and intellectual traditions is, possibly, without equal. This liberty allows him to articulate myth and revolution, politico-religious Andean thought, and politico-secular Western thought.[13]

In Georges Sorel's work, the discourse on myth forms a fundamental part of his syndicalist proposal which is of an anti-intellectual nature and advocates action over theory. The proposal arises in the context of his critique of parliamentary socialism which had lost its revolutionary meaning. Sorelian views on myth should be read in the context of his demythification of the bourgeois idea of "progress", and of the domination of scientific reason and positivism —in short, the belief that all social problems could be resolved by science (1925, 154). One should also bear in mind his critique of the rationalism and intellectualism of social democracy, and his endeavor to maintain links between political ideas and reality: "It is the superstitious respect paid by social democracy to the mere text of its doctrines that nullified every attempt in Germany to perfect Marxism" (141–42). Sorelian syndicalism, which, in fact, had a limited influence on the syndicalist movement in general, was characterized by an emphasis on, "class struggle, direct action, the general strike, the destruction of the state and the avoidance of the practices of parliamentary democracy and social peace". Syndicalism offered the working class an alternative to the moral and religious crisis of bourgeois society and the very decadence of capitalism (Jennings 1985, 117–18 and 122–30).

Within Sorelian thought, the "social myths",

> ..enclose with them all the strongest inclinations of a people, of a party or of a class, inclinations which recur to the mind with the insistence of instincts in all the circumstances of life...and give an aspect of complete reality to the hopes of immediate action by which, more easily than by any other method, men can reform their desires, passions and mental activity. (Sorel 1925, 133–34)

Sorel sets up an opposition between intuition and rationality; the struggle for socialism should be represented by images and, in this way, appeal to the emotions rather than being presented through argument or debate, which are methods which appeal to reason. The function of myth is to move people to act in and have an effect on the present; its effective-

---

[13] According to Rowe (1994, 297–98) Mariátegui's use of the notion of "myth" evokes many meanings, amongst which are the following: "inner life, passion... religious experience freed from dogma or institutional church..., the way [the popular classes] experience the world..., something that can cross social and ethnic divisions..., the entry of artistic experience into politics." Myth, in Mariátegui's discourse, offers "a bridge between indigenous culture and indigenous politics and the great traditions of Western politics, which are traditions of secularisation and freedom, Andean politics being religious in its language and its thinking."

ness can thus be measured according to its capacity to synthesize and represent collective aspirations and to move the masses to action (133–36). Sorel defines the syndicalist myth as a body of images which would appeal to intuition and would evoke the socialist struggle; the general strike, as the foremost revolutionary strategy would constitute the syndicalists' myth (137).

The general strike, therefore, would be a creation of the workers' movement and not of the intellectuals; it would encompass all the fundamental aspects of socialism, but would have a greater capacity for popular mobilization than that offered by mere doctrines (142 and 77). Richard Humphrey sums up the significance of the Sorelian notion of myth for Marxism:

> It was largely through this conception that [Sorel] attempted to replace the utopianism of early socialism by a pragmatic social theory that would give a genuine recognition to historical tradition and that would complete Marx's doctrine of economic determinism by a theory of man's creative freedom in moral development. (1971, 171)

Malcolm Sylvers states that, "...debe reconocerse a Sorel el mérito de haber intuido que en la era moderna el ideal social tenía una capacidad de persuación de las conciencias, similar a la que en la antiguedad ejercían los mitos religiosos" (1980, 55). While it is not our intention to analyze the Sorelian discourse on myth, we would just like to note some central aspects, such as some of the contributions to Marxism which are credited to Sorel, since they act as a framework for the reconstruction we intend to make of Mariátegui's theory of myth and its significance for Latin American thought.

In this connection, it is especially useful to look at both the appropriation and evaluation of the Sorelian myth carried out by Gramsci, that other heterodox Marxist who was labelled irrationalist and voluntarist along with Mariátegui because of the presence of Sorelian ideas in his discourse. With this in mind, Melis calls attention to the critics' schematic approach when dealing with "lo que es un dirigente y un teórico revolucionario", and in ignoring voluntarist attitudes even in Marx, Lenin and Mao (1976, 130).

Like Mariátegui, Gramsci incorporates Sorelian myth into his discourse. In his writings on "The Modern Prince", he uses Sorel's myth for his analysis of Machiavelli's *The Prince*, cataloguing it as a dramatic piece and its protagonist as "mythical". Gramsci writes that this work inaugurated a new form of political discourse which fuses ideology and political science "in the dramatic form of a 'myth' ", taking on the aspect of "fantasy and art". In the book, the protagonist, the "condottiere", personifies and expresses through his values, doctrinal, rational principles and represents "plastically and 'anthropomorphically' the symbol of the 'collective will' ". This form of doctrinal representation through a "concrete" character stimulates "...the artistic fantasy of those he wants to convince and gives a more concrete form to political passions". For Gramsci, *The Prince* can be considered as an historical example of Sorel's myth, inasmuch as it is an expression of,

> ...a political ideology which is not presented as a cold utopia or as a rational doctrine, but as a creation of concrete fantasy which works on a disperse and pulverised people in order to arouse and organize their collective will. (1980, 135)

Myth here is neither a pure abstraction nor just a fictitious creation; it is articulated to a particular historical reality. Machiavelli's *Prince* appeals to a specific, concrete public as an elaboration of their own experience and consciousness. And it appeals to that public on an emotional, non-rational level to move it to action in a certain direction —in this case, the foundation of a new State and a new social and national structure. The Prince identifies with popular consciousness; however, the popular has a restricted meaning here —it does not mean the people in general, but those

> ...people whom Machiavelli has convinced with the preceding tract, whose conscious expression he becomes and feels himself to be, with whom he feels himself identified: it seems that the whole of the "logical" work is only a reflection of the people, an internal reasoning which takes place inside the popular consciousness and has its conclusions in an impassioned, urgent cry. Passion, from reasoning about itself becomes "emotion", fever, fanaticism for action. (135–37)

Gramsci's interest in the Sorelian myth is directly linked to his preoccupation with the tasks involved in political leadership, in particular the conception and shaping of the party and its functions regarding the need to develop and consolidate a collective popular-national will. This is in the context of a country which has experienced a succession of failures in this endeavor, due to a lack of "...an efficient jacobine force, ("...a 'categoric incarnation' of Machiavelli's *Prince*") just such a force which in other nations awakened and organized the popular collective will and founded the modern States". The project of Machiavelli's *Prince* acts as a point of reference for his task of forging the "modern prince" —the party, "...the first cell containing the germs of collective will which are striving to become universal and total". And he defines this will "...as working consciousness of historical necessity, as protagonist of a real and effective historical drama". Any attempt to give form to this collective will depends on the presence of urban groups located in the industrial production sector, with their historico-political culture and, in particular, on a simultaneous invasion of the nation's political arena by the peasant masses. Gramsci sums up the party's function as follows:

> The Modern Prince must and cannot but be the preacher and organizer of intellectual and moral reform, which means creating the basis for a later development of the national popular collective will towards the realization of a higher and total form of modern civilization. (136–39)

Gramsci's main criticism of the Sorelian notion of myth also fits in with his own theorization of the party. Gramsci believes Sorelian myth to be "abstract", which he interprets in connection with Sorel's "ethical" rejection of Jacobinism. He criticizes him for being unable to pass from his conception of myth to the understanding of the needs of the party and for having held onto the idea of the general strike (a "passive activity") as the maximum existing realization of the already existing collective will. For Gramsci, this belief leaves no room for the "active and constructive" stage in the creation of the collective will. Sorel's refusal to accept the revolutionary validity of any "pre-established" plan left him no alternative but to resort to the "irrational impulse" or the "spontaneous" response:

> In Sorel therefore two necessities were in conflict: that of the myth and that of criticism of the myth since "every pre-established plan is utopian and reactionary". The solution was left to irrational impulse, to "chance" (in the Bergsonian sense of "vital impulse") or to "spontaneity". (136–38)

The schematic reconstruction of the Gramscian conception of myth above serves a double purpose: on the one hand, it illustrates the process of resemanticization to which Sorel's notion is subjected when incorporated into Gramsci's discourse, in which it is informed with a historical character. On the other hand, it suggests as a possible parameter for the interpretation of Mariátegui some areas of contact between the historico-political circumstances of Gramsci and the Peruvian critic. Firstly, the fact that they were both engaged in the task of organizing the party and, secondly, that they shared a preoccupation with the national question in connection to the revolutionary project. An approach to the Mariateguian discourse on myth which bears in mind both this framework and the circumstances we have mentioned, should help us to clarify the historical meaning and transforming potential which myth also takes on in Mariátegui's work. Finally, both Gramsci and Mariátegui's interest in the articulation of political project, artistic project and popular imaginary, constitutes a third point of contact between the two thinkers, as demonstrated by Gramsci's reading of *The Prince* and Mariátegui's reading of *indigenista* literature: for Mariátegui, *indigenismo* is a movement which derives its historical meaning from its roots in the culture of the silenced majority in Peru those "...tres a cuatro milliones de hombres autóctonos [cuya presencia] en el panorama mental de un pueblo de cinco milliones no debe sorprender a nadie..." (1985, 333), and from its links with the forces which seek to transform society:

> Basta observar su coincidencia visible y su consanguinidad íntima con una corriente ideológica y social que recluta cada día más adhesiones en la juventud, para comprender que el indigenismo literario traduce un estado de ánimo, un estado de conciencia del Perú nuevo. (327–28)

Mariátegui stresses that the Indian's relevance to the arts does not simply arise from an "intellectual and theoretical" fact, but is the result of an "instinctive and biological phenomenon". The Indian is vindicated by "...las fuerzas nuevas y el impulso vital de la nación" (333). *Indigenista* literature is sustained by this social and cultural movement. Mariátegui's discourse highlights the elements of subjectivity, valuing their power to transform society and culture. This discourse is closely linked with his views on the creativity of the popular imagination and its importance for any artistic and revolutionary project —in short, on the importance of myth as the driving force of history and change— which we will discuss later on. Mariátegui's position does not involve a total rejection of critical reasoning —his work as an intellectual, as one of the most incisive analysts of the culture and society of his time, as well as the enterprise he engaged in with *Amauta*, are ample proof of this. His position is, rather, an expression of his belief in the need to retrieve the imagination, stifled by the cult of Reason, for art and politics.

Mariátegui compares *indigenismo* with "muzhik" literature in terms of its role in the trial and condemnation of feudalism and in its preparation of the terrain for the Russian Revolution, despite the fact that, "...al retratar al mujik...el poeta o el novelista ruso estuvieran muy lejos de pensar en la socialización" (328). "Los indigenistas... [stresses Mariátegui] ... colaboraron concientemente o no en una obra política y económica de reivindicación [de lo autóctono]" (332). This idea of literature's capacity to anticipate change recurs throughout Mariátegui's critical discourse: art is not restricted to representing that which already exists, but assumes the function of imagining new worlds.

We have already indicated how myth plays a key role in Mariátegui's critique of bourgeois rationalism and how it is the basis of his counter-hegemonic project. He believes that rationalism precipitated the crisis within the bourgeois order with its erosion of myth, of a "metaphysical conception of life": "La crisis de la civilización burguesa apareció evidente desde el instante en que esta civilización constató su carencia de un mito"

(1970b, 18–19). The crisis began with the aging of its "renaissance liberal myth" and its incapacity to inspire people now as it did in its time. "Nada más estéril que pretender reanimar un mito extinto." (21–22).

So although at first sight the language which Mariátegui uses to talk about myth might suggest a notion alien to the passage of history, it is, in fact, inextricably embedded in history. It develops historically and corresponds to a vision of the world produced in a particular period. In effect Mariátegui equates myth with, among other terms, "fé", "esperanza", and "una fuerza religiosa, mística, espiritual". And thus he defines socialism, the myth which replaces the defunct liberal myth, as a "religious, mystical, metaphysical" phenomenon:

> La emoción revolucionaria...es una emoción religiosa...[sólo que esos] motivos religiosos se han desplazado del cielo a la tierra. No son divinos; son humanos, son sociables [sic]. (18–22)

As we have said, the use of this language accords with Mariátegui's rejection of a rationalism characteristic of the social-democratic conception of the methods of political action and its subsequent incapacity to reach the masses and satisfy their emotional and metaphysical demands. All these terms go through a process of resemanticization when articulated to a clearly historical vision in Mariáteguian discourse: his revolutionary perspective transforms the religious imaginary into social imaginary and evokes the possibility of changing surrounding reality. The myth of revolution, the religion of "the new times" has no transhistorical validity (23). Every epoch has its "truth". Thus myths and truths are "relative" and never absolute, although they may be experienced as absolute in each stage of history. That is where their effectiveness lies, because "[el] hombre se resiste a seguir una verdad mientras no la cree absoluta y suprema" (21 and 23). As Mariátegui writes in "La lucha final":

> El mesiánico milenio no vendrá nunca. El hombre llega para partir de nuevo. No puede, sin embargo, prescindir de la creencia de que la nueva fórmula es la jornada definitiva. Ninguna revolución prevé la revolución que vendrá después, aunque en la entraña porte su germen...El proletario revolucionario...vive la realidad de una lucha final. La humanidad, entanto, desde un punto de vista abstracto, vive la ilusión de una lucha final. (24)

This very "relativity" of the experience of myth is what enables it to act as the driving force of history and innovation (25–26). In fact, myth in Mariátegui's work —whether he calls it religion, invention of the imagination or utopia— corresponds to a historical project and has a transforming nature. This is well illustrated by Mariátegui's description of the wars of Latin American independence, the myth of the Liberators:

> Los Libertadores fueron grandes porque fueron ante todo imaginativos. Insurgieron contra la realidad limitada, contra la realidad imperfecta de su tiempo. Trabajaron por crear una realidad nueva...La realidad sensible, la realidad evidente, en los tiempos de la revolución de independencia, no era, por cierto, republicana ni nacionalista. La benemerencia de los Libertadores consiste en haber visto una realidad potencial, una realidad superior, una realidad imaginaria. (37)

So the "imagination" for Mariátegui does not operate totally independently of historical circumstances —historical circumstances dictate the limits of the imagination:

> En todos los hombres, en los más geniales como en los más idiotas, [la imaginación] se encuentra condicionada por circunstancias de tiempo y espacio. El espíritu humano reacciona contra la realidad contingente. Pero precisamente cuando reacciona contra la realidad es cuando tal vez depende más de ella. Pugna por modificar lo que ve y lo que siente, no lo que ignora. Luego, sólo son válidas aquellas utopías que nacen de la entraña misma de la realidad. (38)

In conclusion, we should not lose sight of the fact that Mariátegui's reflections on myth constitute, as already stated, a quest for alternatives to a socialism conceived from a positivist perspective, a reshaping of the social democratic and bourgeois vision of politics and an endeavor to formulate a revolutionary strategy anchored in national reality.[14] Myth, which appeals not to reason but to "passion" and "will", is more capable of moving people to action and the construction of a new order:

> La burguesía niega, el proletariado afirma. La inteligencia burguesa se entretiene en una crítica racionalista del método, de la teoría, de la técnica de los revolucionarios. ¡Qué incomprensión! La fuerza de los revolucionarios no está en su ciencia; está en su fé, en su pasión, en su voluntad...Es la fuerza del Mito. (22)

Furthermore, and this is of enormous significance and interest to the current debate, myth is articulated to popular culture and its counter-hegemonic potential. Myth, writes Mariátegui, cannot be a product of reason, or of intelectuals, but is an invention of the people ("multitudes") who outstrip the intellectuals in the forging of a new order:

> Los profesionales de la Inteligencia no encontrarán el camino de la fé; lo encontrarán las multitudes. A los filósofos les tocará, más tarde, codificar el pensamiento que emerja de la gran gesta multitudinaria. (23)

---

[14] On the vacuum of reflections on the national question within Marxist tradition and the counterweight provided by Latin American thought, and particularly by Mariátegui, see especially Terán (1985, 83–85 and 99).

In "La lucha final", Mariátegui insists that the creative power of the "illiterate man" exceeds that of the intellectual, and that the former has a greater capacity to find "su camino" (27). And in Peru, the double project of social revolution and construction of the nation —that popular epic— would have, as has already been stressed, autochtonous roots. It would be articulated to indigenous culture whose outlook, with its traditional connection to the land, would coincide with socialist goals.

It would be fitting here to call attention to the proximity between Mariátegui's views on myth's functioning and social role, and those of Gramsci discussed earlier. There are parallels, for example, between the historico-political junctures to which both theorizations respond. In this connection, it is worth mentioning the similarities which Malcolm Sylvers notes in the two essayists' perspectives in his study of Gramsci's notion of "hegemony":

> Una notable anticipación del concepto gramsciano de "hegemonía" nos parece su observación de que para vencer una guerra moderna como la de 1914 era necesario despertar la conciencia popular y dar a los factores morales, psicológicos y políticos una importancia mayor que a los mismos factores militares. (1980, 39)

Sylvers' comments are based on Mariátegui's analysis of Italy's role in the war in "La intervención de Italia en la guerra" (1964a, 41–53). Although Sylvers does not make the connection explicit, Mariátegui's vision is contained in his very notion of myth. It acquires more clarity in the following extract, taken from the article "El hombre y el mito" which we have been analysing, in which Mariátegui highlights the value of myth and the strength of popular consciousness:

> ..la guerra probó, una vez más, fehaciente y trágica, el valor del mito. Los pueblos capaces de la victoria fueron los pueblos capaces de un mito multitudinario. (1970b, 19)

We will now explore the relationship between Mariátegui's theory of myth and his aesthetic conception. When Mariátegui speaks of "myth", he moves —as we have attempted to show— in a space in which the historical and the "irrational", subjectivity, the imagination and creativity are articulated. Myth operates as a passage which allows communication between artistic imagination and social imaginary, and popular culture. And that interaction is what gives art its transforming potential. As we have said, for Mariátegui, art goes beyond representation. He never ceases to emphasize the power of creative imagination for the forging of alternative realities. This is clear in his interpretation of *indigenismo*, discussed earlier, and also in his reading of the crisis of bourgeois society and aesthetics and the revolutionary role he assigns to art.

The decadence which Mariátegui detects in bourgeois civilization is also shared by bourgeois art. This decadence is confirmed by its "atomization" and "dissolution", in the loss of its "essential unity", and the consequent proliferation of schools that has come about due to the fact that now, "only centrifugal forces operate". But, although this crisis is an expression of the collapse of bourgeois culture, it is simultaneously the seed of a new art:

> Pero esta anarquía, en la cual muere, irreparablemente escindido y disgregado el espíritu del arte burgués, preludia y prepara un orden nuevo... En esta crisis se elaboran dispersamente los elementos del arte del porvenir. (1959, 19)

The various movements converge with their contributions to the proposal of a path of innovation —innovation which, as has been pointed out, cannot be based on technique alone, but "...en el repudio, en el desahucio, en la befa del absoluto burgués". That is where its "revolutionary meaning" lies.

The lack of myth experienced by bourgeois culture is also evident in bourgeois art. "La literatura de la decadencia es una literatura sin absoluto". Avant-garde art records the lack of myth and the need for it: "El artista que más exasperadamente escéptico y nihilista se confiesa es, generalmente, el que tiene, más desesperada necesidad de un mito" (19).

It is up to art to create new myths, new values, new principles, breaking with the defunct myths, values and principles which sustain the bourgeois order (21–22). Time and again, Mariátegui reiterates that the task of art, beyond mere representation, is to use the imagination to invent new aims. Moreover, the double process of rupture followed by the forging of new projects is directly related to Mariátegui's premise that the point of departure for a true aesthetic revolution is the break with the realist principle of bourgeois art. "Liberados de esta traba, los artistas pueden lanzarse a la conquista de nuevos horizontes", in search of new myths which can rescue art from the crisis: "La raíz de su mal [de la literatura moderna] no hay que buscarla en su exceso de ficción, sino en la falta de una gran ficción que pueda ser su mito y su estrella" (23–25). In works which predate the incorporation of the national dimension into his aesthetic reflections, Mariátegui already sketches out a connection between myth and popular culture —that source of creative imagination with counter-hegemonic potential and the power to subvert the rationalist foundations of the bourgeois order.[15] This connection between myth and popular

---

[15] It is suggested, for instance, in his article "Anatole France" (1964b, 166–67); here, Mariátegui reads the French author's position as one of transition between a decadent

culture, however, did not really form an essential part of the critical writings in which an international perspective dominated; it would only be incorporated into his aesthetic parameters in his analysis of the question of national literature, especially in "El proceso de la literatura". Here he elaborates his proposal of articulation between national literature and popular culture which is of unquestionable importance for current criticism. We will discuss this aspect of his discourse later.

Mariátegui's defense of fantasy and the imagination in art as the principal vehicle to erode old realism, corresponds to his conviction that realism is the best guarantee for a separation between art and reality:

> El viejo realismo nos alejaba en literatura de la realidad. La experiencia realista no nos ha servido sino para demostrarnos que sólo podemos encontrar la realidad por los caminos de la fantasía. (1959, 23)

On another occasion he writes that the retrieval for literature of "los fueros de la fantasía no puede servir, si para algo sirve, sino para restablecer los derechos o los valores de la realidad" (178–79). The absurd ("el disparate"), fiction, fantasy and the imagination, with their anti-rationalist function, constitute the instruments used by art, especially literature, for the demolition of the rationalist edifice which supports bourgeois aesthetics.

His note published in *Amauta,* entitled "Defensa del disparate puro", was written on the occasion of the publication of Martín Adán's poem "Gira", and summarizes the essence of both Mariátegui's aesthetic parameters and his vision of the revolutionary task and mechanisms of art. For this reason we feel justified in reproducing this text almost in its entirety:

> Martín Adán toca en estos versos el disparate puro que es, a nuestro parecer, una de las tres categorías sustantivas de la poesía contemporánea. El disparate puro certifica la defunción del absoluto burgués. Denuncia la quiebra de un espíritu, de una filosofía, más que de una técnica...En una época revolucionaria, romántica, artistas de estirpe y contextura clásicas como Martín Adán, no aciertan a conservarse dentro de la tradición. Y es que entonces fundamentalmente la tradición no existe sino como un inerte conjunto de módulos secos y muertos. La verdadera tradición está invisible, etéreamente en el trabajo de creación de un orden nuevo. El disparate tiene una función revolucionaria porque cierra y extrema un

civilization to which he declares himself to be opposed, and a new revolutionary era to which he cannot commit himself "spiritually", but only through an "intellectual act". For all his rejection of bourgeois society, says Mariátegui, France's work nevertheless draws on bourgeois aesthetic values, rather than those of popular culture.

proceso de disolución. No es un orden — ni el nuevo ni el viejo — pero sí es el desorden, proclamado como única posibilidad artística. Y...no puede sustraerse a cierto ascendiente de los términos, símbolos y conceptos del orden nuevo...una tendencia espontánea al orden aparece en medio de una estridente explosión de desorden. (1970a, 155)[16]

So the Mariateguian reading of the avant-garde interpretation of the crisis of values within bourgeois society involves a much more complex conception of the articulation between art and society than, for example, the notion of art as reflection in Lukacsian aesthetics.[17] The Lukacsian notion of reflection is incapable of interpreting the subversive dimension of avant-garde production, its anticipatory character, or its capacity for embarking on the search for alternative projects, which is exactly what Mariátegui's evaluation of the avant-garde consists of. Furthermore, Mariátegui's discourse is notably free of dogmatism and reductionism not only in its analysis but also in the placing of such diverse literary languages and quests, not just within the avant-gardes, but also outside them, as is the case with his reading of Peruvian *indigenismo*. His discourse is thus still relevant to Latin American criticism projects which have frequently encountered difficulties in the treatment of avant-garde literatures.

The national dimension of Mariátegui's aesthetic discourse would only be legitimized from a socialist point of view in his writings dating from 1925 onwards, in particular his article "Nacionalismo y vanguardia en la literatura y en el arte", originally published in *Mundial*, Lima, 4 December 1925.[18] In "Lo nacional y lo exótico" (October 1924), Mariátegui's view of nationalism within the discussion on Peruvian culture, was that it served the conservative idea and assisted in the rejection of modernization and social transformations. For Mariátegui, this nationalism was not only reactionary but also embodied an opportunistic attitude, since it only vetoed as foreign any progressive ideology, while unscrupulously appropri-

---

[16] A clarification: although Mariátegui (1985, 306) does not explain the other two "categorías sustantivas de la poesía contemporánea", perhaps a key to their understanding can be found in a paragraph in "El proceso" in which he says that, "...por comodidad de clasificación y crítica cabe... dividir la poesía de hoy [en tres categorías primarias:] lírica pura, disparate absoluto y épica revolucionaria...".

[17] Lukács (1977).

[18] This article constitutes the second part of the article "Nacionalismo y vanguardismo", initially published in 1925. Later Mariátegui was to combine both articles to produce "Nacionalismo y vanguardismo: en la ideología política, en la literatura y el arte." (1970a).

ating any other which instead strengthened its position. Finally, that nationalism distorted the notion of national reality in that it tried to deny its place within the Western sphere:

> El Perú contemporáneo se mueve dentro de la órbita de la civilización occidental. La mistificada realidad nacional no es sino un segmento, una parcela de la vasta realidad mundial.

The West provided the only cultural space which was left to Peru to construct its nationality, given the destruction of any autochtonous route by the Spanish Conquest (1970a, 25–26).

The retrieval for the left of the nationalist dimension opens up new thematic fields for Mariátegui and provides him with new axes from which to deal with the artistic phenomenon in its double articulation with Latin American and European socio-cultural space. In his article "Nacionalismo y vanguardismo...", he attempts to articulate, on the one hand, the political and intellectual avant-garde through the *indigenista* nationalism of the "new generation" (for Mariátegui all "authentic avant-gardism" would have "national meaning"), and, on the other hand, cosmopolitanism and nationalism in the literature of the Latin American avant-gardes (in his vision, the Argentinean and Peruvian avant-gardes would be informed as much by cosmopolitanism as by nationalism). Mariátegui thus proposes a radically different and much more complex reading of the nationalist phenomenon within the debate on Peruvian culture. The nationalism, of a conservative, colonialist and *pasatista* elite, tied to its Hispanist and —through Spain— Latinist roots, is discredited by Mariátegui for its lack of popular support and its denial of the traditions of the bulk of the population. Mariátegui sets up an opposition between this and an avant-garde nationalism which vindicates indigenous history and culture —the pillars for the construction of a legitimate Peruvian nationhood as a living patrimony "...de las cuatro quintas partes de la población del Perú" (72). The revolutionary strength of *indigenismo* would lie in its potential to construct a national movement which would offer an alternative to, "...las viejas tendencias [satisfechas con] representar los residuos espirituales y formales del pasado", which lack the power of invention and national content. "La nación [writes Mariátegui] vive en los precursores de su porvenir más que en los superéstites de su pasado" (76).

Moreover, far from presenting cosmopolitanism as in opposition to nationalism, Mariátegui unites them in a single Latin American avant-garde phenomenon which would act as an innovator of Peruvian and Latin American culture. He also finds a way into "lo nacional" through a cosmopolitanism which would be illustrated by both the Argentinean and Peruvian avant-gardes. Thus Mariátegui concludes,

...por estos caminos cosmopolitas y ecuménicos, que tanto se nos reprochan, nos vamos acercando cada vez más a nosotros mismos. (1970a, 79)

In fact Mariátegui confirms, rather than explains, this bridge between cosmopolitanism and nationalism in the Latin American avant-garde. Nevertheless, there are various ideas in the article we have been commenting upon which enable us to trace the key to that explanation. It must be found in the articulation between cosmopolitanism and popular culture which is never made explicit by Mariátegui. It must not be forgotten that Mariátegui justifies nationalism from a socialist perspective through his analysis of imperialism and the national independence movements in the colonial countries. For him, these movements always receive "...su impulso y su energía de la masa popular" (1970a, 74–75). The nationalism vindicated by Mariátegui is of a revolutionary and popular nature, legitimized as a progressive phenomenon by its popular character. On the artistic and literary level, Mariátegui is interested in an innovation which incorporates the culture of the majority of the population, popular culture, national culture. Those "...cosas del mundo y del terruño...", the popular, are precisely what would build a bridge between the cosmopolitan and the national (79). The national character of Latin American literature arises from the writer's capacity to appropriate popular culture without disowning his cosmopolitan education. Later we will look at how Mariátegui develops these concepts in "El proceso de la literatura" (1985).

Mariátegui's interest in the national element in no way implies the imposition of a single nationalist program articulated to *indigenismo* upon the literary and cultural production of Peru. On the contrary, as we have pointed out, if anything characterizes the Peruvian critic, it is his capacity to handle a plurality of languages and literary quests as can be seen in his writings which cover works as diverse as those of Eguren, Martín Adán and the *indigenistas*.[19] Furthermore, in his polemic with Luis Alberto Sánchez on the subject of *indigenismo*, Mariátegui clarifies that, far from being a program, *indigenismo* is, above all, an open debate, a part of the cultural innovation of Peru. And, he adds emphatically, rather than "imposing a criterion", he is interested in "contributing to its formation" (1980, 215). This attitude is in harmony with his efforts for the hegemonization of the innovative forces within both political and cultural spheres.

---

[19] On Eguren, see Mariátegui (1985, 293–303) and (1970a, 158–61). For writings on Martín Adán, see Mariátegui (1970a, 155), and on indigenismo (1985, 327–348 & 1980, 214–23). This article combines two parts, originally published in *Mundial*, Lima, Feb and Mar 1927; it constitutes a response to Luis Alberto Sánchez in the debate between the two critics on indigenismo.

We would be doing Mariátegui a disservice if we took "El proceso de la literatura" to be a paradigm and synthesis of his critical discourse, given that this does not display the critic's attention to the multiple forms of innovation found in the literature of his time. In order fully to appreciate Mariátegui's approach, one must look at the whole body of his work. In "El proceso", Mariátegui proposes a re-reading of the development of Peruvian literature which challenges the traditional and monolithically Hispanist vision of oligarchical discourse dominant, until that time, in Peruvian criticism —a paradigm of which is the work of Riva Agüero: "La generación de [éste ultimo habría realizado, en opinión de Mariátegui] la ultima tentativa para salvar a la Colonia" (1985, 349). Against this view he proposes, from a nationalist perspective and with a dualist conception of the cultural composition of Peruvian society, a literary process which seeks to give expression to the majority of the population, marginalized and silenced since the Conquest.[20] For Mariátegui, the study of national Peruvian literature cannot afford to ignore the intervention of the conquest, which implies in the first place the unresolved conflict between Andean and Spanish cultures.

> El dualismo quechua-español del Perú, no resuelto aún, hace de la literatura nacional un caso de excepción que no es posible estudiar con el método válido para las literaturas orgánicamente nacionales, nacidas y crecidas sin la intervención de una conquista. (1985, 236)

According to Antonio Cornejo Polar, one of his most eminent critics, this view constitutes a conceptual leap regarding the generalized quest on the part of Mariátegui's contemporaries for a unitary formula for literature and the national question. This unitary formula can be found in Riva Agüero's Hispanicism, the numerous proposals structured around the theory of *mestizaje*, Sanchez's attempt to incorporate pre-Hispanic literature and folkloric tradition into the Peruvian literary corpus, and even in More's aggressively *indigenista* proposal which holds that the national matrix is, and must continue to be, Quechua, even though historical development may have muddied its purity with Western elements (1982, 20 and 1980c, 50–51). Mariátegui, on the other hand, introduces an element of relativism to the principle of unity of Peruvian literature, revealing its "múltiple y conflictivo proceso". For him, the notion of cultural plurality in the composition of society is the basis of that literature and is itself the result of, "...la invasión y conquista del Perú autóctono por

---

[20] For an analysis of Mariátegui's racist reading of the other ethnic groups in Peru, such as the population of African origin, and Chinese immigrants, see Garrels (1982).

una raza extranjera que no ha conseguido fusionarse con la raza indígena, ni eliminarla, ni absorverla..." (1982, 23). This plurality would have its correlative in the "no orgánicamente nacional" character of Peruvian literature. Although, as Cornejo Polar reminds us, Mariátegui does not further develop this last premise, he nevertheless leaves some notes of crucial importance to criticism, such as his differentiation between indigenous and *indigenista* literature; most importantly, he opens the road "para comprender nuestra literatura sin mutilar su pluralidad" (1980c, 55). In fact, to a great extent Cornejo Polar's project itself uses these Mariateguian proposals as a point of departure. The heterogeneity of Peruvian literature and society constitutes a central axis of his critical discourse, as we shall see in the chapter dedicated to his work.

The unity so coveted by Mariátegui's contemporaries not only fails to materialize but, as Cornejo states, it actually comes to lose its legitimacy as an "objeto deseable".[21] Thus, stresses Cornejo, Mariátegui's promotion of the concept of plurality brings to a close "...todas las opciones que a nombre de una falsa unidad cercenaban el proceso y el corpus...[de la literatura peruana]". Cornejo describes the implications which the incorporation and development of Mariátegui's proposal has for Peruvian criticism in the following terms:

> ...la aceptación de la heterogénea multiplicidad de la literatura peruana implica, de una parte, la reivindicación del carácter nacional y del estatuto literario de todos los sistemas de literatura no erudita que se producen en el Perú; de otra, permite desenmascarar la ideología discriminadora, de base clasista y étnica, que obtiene la homogeneidad mediante la supresión de toda manifestación literaria que no pertenezca o no pueda ser asumida con comodidad por el grupo que norma lo que es o no es nacional y lo que es o no es literatura. (1982, 23–24 & 1980c, 55–56)

These projections of Mariateguian discourse are unquestionably useful, with the necessary adjustments, to the particular historico-cultural context of the various regions of the continent. Cornejo himself extends this

---

[21] Some clarification of Cornejo's interpretation is necessary here, since it appears to overlook the fact that the ideals of unity and integration are not alien to Mariátegui's perspective. Cornejo is correct in highlighting the category of plurality as a fundamental dimension of his interpretation of Peruvian society, culture and literature of the period. However, as a possibility projected to the future, that longed-for goal of unity is evident at various points in his writings: "El pasado...dispersa...los elementos de la nacionalidad, tan mal combinados, tan mal concertados todavía. El pasado nos enemista. Al porvenir le toca darnos unidad" (1970a, 24). "He constatado la dualidad nacida de la conquista para afirmar la necesidad histórica de resolverla. No es mi ideal el Perú colonial ni el Perú incaico sino el Perú integral..." (1980, 222).

perspective to the interpretation of literatures which express other kinds of heterogeneity, such as "las que surgen de la implantación del sistema esclavista, por ejemplo". He also proposes the *indigenismo* of the other Andean countries, and Mexico or Guatemala, as well as the "negrismo" of Central America and the Caribbean, gaucho literature and the poetics of "lo real marvilloso", as variations of the phenomenon of heterogeneity, since all of them constitute "literaturas situadas en el conflictivo cruce de dos sociedades y dos culturas" (1980b, 3–4).

Returning to Mariátegui's discourse, it is clear that against a literature without a nation and without popular content he seeks to set a literature which is capable of eradicating colonial thought and of acting as a foundation stone for a truly national literature. As Cornejo rightly points out, Mariátegui sees "...en Vallejo y los indigenistas de la época a los fundadores del período nacional...[de la literatura peruana]" (21). Mariátegui's critical endeavor is interwoven with a political one in that he is simultaneously proposing a social project as an alternative to the prevailing regime. *Indigenismo* —the consciousness of a "new Peru"— would, in fact, prepare the way for social revolution (1985, 327–28). Mariátegui evaluates Riva Agüero's Hispanicism as follows:

> Riva Agüero enjuició la literatura con evidente criterio "civilista". Su ensayo sobre "el carácter de la literatura del Perú independiente" está en todas sus partes, inequívocamente transido no sólo de conceptos políticos sino aun de sentimientos de casta. Es simultáneamente una pieza de historiografía literaria y de reivindicación política. El espíritu de casta de los encomenderos coloniales inspira sus escenciales proposiciones críticas que casi invariablemente se resuelven en españolismo, colonialismo, aristocratismo... (231–32)

Cornejo Polar adds that Riva Agüero and his followers' discourse, produced from a position of power by "una clase que también era una casta",

> expulsó de la nación y de la literatura nacional a todo componente que no fuera hispánico en su raíz, forma y espíritu! Lo indígena resultaba ser lo "exótico" — es decir: lo no nuestro — y su literatura — en el mejor de los casos — un quehacer primitivo sin rango estético y sin vínculo posible con la literatura nacional. (1982, 20 and 1980c, 51)

The strategy which governs the writing of Mariátegui's "El proceso" can partly be attributed to the need to break the conservative hegemony of national literary history, as well as to the political pressures acting on Mariátegui. In Cornejo Polar's accurate opinion, in "El proceso", Mariátegui is basically interested in "las relaciones de las clases sociales con el tipo de literatura que producen, con la crítica que generan sobre su propia literatura y sobre la que corresponde a otros estratos y con el modo como —literatura y crítica, productos obviamente ideológicos— se inscriben dentro de diversos y contradictorios proyectos sociales" (1980c, 52). This essay of Mariátegui's should be considered as just another aspect within the whole of his aesthetic reflections, rather than as the definitive text of his critical proposal. Without losing sight of this observation, we will now examine both his views on the relationship between the popular-national model and aesthetics, and his ideas on *indigenismo* and its place within the Peruvian literary process. From this perspective we should also look at the potential tension which could arise within his critical discourse, between, on the one hand, his thoughts on realism and, on the other, its role within the *indigenista* movement. This last theme, however, would never be developed by Mariátegui.

In his "process" to "national" literature and his unfavorable verdict, Mariátegui departs from the lucid premise that the mediocrity of Peruvian literature and its incapacity to endure is due to the absence of links to popular tradition and its insistence on remaining in the orbit of Spanish literature:

> Los pocos literatos vitales, en esta palúdica y clorótica teoría de cansinos y chafados retores, son los que de algún modo tradujeron al pueblo. La literatura peruana es una pesada e indigesta rapsodia de la literatura española, en todas las obras en que ignora al Perú viviente verdadero. (1985, 244–45)

Furthermore, this literature, disconnected from the people, would never have attempted to "...traducir el penoso trabajo de formación de un Perú integral, de un Perú nuevo. Entre el Inkario y la Colonia, [optaría] por la Colonia" (242). In fact, it is impossible to speak of national literature where the popular imagination has not intervened, since, for Mariátegui, this always precedes artistic imagination. Argentinean literature would testify to this —Mariátegui sees it as an example of a literature which is capable of absorbing all kinds of cosmopolitan influences without renouncing its national spirit (243–44).[22]

---

[22] This association between the national and the popular has already been noted by Cornejo in his analysis of the periodization of Peruvian literature proposed by Mariátegui in "El proceso". See Cornejo (1980c, 57–58 and 1983, 42). That analysis will be examined in the section of this study dedicated to Cornejo Polar, as it sheds light on an important aspect of his theoretical perspective. On Mariátegui's defence of *indigenismo*, his defence of Sarmiento and his incapacity to detect Sarmiento's anti-*indigenismo*, see Garrels (1976). Garrels critically analyzes Mariátegui's reading of the national project of Argentinian literature.

We have already seen that Mariátegui believes cosmopolitanism and nationalism to be compatible. He even states that *indigenismo* "...encuentra estímulo en la asimilación por [la literatura peruana] de elementos de cosmopolitismo" (1985, 329). Similarly, he sees no conflict between *indigenismo* and the avant-garde; he believes *indigenismo* to be a part of the avant-garde. Mariátegui does not conceive of one single route to innovation. We have looked at that other proposal which plays such an important role in his writings —the advocacy of the "disparate puro". Mariátegui does not intend *indigenismo* to monopolize the process of literary and cultural transformation in Peru. He describes in the following terms the place he assigns to *indigenismo* in the task of innovation within the Peruvian cultural field:

> El desarrollo de la corriente indigenista no amenaza ni paraliza el de otros elementos vitales de nuestra literatura. El "indigenismo" no aspira indudablemente a acaparar la escena literaria. No excluye ni estorba otras manifestaciones. Pero representa el color y la tendencia más característica de una época por su afinidad y coherencia con la orientación espiritual de las nuevas generaciones, condicionada, a su vez, por imperiosas necesidades de nuestro desarrollo económico y social. (334–35)

As we have stated, the Mariateguian reading of the *indigenista* project is ultimately the clearest illustration of his theory of myth and of the articulations not just between the political and cultural avant-gardes, but between art and the popular imaginary.

Mariátegui's reflections on *indigenismo* lay the foundations for the most important study of this subject produced within contemporary Peruvian criticism. As we shall see in the chapter dedicated to Antonio Cornejo Polar, his project develops the following Mariateguian proposals:

Firstly, Mariátegui departs from the recognition of the non-national character of Peruvian literature, and of its roots in the fracture and the unresolved conflict between the Andean and Spanish worlds brought on by the Conquest. Cornejo's vindication of autochtonous culture and his support for *indigenismo* as the first movement within Peruvian "erudite" literature to attempt an articulation to popular culture, is derived from this Mariateguian perspective. The defense of *indigenista* literature in "El proceso" includes a warning about the inevitable "...falta de autoctonismo integral o la presencia más o menos acusada en sus obras, de elementos de artificio en la interpretación y en la expresión...". It is clear to Mariátegui that *indigenismo* is "una literatura de mestizos" and, for this reason, "no puede darnos una versión verista del indio...[así como] no puede darnos su propia ánima". On the contrary, the external nature of *indigenista* literature regarding the Indian (the writer not being part of the referent) is an intrinsic characteristic of that literature: it can only "idealizar y estilizar [al indio]." Mariátegui points out that this external nature of *indigenismo* cannot, then, be used as a devaluing criterion from an aesthetic point of view. Mariátegui lucidly makes the distinction between indigenous and *indigenista* literature: "Por eso se llama una literatura indigenista y no indígena. Una literatura indígena, si debe venir, vendrá a su tiempo. Cuando los propios indios estén en grado de producirla" (335). It should be added, however, that this last statement is less accurate, since indigenous literature has evidently never ceased to be produced. However, his distinction between the two literatures and his legitimization of the external character of *indigenismo* would become extremely fruitful perspectives for Cornejo Polar's retrieval of *indigenismo* some decades later.

Mariátegui's responses to the question of an art and literature produced in a society of colonial origin, with the subsequent conflicts occasioned by its heterogeneous composition derived from the trauma of conquest and the violent imposition of one cultural formation over another, clear the way for an important part of Latin American criticism. These responses also merit examination with a view to offering alternatives to some of the theoretical and methodological problems faced by the projects towards an autonomous Latin American criticism, problems which will be discussed in the following chapters of this study. One of these problems is the conflictive articulation between aesthetics and cultural nationalism, with the risk of oversimplification and polarization in the interpretation of the literary phenomenon and its traditions, which Mariátegui seems capable of avoiding. Mariátegui refuses to simplify the concept of national identity, or to stigmatize cosmopolitanism and set one aganist the other as two antagonistic or mutually exclusive categories. This undoubtedly produces a much more complex and subtle discourse on the plurality of the aesthetic quests in the Latin American literary corpus than some of the views which have dominated nationalist criticism in recent decades. Amongst them is the insistence upon classifying the literary corpus of the continent around two axes, one "national" —which the said criticism legitimizes— and the other "cosmopolitan" —which it either stigmatizes or finds itself unable to interpret. Contemporary Latin American criticism has much to gain from the Mariateguian perception of the multiple connections between the cosmopolitan components of Peruvian, and even Latin American, culture and its national elements. His subtle project of articulation of artistic and social imagination is another fertile area, as are his views on the creative and prefigurative capacity of art, as opposed to its simply serving to represent or reproduce social reality.

CHAPTER 2
ANGEL RAMA: LITERATURE, MODERNIZATION AND RESISTANCE

The work of the Uruguayan critic Angel Rama is a cornerstone of the innovation which has taken place within contemporary literary criticism in Latin America. During the years in which he was in charge of the literary section of the weekly paper *Marcha* (1959–1968), one of the continent's most progressive and influential publications at that time, he was already filling an important theoretical vacuum within the discipline by promoting a socio-historical perspective for the approach to Latin American reality and the artistic and literary production of the continent. The significance of this contribution could be overlooked if one fails to take into account the fact that this offers an alternative to a discipline hegemonized up to that point by the immanent methodology of Stylistics, which had proved incapable of accounting for any literature that incorporated a dimension of social and political commitment (Portuondo 1975, 45).

As with much of the intellectual left of the time, and in accordance with the libertarian, anti-imperialist and Latin Americanist sentiment radiated by the Cuban Revolution, Rama's work, marked by a clear commitment with regard to cultural matters, was centered on the question of Latin American societies' dependency and their subordination to foreign development models, and on the consequences resulting from these circumstances in the cultural sphere. Several issues were to form the core of Rama's discourse: the exploration of the problem of Latin American cultural identity, the tracing of the diverse quests for autonomy on which Latin American literature was to embark following Independence, and the formulae of resistance to domination proposed by literature. In this context, transcultural narrative was to constitute the prime expression of the Latin American emancipatory tradition.

The term "transculturation", taken from the Cuban Fernando Ortiz, challenges the concept of "acculturation". The latter term describes the behavior of the dominated party as passively receiving the culture imposed by the dominant party upon cultural contact, while the term transculturation stresses the active and creative role of the dominated culture in the processes of appropriation of discourses. This highlights the dominated culture's capacity for resistance and tenacity in preserving and reworking its identity (Rama 1987, 32–35).

Furthermore, the object of his studies transcended national borders and assumed a continent-wide dimension, thus reshaping the compartmentalized vision which had characterized literary history and criticism in Latin America up until then. In Rama's view, national division of the continental literary process not only distorts the reality of its development and functioning, but is also illegitimate in that it overlooks the fact that, in the majority of Latin American countries, nationality was no more than the unfinished enterprise of the Liberal project. In place of the arbitrary fragmentation of the continent into "national" constructs which do not correspond to its cultural configuration and which originate in a history of colonial and neo-colonial domination, Rama offers the category "Latin America", with a view to the reformulation of the cultural and literary systems of the region. This Latin Americanist vision involves a proposal for continental integration which is not only articulated in Rama's critical work, but also manifests itself in his work as cultural promoter and disseminator. The "Biblioteca Ayacucho", of which Rama was director from its foundation in 1974 and the journal *Escritura*, which he founded in 1976 and co-directed with Rafael Di Prisco until his death in 1983, are both cited by Rama as playing an important part in the realization of that project of integration.[1]

Rama's aim is to increase understanding of the Latin American continent and to approach its literature in a manner which goes beyond the simple handling of the most prominent texts and figures of the various regions; his objective is the broad outlining of literary movements and projects, thus allowing both the recomposition and re-evaluation of the continent's literary corpus and a grater awareness of the historical and cultural processes which give it meaning. According to Rama, the purpose of criticism is not only the constitution of a literature —the construction of an organic system of literary works— but must also be the restoration of the ties between literary works and the culture of which they are an expression.

His research, particularly from the 1970s on, focused upon the specificity of the Latin American context, and at the same time discarded

---

[1] The "Biblioteca Ayacucho" project constitutes the most important collection of Latin American classics currently in existence. For a synthesis of the principles that serve as the basis of this project, see Rama (1981). These criteria would govern the selection of the texts while Rama acted as literary director until his death. The journal *Escritura*, specializing in literary theory and criticism, was conceived initially by Rama as a means to fill a vacuum within the Venezuelan cultural sphere; it was also an expression of his Latin Americanist conception, as it attempted to break with the traditional lack of intellectual communication between the different regions of the continent (Interview with Rafael Di Prisco, Caracas, 21 February 1992).

homogeneous and elitist visions of the literary production of the continent. Rama questions the supposed universal validity of metropolitan theoretical and methodological models and the tendency within the discipline mechanically to transpose them, ignoring the fact that, in reality, those models were shaped in other contexts and around literatures whose development is alien to that of Latin American writing. Rama pursues the formulation of parameters which, derived from Latin American literary production, allow its peculiarities to be explored and restore its historical/cultural articulations. The Uruguayan critic thus stresses the need for a treatment which combines a class reading with a culturalist perspective (n.d. and 1968). Rama's proposed methodology consists of the observation of two "axes": a "horizontal" axis which corresponds to the various cultural regions of the continent and a "vertical" axis which gives account of the socio-cultural variants within those regions (1975a, 1976c, 1984a, 1987). Rama is interested in discussing the "density" of literature, in other words, the plurality and multiplicity of its socio-cultural articulations. For Rama, "la complejidad de la estructura social y cultural" in Latin America is, moreover, an indication of the resistance that the structure puts up to "...la homogenización que el sistema económico y sus instrumentos de comunicación, procuran" (1976c, 63). Amongst the central functions which Rama assigns to his critical practice are, firstly, his emphasis on a redesigning of the region's literary corpus and its de-elitisization through the recognition of the contributions of popular culture, in particular that of peasant culture; and, secondly, his search for foci of resistance and alternative projects to the modernizing model within the Latin American literary process, above all where that literary process is connected to popular culture.

With the exception of the two articles referred to above, "Sistema literario y sistema social en Hispanoamérica" and "Literatura y clase social", Rama does not theoretically isolate or systematize his critical theory. In general, his theoretical framework must be deduced from his analyses of concrete literary works and movements, pre-eminently his writings on Gaucho poetry, Venezuelan narrative, the two avant-gardes or the two routes of innovation proposed by Latin American letters, his reconsideration of the literature of the "boom" period, his analysis of the dictatorship novel, his incisive interpretation of Darío and *Modernismo* in the light of the modernizing process experienced by Latin American societies at the time and, finally, his writings on Arguedas' work and transcultural narrative (1976a, 1976b, 1982a, 1984d, 1985a, 1985c, 1987). These works constitute Rama's attempt to provide a foundation for a social history of Latin American literature.

Towards the end of his work, Rama began a new line of research, albeit still within his general scheme of clarification of the specificity of Latin American historical and cultural development; the results of that research were set down in his last book, *La Ciudad Letrada* (1984b). This dealt with the role played by the city and the intellectual in the cultural shaping of Latin American societies from the colonial period up until the beginning of this century. The Latin American city, in contrast to the European city –writes Rama— did not emerge as a consequence of the demands imposed by agricultural development; on the contrary, the city implanted itself as a center of control and domination over the conquered agrarian sphere, and determined not only the historical development of Latin America, but also, to a certain extent, the ideology and elitist behavior of its intellectuals, distanced as they were from popular culture and popular language. In short, the city leaves its mark in the separation between "high" and popular production, between writing and orality —a situation which was to remain unmodified following Independence and throughout the nineteenth century, and which would only begin to alter immediately after the transformations introduced by the revolutions which took place at the beginning of the twentieth century. This work raises questions for Latin American cultural criticism which are still absolutely relevant today.

Rama's writings lie at the root of the movement towards the construction of an autonomous Latin American criticism liberated from the weight of ethnocentric schemes which had gained momentum in the continent during the 1970s. Of the various paths explored by the Uruguayan, his discourse on narrative transculturation stands out as one of the most fruitful contributions to the said project. His transculturation theory, making use of anthropological approaches, redraws the Latin American cultural map, emphasizing its multiplicity and density and promoting a retrieval of literatures articulated to regional and peasant cultures. These had up until this point, been ignored by dominant critical models; Rama was now to claim them for the corpus of modern Latin American writing. Furthermore, his retrieval of Arguedas' narrative for Latin American avant-garde literature opens the way for an overall reconsideration of the counter-hegemonic potential of literatures grounded in traditional cultures which offer alternative forms of innovation —specifically Latin American alternatives— as is the case with the work of Gabriel García Márquez, Juan Rulfo, Augusto Roa Bastos or the Brazilian João Guimarães Rosa.

Angel Rama's writing on transculturation has given criticism a new perspective on, and a re-evaluation of, rural popular cultures, wresting them from the fossilized precincts of the "folkloric" to which they had been relegated until then, in order to articulate them to modernity, uncovering their creativity and proven capacity for resistance to the dictates of hegemonic discourses. Rama's interpretation of the appropriation of the cosmovisions of popular regional cultures by the aforementioned transcultural authors constitutes, in fact, a novel and revolutionary contribution to the discipline. This new critical strategy, explains the Uruguayan critic, "se situa en el plano artístico para desentrañar cuál es la aportación estética que se alcanza por [la] vía [de la transculturación], cuál es su originalidad y cuál es la especificidad latinoamericana que se trasunta en estas operaciones". The contribution made by the transcultural authors to the search of artistic and cultural autonomy in Latin America is summed up by Rama himself in the following terms:

> Porque de estas obras podría decirse que se instalan en la intrarrealidad latinoamericana, cumplen un ingente abarcamiento de elementos contrarios cuyas energías buscan canalizar armónicamente, rescatan pasado y apuestan a un futuro que acelere la expansión de la nueva cultura, auténtica e integradora. Son por lo tanto obras que nos develan el orbe original de la cultura latinoamericana en una nueva etapa de su evolución. (1982a, 229)

Furthermore, although Rama always discusses the concept of transculturation in the context of the modernization of Latin American societies, it is possible to project that notion onto all literature produced at a point of conflictive intersection between two cultures. The transcultural perspective opens the way both for a re-reading of Latin American history and literature, from the earliest works of colonial writing onwards, and for the understanding of the counter-hegemonic processes which may have been generated by that literature.

The object of this chapter is to examine Angel Rama's discourse on transculturation, a discourse which undoubtedly constitutes one of the most fruitful contributions to the debate on Latin American culture. Nevertheless, the acknowledgment of its significance with regard to the advance of the discipline does not prevent the recognition of the theoretical and methodological problems which underlie this critical proposal. Most of these problems are connected to some of the dominant perspectives within the intellectual production of the left at that time, and in particular within historical/cultural criticism where it touches on the relationships between nationalism and culture and between art, politics and ideology; in fact they are also present, to various degrees, in the work of Alejandro Losada and Antonio Cornejo Polar, who are discussed elsewhere in this book. These problems deserve to be analyzed, with a view to looking for alternatives. In this sense, the writings that Beatriz Sarlo dedicated to the analysis of the modernization of the Argentinean cultural field, and to the questioning of cultural nationalism and the subordination of aesthetics to politics and ideology within her country, provide an invaluable contribution to Latin American criticism. These writings, which will be discussed in the last chapter, shed light on processes which transcend Argentinean borders and which were experienced by the majority of intellectuals of the continent from the 1970s onwards.[2]

From National Criticism to Latin American Criticism

Little has been written about the process of Latin Americanization which continental criticism has undergone in the last few decades, or about the various levels on which this operates, and even less has been written on the significance of Angel Rama's work within that process.[3] Perhaps the first thing that occurs to us when we think of the Latin Americanization of criticism is the extension of the subject matter and corpus beyond "national" confines within which criticism had traditionally developed. In fact, this is one of the most important and pioneering contributions with which Rama is credited (Losada 1985, 45).

No less important to the Latin Americanization of criticism is the formulation of an autonomous perspective for the treatment of the literary phenomenon which takes account of its historical and cultural specificity. Rama dedicated the most important part of his work to this objective. Our intention is to sketch a map of the principal paths of inquiry followed by the Uruguayan, in an attempt to define and analyze the various discourses to which this inquiry is articulated and the implications which these articulations have for his project.

We shall briefly examine some of the interpretations that have been offered of Rama's Latin Americanism, firstly, the Chilean critic Nelson Osorio's interpretation, in which he links Rama's ideas with both the anti-imperialist discourse of the Cuban Revolution —and its effect on Latin American intellectuals of the 1970s— and the integrationist tradition stemming from Bolívar:

> Como se puede apreciar, en el proyecto y la tarea cumplida por Angel Rama vemos conjugarse dos vertientes. Por una parte, en la crisis de la conciencia intelectual de América que se produce en los años 60 a partir

---

[2] Principally her book *Una modernidad periférica: Buenos Aires 1920 y 1930* (1988), but also her articles published in *Punto de Vista* between 1983 and 1989.

[3] For literature written on Angel Rama's work in general, see especially: Candido (1993), Franco (1984), Leenhardt (1993), Losada (1985), A. Martínez (1983), T. E. Martínez (1985), Moraña (1997), Osorio (1985), Pizarro (1993), Prego (1984), Ruffinelli (1983) and Sosnowski (1985).

de la Revolución Cubana, el marxismo —filtrado o no por Sartre, pero indudablemente vinculado a él— fortalece teóricamente una búsqueda renovadora, antimperialista y antiburguesa. Y ésta se fertiliza en la tradición integradora, continentalista, cuyas raíces se encuentran en Bolívar y se proyecta al estudio de la producción literaria latinoamericana. (Osorio 1985, 158)[4]

As part of this integrationist tradition and as an antecedent to Rama's autonomous Latin American criticism project, Osorio quotes Pedro Henriquez Ureña in the same article (57). This is certainly not the only point of contact between the two critics. Rama is interested in many other aspects of Pedro Henriquez Ureña's work and incorporates them into his discourse; these aspects include his Latin Americanist thought, his reading of the quest for autonomy upon which Latin American letters had embarked following Independence, and his reflections on the culture of the continent.[5] Although we do not propose to go into this matter here, we would like to take this opportunity to make a methodological observation about Osorio's statement; he appeals to the mere existence of intellectual traditions to legitimize a project, in this case that of the Latin Americanization of critical discourse; we consider this useful to note, because this process leads to homogenizing and ahistorical perceptions of cultural manifestations. For the understanding of those cultural manifestations, it would surely be more useful firstly to ascertain the historical reasons which accounted for the motives of the "discovery" or interest in discourses and projects of the past. Secondly, one should establish both the new directions which those discourses and projects take upon being appropriated and rearticulated from a necessarily different juncture, and also the contradictions which can result from that process. Moreover, becoming aware of such reformulations can help us to clarify the circumstances leading to the appropriation itself.[6] The Latin Americanization project in Rama's work is, in fact, much more complex and conflictive than Osorio would have wished; for now, we will just state that the

---

[4] Losada (1985, 52) considers events such as the Cuban Revolution, the Peruvian Revolution and the dictatorships of the Southern Cone countries in the 1970s to be the source of the political and cultural Latin Americanization of the River Plate intellectuals and Rama in particular.

[5] See especially Henríquez Ureña (1960).

[6] Taking a similar approach to that of Osorio, A. Martínez (1983, 8) places Rama within the culturalist tradition of Latin American criticism; his confirmation of the existence of that tradition is virtually presented as the ultimate legitimization of the project in question. Apart from this, the article sheds little light on the said tradition.

attempt to fuse an intellectual project —that of a continent-wide criticism which transcends national frontiers— with the political project of continental integration raises various problems which will be discussed later on.

Alejandro Losada interprets this dimension of Rama's work in another way. Losada sees Latin Americanization operating on two levels; on the one hand, the object of research; and on the other, the interpretive perspective that seeks to read works from within a cultural context. Thus, Rama's works,

> ...significan la constitución progresiva de un nuevo *OBJETO* de investigación —la literatura contemporánea elaborada como un conjunto *latinoamericano*—; y sus interpretaciones parten de la observación de un nuevo *CAMPO* de relaciones —el desarrollo literario de la región, la práctica cultural de los intelectuales y la identidad histórica de la sociedad global. (1985, 46)

Nevertheless, Losada expresses some reservations over Rama's modernizing criterion that governs the construction of both the subject and the corpus of Latin American literature and which Losada seems to believe would have led Rama to ignore all that literature which did not fit within the new canons. In fact, Losada attributes this criterion not just to Rama, but to much literary criticism of the time in which the opposition between the modern and the traditional was to dominate as the central issue within the analysis of Latin American literature, and in which modernization was the aspiration. In Losada's view this implied opting for "UNA [in capitals in the original] determinada literatura internacionalizada que provenía de la América Latina", in detriment to the literature which, up until then, had been labeled "regionalist" and which had to be discarded (56).

In order to appreciate the intellectual atmosphere of the time, it is useful to note the connection drawn by Losada between the commitment among Latin American intellectuals of the 1960s, including progressive intellectuals, to material and cultural modernization and, "...la expectativa que despertó [sic] el desarrollismo norteamericano y los programas de la Alianza para el Progreso..."; la"...'modernización' significaba [así para aquellos] liquidación crítica de los valores culturales tradicionales y compromiso con el desarrollo social latinoamericano" (50–52). Pedro Morandé also testifies to this pro-modernization current within the intellectual sphere at the time: "La sociología luchaba por la posibilidad de elegir entre alternativas distintas de modernización, pero no puso en tela de juicio a la modernización como tal... Algunos querían desarrollarse hacia un 'capitalismo a la latinoamericana' otros hacía un 'socialismo a la latinoamericana', donde lo importante no era, naturalmente, el adjetivo sino el sustantivo" (Morandé 1987, 11–12).[7]

Nevertheless, Losada's interpretation of Rama overlooks Rama's project to clarify the specific processes of Latin American cultural modernization, and to re-evaluate the traditional in order to retrieve it for modernity; his discourse is, in fact, a response to those who endorse a modernization which ignores the traditional Latin American cultures. This leads on to Rama's discourse on "the two avant-gardes" which questions the homogenizing character of the concept of the avant-garde maintained by the modernizing parameters that formed the basis of criticism up to the beginning of the 1970s:

> En un ensayo, escrito a comienzos de los años setenta, llamé la atención sobre los perjuicios que para la recta apreciación de la cultura latinoamericana entrañaba la simplificación del concepto de vanguardia que venía manejando la crítica, la cual lo establece exclusivamente en oposición a las corrientes tradicionales o regionalistas. Si así se conseguía conferirle claridad y rotundidad, fijando una oposición tajante blanco / negro, pagaba estas ventajas con un empobrecimiento de la visión del vanguardismo, cuya pluralidad de caminos era borrada, unificándolos bajo su común denominador: *modernización*. (1982a, 338; emphasized in the original)

Although Losada is correct in affirming that Rama was only interested in the movements of innovation of our literature, and, more precisely, in our narrative, Losada is not correct in affirming that the Uruguayan critic excludes *all* literature connected with traditional cultures. In fact, he recognizes currents within that literature —for example the case of transcultural narrative, which at one point he referred to as "new regionalism" (1987, 96)— which incorporate processes of innovation, calling upon both elements originating from internationalized modern culture and "archaic" elements which indeed originate from traditional cultures (1982a, 333). Having made these clarifications, it must also be said that, in reality, Losada's and Rama's view of Latin American literary production is not as far apart as Losada would have it: in fact, they both classify the literatures of the region in two opposing paradigms —"cosmopolitan" or "internationalized" literatures on the one hand, and literatures articulated to regional cultures on the other.

The idea of the two avant-gardes, Rama contends, summing up the hypothesis he offered in the article mentioned,

---

[7] On the new approaches of Latin American social sciences and on the emergence of sociology of culture in the region and its contributions to Latin American cultural studies, see García Canclini (1991, 41-48).

> ...nos permitiría una más precisa visualización de las diferencias existentes entre las áreas culturales latinoamericanas, pero sobre todo patentizaría la existencia de dos diálogos culturales simultáneos que se tramaban entre términos distintos: uno, interno, religaba zonas desequilibradas de la cultura del continente, pretendiendo alcanzar su modernización sin pérdida de los factores constitutivos tradicionales, por lo cual procuraba enlazar términos tan dispares como Trujillo-Lima-el mundo; y otro, externo, establecía una comunicación directa con los centros exteriores de donde manaban las pulsiones transformadores a partir de puntos latinoamericanos ya modernizados, lo que se traducía en el enlace Santiago de Chile-Paris-el mundo. (339)[8]

Rama's retrieval of this second avant-garde undoubtedly constituted at the time an enriching contribution to Latin American criticism and urgently called attention to the tendency acritically to celebrate modernization and to regard it as the exclusive parameter for aesthetic evaluation. Nevertheless, it is also true that this bi-polar interpretation would introduce problems insofar as each pole supposedly expressed different concepts of national identity, but we will leave this discussion for the next section of this chapter.

Before going any further, there is one other note to be made on Losada's interpretation of the role of modernization in Rama's writings. Although modernization is at the core of his work, it would be wrong to consider it as having been unmodified throughout; on the contrary, the notion of modernization is reformulated around the various nationalist discourses which are articulated in Rama's work, and which we shall examine later. Essentially, Losada's interpretation has more to do with the Rama of the 1960s than with the Rama who wrote on narrative transculturation in the following decade.

Returning to Rama's Latin Americanism, we note that, for him, criticism must have recourse to a double perspective that combines a continental focus with a regional one, in order to account for, "...esas dos fuerzas, [unidad y diversidad] esos dos polos, [que] actúan permanentemente en nuestra cultura..." (1985b, 85).[9] For Rama, the history of Latin American society and culture is in effect marked by this unresolved tension between unifying processes and diversifying processes:

> La unidad de América Latina ha sido y sigue siendo un proyecto del equipo intelectual propio, reconocida por un consenso internacional. Está

---

[8] For the essay the critic refers to, see Rama (1973).

[9] The terms unity and diversity refer to José Luis Martínez's well-known book, *Unidad y diversidad en la literatura latinoamericana* (1972).

fundada en persuasivas razones y cuenta a su favor con reales y poderosas fuerzas unificadoras. La mayoría de ellas radican en el pasado, habiendo modelado hondamente la vida de los pueblos: van desde una historia común a una común lengua y a similares modelos de comportamiento. Las otras son contemporáneas y compensan su minoría con una alta potencialidad: responden a las pulsiones económicas y políticas universales que acarrean la expansión de las civilizaciones dominantes del planeta. Por debajo de esa unidad, real en cuanto proyecto, real en cuanto a base de sustentación, se despliega una interior diversidad que es definición más precisa del continente. (1987, 57)

With respect to this project of unification which Latin American intellectuals had pursued, Rama refers to the lack of communication with Latin America, a situation which prevailed during the Colonial period and was only to see hesitant, incipient changes at the end of the nineteenth century; it was then that the first integration movements of our cultural production began to be attempted through the circulation of authors and works. That movement towards integration constituted an evolutionary process which was to continue throughout the twentieth century and was either driven from "centros de religación externa" such as Paris, New York or London —principally as a consequence of emigration and exile— or from "centros de religación interna", for example Mexico and Cuba, as a result of their revolutions. These revolutions, Rama stresses, "...agitaron, conmovieron el imaginario de los intelectuales y efectivamente entonces...[condujeron a la producción de] vinculaciones y relaciones" (1985b, 86).[10] But this search for unity, Rama insists, takes place within a context of cultural fragmentation. Rama rejects the vision of Latin America as a "block". In fact, he states that, "...la realidad es más compleja, la realidad es de más plurales centros, de áreas diferenciales, algunas asociadas entre sí" (86–87).

The various national formations of the continent testify to that diversity, as do, to an even greater degree, the different "regional cultures" within them which often challenge their supposed "national unity" and political borders; thus Rama's interpretation recomposes the Latin American map. "Este segundo mapa latinoamericano es más verdadero que el oficial cuyas fronteras fueron, en el mejor de los casos, determinadas por las viejas divisiones administrativas de la Colonia y, en una cantidad no menor, por los azares de la vida política, nacional o internacional" (1987, 57–58). Based on a point of view which is both anthropological and linguistic, Rama proposes the following division by cultural zones in his article,

---

[10] See also (1985b, 85 and 90).

"Medio siglo de narrativa latinoamericana (1922-1972)": "...zona rioplatense y chilena, zona andina, zona Caribe, zona del nordeste de Brasil, y centro o sur de Brasil, zona de México y, finalmente, zona de Mesoamérica" (1982a, 144).

The acknowledgment of the cultural plurality of Latin America supports his reflections on the literature of the continent and allows that literature to be understood in terms of its articulations to the diverse cultural systems; in this way, in proposing multiple literary processes, Rama challenges the unitary vision which had, until then, dominated the discipline. It is on the basis of this new conception of Latin American reality that Rama re-reads José María Arguedas' narrative; his theoretical and methodological proposal dealing with narrative transculturation is a result of his research into a specific region —the Andean area. This proposal is, in fact, applicable to various other regions of the continent in which traditional cultures coexist with modernized social spheres. His writings on García Márquez and Roa Bastos, for example, were to follow on from here.

In his book on narrative transculturation, Rama stresses the persistence of the character particular to the regional cultures, despite the homogenizing pressures introduced by the advance of modernization. In fact, through transcultural operations these local cultures resist that advance, preserving their particularity. Furthermore, writes Rama, neither the historical circumstances, nor the aspects that the numerous Latin American regional cultures have in common with each other and, indeed, also share with other Third World areas,

> ...[permiten] disolver un componente irreductible que pertenece a los orígines étnicos, a la lengua, a las tradiciones, a las circunstancias siempre propias y originales de su desenvolvimiento...podemos encontrar similares operaciones literarias y ejercicios comunes de un cierto imaginario popular afín, pero jamás podríamos equipararlas estrictamente. Lo original de cualquier cultura es su misma originalidad, la imposibilidad de reducirla a otra, por más fundamentos comunes que compartan. (1987, 97)

His discourse on transculturation, one of his greatest critical contributions to Western theories of culture, constitutes a model for multicultural counter-hegemonic interpretation; with his recomposition of the Latin American "map", mentioned above, which displays the diversity of regional cultural formations which transcend state borders, he reveals the failure of the Liberal project, both in its initial attempts to draw up proposals for national cultures, and in its efforts towards integration through the modernizing process. This new cultural map reveals the transculturation processes by which Latin America has tenaciously opposed domination and the imposition of homogenizing cultural models. Through these processes it also proposes alternative routes to modernization which are underpinned by formulas of regional identity:

> ...las regiones se expresan y afirman, a pesar del avance unificador...hay, un fortalecimiento de las...culturas interiores del continente, no en la medida en que se atrincheran rígidamente en sus tradiciones, sino en la medida en que se transculturan sin renunciar al alma, como habría dicho Arguedas. Al hacerlo robustecen las culturas nacionales (y por ende el proyecto de una cultura latinoamericana) prestándoles materiales y energías para no ceder simplemente al impacto modernizador externo en un ejemplo de extrema vulnerabilidad. La modernidad no es renunciable y negarse a ella es suicida; lo es también renunciar a sí mismo para aceptarla. (71)

For Rama, transcultural narrative embodies that sought-after formula for autonomous literature that grounds his discourse in a "national identity" which is itself based upon traditional popular cultures, a formula which nevertheless incorporates a modernizing perspective. Transculturation is an alternative modernizing model inasmuch as it does not evade the challenge of the Liberal hegemonic project; on the contrary; it proposes the "national" formula, resisting the aggressive universalist formula of Western culture. As Rama states, in reference to Arguedas, transcultural narrative seeks to "...insertarse en la cultura dominante [para] imponer en tierra enemiga su cosmovisión y su protesta..." (207).

However, Rama's concept of "national culture", explained in the passage quoted above, introduces certain problems. As we have said, the transcultural project points towards the redefinition of Latin American culture on the basis of regions, which represent the reality of the continent with more accuracy than political borders and which testify to the resistance to the homogenizing pressures of the dominant model. In this sense, the concept of "the nation" is identified with the region and, as a cultural entity, invalidates that proposed by the dominant elites of the Latin American Liberal states. Rama paradoxically states, nevertheless, that the strengthening of the region has as a logical consequence the strengthening of the "national" culture.[11] But which national culture is he referring to? To the state's own view of what the nation consists of? The prolongation of this chain of "causality" is equally paradoxical: the region is supposedly

---

[11] In fact, as will become clear, "lo nacional" in Rama refers to the production of contestatory local identities (be they regional, national or continental), which are distinct from the construction of "lo latinoamericano" as part of phenomena which are either internationalized or of universal nature.

the key to making the integration of Latin American culture finally possible! This line of reasoning is curious to say the least, when, in effect, it involves irreducible cultural projects, while the idea of a "national" culture, and of a Latin American culture, involves an intention to integrate, and integration occurs at the expense of plurality, even if carried out with the region as starting point. In fact, Rama never manages to break with the idea of unity itself; thus his ideal is that of an alternative formula for unification to that of the Liberal model, resting in:

> ...la superior potencia integradora que caracteriza a la cultura regional, incomparablemente más fuerte que la que puede vincular a las diversas clases de una cultura urbana, por lo mismo que tiene un desarrollo histórico que puede remontarse a siglos y se ejerce sobre comunidades de muy escasa movilidad social, donde los patrones de comportamientos han sido internalizados, convalidados y aceptados, de padres a hijos, durante generaciones. (66–67)

Rama does not tackle this problem, however. The use of this "integratory potential" would imply the reduction of the diverse coexisting cultures, firstly within each national space, and, secondly, within the continent. If the legitimacy of the reclaiming of regional popular cultures is indisputable, their imposition as a new hegemonic model is less so. Nor is it clear which regional unit would serve as the basis for this integration; this integration questions certain hierarchical views, but ultimately it does not challenge them; the multi-cultural map, on the other hand, offers the possibility of erasing them altogether.

The problems identified in Rama's "national" project are, in part, explained through the confluence of different discourses and the difficulty of conciliating them. On the one hand, even if his regional model demythifies the liberal national model, it assumes the task of "completing" what that very liberal project did not complete; in fact, as Jorge Castañeda points out, it is the Latin American Left in general which has, historically, committed itself to conclude this unfinished project of the building of nation and nationhood, initiated by the liberal elites in the nineteenth century (Castañeda 1994, 272). If, on the one hand, Rama proposes a pluralistic approach for the conceptualization of "lo nacional" —through his "discovery" and retrieval of ethnic and regional popular identities— on the other, he endorses a homogenizing project and resorts to an essentialist discourse that reduces plurality.

At the same time, his transculturation formula for the construction of nationality takes on echoes of an integratory utopia on a cultural and political level, which is an heir to the Americanist discourses of the nineteenth century; that utopia would, in effect, be appropriated and rearticulated from an anti-imperialist perspective, and would be associated with the Latin Americanism of the Cuban Revolution which had so much influence on the intellectual left of the continent during the 1960s and '70s. Rama's project of "a Latin American culture" is a response to imperialism; that culture would have more chance of success in confronting the unifying advance of modernizing forces than the vulnerable, fragmented regional cultures. One problematic aspect of the formulation of this integratory utopia as a reaction to imperialist aggression has to do with a lack of clarity regarding the relations and mediations between the political field and the cultural field, which could lead to the imposition of a political project on the interpretation of cultural processes; the imposition of the logic that dictates political thought over the logic which holds sway over cultural processes would distort the nature of their dynamic. Occasionally Rama loses sight of that which he himself has already shown us: that the persistence of Latin American cultural fragmentation is the strongest expression of our regional cultures' capacity for resistance and creativity: it is in the sphere of "... las culturas internas del continente ... [donde] se juega la resistencia y la neoculturación..." (73).[12]

Nevertheless, by this we do not mean to disregard the areas of intersection which do exist between culture and politics, or to deny legitimacy to any conception or action resulting from the recognition of that intersection. In fact, it must be stressed that the rise of continentalist visions is stimulated by the interventionist policies of the United States throughout the region, and particularly in Cuba which it not only subjects to an economic blockade, but which it is also seeking to isolate culturally from the rest of the region by pressurizing Latin American governments to break diplomatic relations with the island. The cultural sphere is perceived as a theater of confrontation between imperialism and Latin America, and intellectuals feel committed to that struggle. The Latin Americanist perspective is one of the dimensions in which this committment is embodied, but, as we have already seen, this committment can be taken on in various ways, including the conception of integration as a measure

---

[12] Ortiz-Márquez also discusses a project of integration in Rama, although she does not look into the problematic aspects examined here. Her emphasis is rather on Rama's combination of conflicting proposals in his book on transculturation: on the one hand, one of national integration (which she associates to the impact of the nineteenth-century *artiguista* discourses on some of the intellectuals linked to *Marcha*), and, on the other, an anticipation of elements of the postmodern critiques of modernity that would be articulated in the 1980s in Latin America and that Rama would develop in *Máscaras democráticas del modernismo*. See Moraña (1997, 193–94 & 207).

against lack of communication, especially if that lack of communication is imposed from outside. The following paragraph is from issue 26 of *Revista Casa de las Américas* (1964), a journal which played a crucial role in the effort of intellectuals to produce links between different national spaces at the time. This piece testifies to the siege-like atmosphere experienced by the intellectual left, and to the significance they attached to gestures of cultural integration as an act of resistance:

> Mientras en Washington se preparaba este bloqueo cultural, nosotros preparábamos este número sobre la nueva novela latinoamericana, recogiendo algunos textos de grandes escritores del continente, para mostrar cómo han contribuido a través de su arte a liberarnos del subdesarrollo intelectual en que se nos ha pretendido mantener, a crear las condiciones de la independencia cultural, a proporcionar obras que enriquecen la vida espiritual de los pueblos. Mientras en Washington se acrecentaba la política de división, nosotros trabajábamos por la comunicación, mutuamente enriquecedora, de las culturas nacionales. De esta política no nos apartaremos.
> El bloqueo cultural que intenta imponer Washington no prosperará. Este número de la revista es nuestra respuesta. (2)

In passing, we would like to point out another interesting fact about this editorial note, which is that Rama not only contributed an article to this issue of the journal ("Diez problemas para el novelista latinoamericano") but he was also involved in its preparation.[13]

Towards an Autonomous Criticism: Angel Rama's Nationalist Discourses

The search for formulae to develop an autonomous criticism is a constant feature of Angel Rama's extensive work. Up to now we have largely been referring to his project of cultural criticism, which he structured around his "discovery" of the transcultural operations which he himself labeled "new [Latin American] regionalism". This project in fact constitutes his most solid contribution to a criticism determined to free itself from universalist theoretical and methodological models. Nevertheless, it would be a mistake to consider this representative of all his work. He had explored other paths before realizing that criticism could only escape simple rhetoric on autonomy through the reading of literary processes within their cultural contexts, in order to understand how they

---

[13] For another interesting illustration of left-wing Latin American intellectuals' call for integration in response to imperialism, see the "Declaración del comité de colaboración de la Casa de Las Américas" in *Revista Casa de Las Américas* (1967).

had been constructing the "Latin American personality" (1985b, 91).

During the last few decades, other disciplines within the social sciences have followed similar trajectories in Latin America. It is interesting to note what Pedro Morandé has to say on this: he considers the failure of sociology in its endeavor for Latin Americanization to be due to a lack of

> ...[una] reflexión acerca de la cultura... el concepto de cultura representa la única puerta para pasar del universalismo al particularismo, no sólo de la "situación" latinoamericana, sino lo que es todavía más importante, de la 'identidad' latinoamericana. Para quien domina la identidad es un problema nada más que aparente. Lo resuelve por vía tautológica, es decir, por la pura autoafirmación de sí sustentada en el poderío. Pero no le ocurre lo mismo a quien se encuentra en la " periferia" . El problema de su identidad se confunde con su misma posibilidad de sobrevivir y alcanzar alguna vez la autonomía. (Morandé 1987, 12)

For Rama, the purpose of criticism is very much bound up with this perspective; criticism must reclaim and reveal what is specific to Latin American arts and culture and use this as a base for any project for social transformation. This was always the Uruguayan critic's motive —to contribute to the production of the profile that Latin America demanded. That is why he says that one of his reasons for founding the Biblioteca Ayacucho was:

> ...el espectáculo desconcertante de un continente intelectual reclamando su identidad y su originalidad, sin citar las espéndidas obras que en siglos se habían acumulado en esta misma tierra americana, pacientemente rearticuladas por el pensamiento crítico de nuestros antecesores. (1982a, 16)

Commenting on the function that Rama assigns to criticism, Losada states that the Uruguayan "[i]magina la vida de la cultura como un territorio privilegiado en donde se elaboran y superan las contradicciones, donde se armonizan los conflictos, donde toda la sociedad de América Latina podía reconocerse en un sentido afirmativo de la existencia y de donde le venía también el admirativo reconocimiento de la cultura mundial" (Losada 1985, 48). It is true that Rama's project seeks to give Latin American culture the possibility of defining itself in its own terms rather than as a defective reproduction of metropolitan cultures. It is also true that there is a harmonizing dimension to the Uruguayan critic's discourse: this is evident, for example, in the passage quoted at the start of this chapter, where he tells of the effort of transcultural narrative to "canalizar armónicamente" the "elementos contrarios" which it embraces, thus contributing to the integrating function of "la nueva cultura" in its gestation (Rama 1982a, 229). However, what is missing from this observation is that this vision of Rama's coexists with another vision of his which goes beyond "armonización" or "superación" of the contradictions within transcultural works; furthermore, he conceives of the latter as an attempt to articulate counter-hegemonic discourses precisely on the basis of the acknowledgment of the conflicts and not of their denial. Thus, the formal particularities of Arguedas' narrative, for example, reveal the confrontation between two cosmovisions, two languages, two cultures. Arguedas' struggle is, "...insertarse en la cultura dominante, apropiarse de una lengua extraña [el español] forzándola a expresar otra sintaxis [quechua]...", and he does this using the novel, a genre originating from Western tradition, which he adapts with difficulty "...a los sistemas de pensamiento y a las formulaciones artísticas de la cultura indígena peruana"; Arguedas' project involves the attempt to conquer the novel, "...una de las ciudadelas mejor defendidas de la cultura de dominación...". "Por más que Arguedas llegue a organizar una novela apoyándola en los textos de los huaynos populares —writes Rama— por más que adecúe la lengua para dar las equivalencias del quechua, sin cesar *tropieza con una conformación literaria que es radicalmente hostil a su proyecto...*" (1987, 207 and 210–11; my italics).

Antonio Cornejo Polar, for his part, problematizes the notion of transculturation itself. Although he recognizes the great "aptitud hermenéutica" of this notion in the critical discourse of Rama, he wonders to what extent it might ultimately imply "la resolución (¿dialéctica?) de las diferencias en una síntesis superadora de las contradicciones que la originan...", a synthesis that would take place in the space of "la cultura-literatura hegemónica" and which would tend to erase the "alteridades" (1994a, 369). We have already seen that, while this wish for a synthesis is present in Rama's discourse, at the same time it does not cancel his own emphasis upon the permanence of conflicts and differences of socio-cultural origins in the new forms generated by transcultural literatures. The ideal of harmony is absent from his description of the new forms whose gestation is presented through images which emphasize confrontation and tension.

Rama's analysis favors the field of processes of cultural production and, more specifically, that of production of artistic forms as the arena for confrontation between the various cultural formations within Latin America. The resulting forms of those confrontations are the very expression of the creativity and inventiveness of the popular cultures which nourish the literature of the continent, as illustrated by Arguedas' novel *Los ríos profundos*, brilliantly characterized by Rama as the "novel-opera of the poor" in *Transculturación narrativa en América Latina* (1987).

Rama's reading establishes the aesthetic singularity of this Peruvian work and places it beside the narrators who, in the 1950s and 1960s, were recognized as innovators of Latin American literature, "...en tanto invención artística original, dentro del campo competitivo de las formas literarias contemporáneas de América Latina" (229). According to Rama, the originality of *Los ríos profundos* stems from the fact that the writing happens at the intersection between the novel of social criticism, derived from the "gran instrumento narrativo de la burguesía", and a pre-bourgeois genre —the popular opera– preserved by traditional Andean culture (257–58). Furthermore, both the originality of this "ópera de pobres" and its protest character, stresses Rama, originate in the unusual nature of the materials from which it is composed:

> porque... [esta "ópera de pobres"] está construida a partir de los materiales humildes que componen una cultura popular; por momentos, se diría que con los desechos de grandes culturas, tanto la incaica como la española, conservados y elaborados en ese "bricolage" que intentan las comunidades rurales con las migajas que caen de la mesa del banquete de los señores. Toda la acción transcurre en la pobreza, en la basura, en los harapos, en cocinas de indios, caminos lodosos, chicherías de piso de tierra, letrinas de colegios, baldíos, desartalados refectorios. Ningún indicio de educación superior...ninguna presencia de las mayores culturas de las que estos seres son los últimos desamparados herederos...
> Ninguno de los componentes pobres con que [Arguedas] trabaja ha sido recubierto de cosmética y, al contrario, se ha acentuado el desamparo y el horror...Es justamente esta aceptación muda de una materia no prestigiada pero fuerte, la que sostiene el resplandor espiritual de la obra. Da origen a una suntuosa invención artística, hace de una ópera de pobres una joya espléndida. (267–69)

In his proposal for an autonomous criticism, Rama feels himself to be part of a collective enterprise which includes critics of the past. His work is undoubtedly linked to that long tradition within Latin American arts which searches for autonomy, dating back to the contradictory processes of independence at the beginning of the nineteenth century. This tradition was revitalized with the repeated failures of the Liberal project in its attempt to organize the modern American states. But before going into a more detailed interpretation of Rama's discourse on transculturation, it is important to pinpoint its position within Rama's works and its relation to his initial quest for critical autonomy.

More than one discourse on "the nation" exists in Rama's work. In fact, one can identify two perspectives, with the years 1973–1974 acting as a dividing line. We have used his book *Darío y el Modernismo* (1985c) as the paradigm of his first discourse. The approach to the concept of nation in this book is articulated around a problematic notion of autonomy in the work of Darío and the *modernistas*. This notion converts "the nation" into a romantic rhetoric rather than an alternative discourse which could be used by Latin American criticism in its search for intellectual independence. The nationalist discourse of Rama's second period was to be very different; it was built upon his ideas on the processes of transculturation, which we shall discuss later. First we would like briefly to comment upon the conceptual framework which governs Rama's proposal for autonomy in his book on Darío.

In this book, Rama's reading of the enterprise of literary innovation attempted by Darío and *modernismo* establishes a relationship of symmetry between that innovation and the economic and technological modernization of Latin American societies which began in the last decades of the nineteenth century as part of the Liberal hegemonic project, and which is still in force today. In other words, only social modernization made the new aesthetic conception introduced by Darío and the *modernistas* possible: "...Donde se impone con decisión, [el sistema económico liberal]...también se intensifica la corriente modernista..." (31). In fact, Rama also explains the internal diversity of *modernismo* in terms of the varying pace at which modernization penetrated different Latin American societies (28-29). Although for Rama modernization constitutes a new model of imperialist domination, at the same time it enables Latin American literature to enter into a dialogue with European —and in particular French— literature, which would finally allow it to throw off the burden of Hispanic tradition (24). Similarly, only modernization, with its processes of urbanization and social transformations, would create the conditions for the production of an "adult" literature, increasingly contemporary with metropolitan literature and capable of competing with European models: "...A la concepción de la poesía ingenua, que alimentó la estética romántica, [el modernismo] opuso la concepción rígida de una poesía culta como expressión de una sociedad que había alcanzado su primer estadio urbano considerable" (7). In this early discourse of Rama's, there is something of the old Latin American "backwardness" complex, of the need to reduce the gap with Europe.

However, to do Rama justice, this is just one of his interpretations of Darío's work. In later studies his discourse is articulated around different parameters to those on which this book is founded. In fact, he becomes more interested in clarifying Darío's poetic conception, his challenge to Romantic aesthetics, his role as promoter of the professionalization of the Latin American intellectual, or the problems which both Darío and the *modernistas* had to solve in their attempt to renew the literatures of the region. In short, as noted in his prologue to Darío's poetry, in his second interpretation, Rama focuses on the process and circumstances of the actual production of the writing of the Nicaraguan and his contemporaries (1977b). Furthermore, in his book *Las máscaras democráticas del modernismo* (1984d), Rama calls attention to the specificity of Latin American modernization, stressing the essential internal contradiction which this process had for the continental elites : on the one hand they were committed to the stimulation of economic and material development, while on the other, they found themselves trying to contain the democraticizing wave which the modernizing process precipitated not only on the social and political level, but also on the artistic and intellectual level. This is the context in which he examines the *modernistas'* innovatory project and the particular aesthetic solutions with which they responded to the internationalist moment initiated by their literary production in Latin America.

In *Rubén Darío y el modernismo* (1985c), however, Rama applies an economistic perspective, somewhat problematically, to two distinct processes —the social and the cultural. Latin American societies are articulated to the metropoli in terms of domination and dependency, and their culture, "a imagen de su economía", is equally dependent —Rama would say "colonial". According to him, then, "...la historia de la cultura hipanoamericana... [constituye] la sombra obediente de la historia de la cultura europea" (1985c, 20). This vision enters into conflict with his quest for autonomy, given that ultimately it sets up the European model as the exclusive historico-cultural model to which no alternatives, only variants, are offered.[14] Thus, Latin American history is converted into a replica of metropolitan history —and, generally, a poor one— and the quest for autonomy is always carried out within those limits: "...el afán autonómico funcionó [desde la Colonia] adaptándose a la estructura general de las influencias extranjeras..." (20), whilst at best, as for example in the case of Darío, it manifests itself in variations of the matrixes originating from the centers of domination, and reproducing the power structures that characterize the relations between the metropoli and the periphery: the society in which the Nicaraguan poet had to live under tension, "...sin que ambicionara o pudiera [resolver esta tensión]", between the drive for modernization and the brakes of conservative traditionalism. Correlatively, Darío "...nunca pudo resolver el conflicto y vivió tironeado por sus elementos contrastantes". That is why his work proposes, "...una solución estratificadora, que mantenía en capas separadas y escalonadas jerárquica-

---

[14] This statement does not intend to overlook the fact that Rama believed in a revolutionary alternative for Latin America, embodied in the Cuban experience.

mente una concepción moderna, urbana, inyectora de extranjerías, que coronaba la sociedad, y otra tradicionalista, de inserción rural, españolista y conservadora, sobre la que se ejercía el dominio de la primera" (23).

The conditions of dependency in which Latin America is articulated to the bourgeois universalist project condemn Latin American history, according to Rama, to reflex processes which reproduce stages already experienced by European societies, but modified by the peculiar nuances which immediate circumstances confer upon them:

> ...aun en aquellos casos en que las similitudes son muy flagrantes entre los modelos franceses y las imitaciones hispanoamericanas, cabe reconocer que en estas últimas se registra un acento de autenticidad que faltaba en sus antepasados. En los hechos el poeta no copia fórmulas verbales: también acomete experiencias concretas, reales, de tipo similar; se enfrenta a situaciones semejantes, aunque más pálidas que las primigenias del otro lado del océano; comienza a tantear una creación más perdurable por más verdadera. (36)

This is the margin for maneuver that Rama initially leaves to projects of autonomy. It does not allow for either a challenge to the model or recognition of the creative potential of Latin American cultures, and even less for their capacity to articulate counter-hegemonic discourses. In this sense it can be suggested that Rama himself deprives his own project of this possibility, in contrast to what was to happen with his discourse on transculturation in which, in spite of the continued presence of some of these perspectives, he opens new paths to the advance of Latin American criticism towards independence.

Other theoretical problems arise from the symmetrical relationship which Rama establishes between social structure and aesthetic processes. To start with, as has already been said, he states that without modernization there can be no literary innovation, and no possibility of articulating a national project. Furthermore, Rama's discourse suggests that the "bringing up to date" of the socio-economic organization and the cultural coordinates of Latin American countries could eventually lead to the elimination of the distance between metropolis and periphery, between "model" and "copy". But at what cost? Evidently the homogenizing processes in the wake of modernization are not perceived as a threat to Latin American identity at this stage of the Uruguayan critic's work: "Si en el modernismo aún se prolonga la imitación, el hecho de que el patrón oro de la poesía sea la originalidad y la búsqueda de la novedad, comienza a establecer una contención al proceso mimético" (36). This perspective leaves Rama no alternative other than to resort to Romantic mythical categories, such as "authenticity" or "originality", in order to support the *modernista* formula of Latin American identity. The transposition of the concept of dependency of Latin American societies onto literary production is equally problematic: Rama states that Latin American literature, condemned to dependency due to its colonial origin, had always been destined for the servile imitation of European models. This reading of literature as imitation not only undermines his autonomy project, it also implies seeing dominated societies as mere passive receptacles for discourses and forms —in short, for the "original models"— upon which they scarcely leave their personal impression. This is a dubious scenario which makes it difficult to ignore the echoes of a mechanical transposition of the international division of labor onto artistic production.

The incorporation of an anthropological perspective which supports the culturalist dimension of Rama's discourse and which informs his works on transculturation, opens new and more promising routes to the old search for the independence of Latin American criticism. This new approach enables the formulation of a multicultural interpretation which redesigns the cultural contours of the continent, and which reveals not only the resistance of Latin American rural popular cultures in the face of the homogenizing pressures of the modernizing model, but also their capacity to articulate counter-hegemonic discourses and to forge themselves into alternatives to modernization.

The autonomist project of Latin American literature continues to function as the core of Rama's critical discourse, but it is now approached in a different way: autonomy can only be constructed on the basis of the cultural specificity of Latin America. Since its Republican beginnings, the literature of the continent had intended to establish the singularity of Latin America with regard to the various metropoli which had successively dominated it. Such a perspective opened a discourse different from that on Darío, where Latin American autonomy occured only as a variant of the model. Cultural and aesthetic processes are virtually reduced to replicas of the "original".

Furthermore, in his first book on Darío, there is no concept of plurality of cultural projects. There is only a universal metropolitan project, with its pale peripheral imitations. This contrasts with the transcultural project articulated to the regional cultures which resist assimilation; this project proposes alternatives to the hegemonic model; this way of dealing with the cultural specificity of Latin America leads to the affirmation of plurality. The transcultural project also involves a rejection of the idea of the Liberal metropolis as a national model, of which Sarmiento's project represents the classic paradigm (that is, his attempt to impose upon the rest of the country a socio-cultural model derived from an urban space in process of modernization). Constructing autonomy based on the singularity of the regions thus means a rejection of the metropolitan Liberal project and a reaffirmation of the plurality of cultural projects.

The recognition of Latin America's difference from the centers of domination is the starting point of a discourse which distances itself from that which runs through his first reading of Darío, in which Latin American aesthetic processes are conceived as mere re-creations of a universal model of history and culture. Rama's new position breaks with a eurocentric vision, and can be described as a step towards an autonomous Latin American criticism. As has already been shown, the leap from one autonomous project to another begins with the new function which Rama assigns to critical discourse, a function which, up until then, had been neglected by criticism: in other words, the reconstruction of the way in which works enter into dialogue with the cultural space in which they are produced and the results of that interaction.

> Restablecer las obras literarias dentro de las operaciones culturales que cumplen las sociedades americanas, reconociendo sus audaces construcciones significativas y el ingente esfuerzo por manejar auténticamente los lenguajes simbólicos desarrollados por los hombres americanos, es un modo de reforzar estos vertebrales conceptos de independencia, originalidad y representatividad. (1987, 19)

With the incorporation of an anthropological conception of culture in his critical discourse, Rama becomes aware of the survival of cosmovisions, rituals, in short, the significant practices of the traditional social conglomerates of the various regions of the continent and the interaction of literature with those local cultures. On the one hand, the focus is shifted away from the notion of a universal culture towards local culture. On the other hand, the critic's interest now extends to all kinds of symbolic creation within those communities, as elements which are drawn upon by literary production and also as sources of the specificity of the symbolic creation. Through this treatment, Rama frees Latin American literature from a perspective which denies its "otherness" and subjects it to the paradigms of metropolitan literatures.[15]

The idea of originality takes on new meanings in Rama's transcultural discourse: Latin American cultural and aesthetic processes are now read as being active and productive, and not just as reproductive. We can no longer speak of dominated societies, forced to play the role of passive

---

[15] For a discussion of the contributions of anthropology to the project for critical autonomy, see Rama (1984c).

receptors with only the capacity to imitate models. Yes they are dominated, but they are attempting to affirm their distinct identity and independent existence despite that domination, and that effort alone is an indication of resistance to domination. Originality thus comes to mean the attempt within Latin American literature to affirm its "otherness", which had in fact been taking place ever since the beginnings of the Republican period, although at that time it was manifested through the rupture with the colonial past and a rearticulation to Western traditions other than those of Spain and Portugal. This movement does not guarantee autonomy, writes Rama, but it is nevertheless a gesture of independence. Ultimately, originality also comes to be something more than that gesture "...obra de...sus élites literarias" —it becomes an act of independence embodied in a literature which is sustained by the cultural production of that popular rural conglomerate, which Rama resists naming directly and which he refers to in general as internal cultures or, "culturas desarrolladas en lo interior". Transcultural narrative belongs to this latter tradition (1987, 12).

Rama's establishment of two formulas for autonomy bears the mark of another central aspect of his criticism: his aforementioned classification of twentieth-century Latin American literature into two opposing paradigms, the first one of "national" literature, "...[integrada] a procesos de recuperación antropológica de los elementos que forman la nacionalidad..." and the second one of "cosmopolitan" literature, "...totalmente [inserta] en la corriente europea..." (1985b, 39). Rama opts for the first.

This bi-polar view of Latin American cultural production is characteristic not only of Rama's discourse, but also, in varying degrees, of the discourses of Losada and Cornejo Polar (as will be seen in the sections dedicated to their work). An explanation may be found in Jorge Castañeda's interpretation of the nationalism of the region's Left (1994, 273–74). The Left has analyzed "lo nacional" as emanating from "the people"; it has identified the "nation" with "the people" (the descendants of the vanquished of the conquest); the people are "the real nation", the majorities "ethnically differentiated" and treated as minorities for five hundred years by the minorities of colonial origin in power. The white elites are consequently perceived as alien, as "other", as not participating in "lo nacional", as usurpers. The left-wing intellectual thus finds him/herself in a contradictory situation: because of their origins they are invariably ethnically and socially linked to the casts in power, while ideologically moved to solidarity with those marginalized from power. As a response to this paradoxical position the left-wing intellectual has been determined to become "nationalized" through a double maneuver: on the one hand he/she seeks to break his/her class links and in some way to expiate the guilt of his/her "anti-national" origins, working in solidarity with the dispossessed and engaging with the cause of social emancipation, and on the other hand, he/she seeks to restore the "nation" to those from whom it has been usurped, without leaving room within it for the usurpers. The reductionism involved in the bi-polar readings of the Latin American literary process, and the stigmatization of the urban space can, to a certain extent, be understood as deriving from the paradigm of the nationalist Left.

Rama's national discourse excludes all literary and cultural production articulated to the "internationalist" or "cosmopolitan" axis, which can ultimately be assimilated to the modernized, internationalized, and thus "denationalized", urban sphere. The literatures produced in this context would be exclusively receptive to "European influences" (1985b, 39). It is interesting that, when speaking of cosmopolitan literatures, Rama uses the term "influences", which suggests a passive attitude, while when speaking of transcultural literatures, he refers to its "recuperative" role, which implies an active conception of the writing process. Following his "discovery" of transcultural narrative and his re-evaluation of tradition, Rama also reformulates his vision of the modernization and the internationalization of the literature of the continent: in contrast to the first period of his critical work, which celebrates Latin American literature being brought up to date with the European avant-garde, his interest now turns to the examination of, "... la producción de las últimas décadas para ver si no había otras fuentes nutricias de una renovación artística que aquellas que provenían simplemente de los barcos europeos...". The only way towards "descolonización espiritual" is given by the "...reconocimiento de las capacidades adquiridas por un continente que tiene una ya muy larga y fecunda tradición inventiva, que ha desplegado una lucha tenaz para constituirse como una de las ricas fuentes culturales del universo" (1987, 20).

Rama's book, *La ciudad letrada* (1984b), sheds light on the historical vision which laid the foundations for his re-evaluation of the two axes of his bi-polar system. This book gathers together the results of his research on Latin American urban cultures, from their genesis in the colonial period up to the processes of modernization initiated in the last decades of the nineteenth century. For Rama, ever since its origins, the Latin American city has been the classic expression of a project of Conquest; the city is the ideological, cultural and material implantation of the project of exterior domination —domination by the Metropolis. It is the physical space of the invader— the invader's social and cultural model. It is transplanted, the alien, imposed on the autochtonous, the internal, the rural, and, in contrast to European cities born out of rural agricultural development and mercantile necessity, was intended to operate as their controllers. With Conquest, he writes, "...quedó certificado el triunfo de las ciudades sobre un inmenso y desconocido territorio, reiterando la concepción griega que oponía la polis civilizada a la barbarie de los no urbanizados" (14). And that same concept of "ciudades como focos civilizadores", opposed to "los campos donde veía engendrada la barbarie", was to be prolonged in Sarmiento's model, with the city as the cutting edge of the nineteenth century modernization project (16). Such a model constituted a deepening of the Conquest and a continuation of the destruction of the native American cultures. It is not difficult to establish a relationship between this interpretation and that found in *Transculturación narrativa* (1987), in which cities function as modernizing poles, radiating contemporary forms of colonization —one more phase in the imposition of external cultural models on the "internal", the bearers of Latin American identity.

Evidently, the Uruguayan critic's work constitutes an important contribution to a literary history which seeks to clarify the specific development of a literature born out of the violence of the Conquest, particularly as it enhances the understanding of the conflictive relationship between countryside and city, orality and literacy, popular culture and "high" culture. Although it clarifies the reason for the difference in Rama's perspective regarding the literatures of the avant-garde which he conceives of as simple reproductions of the dominant model in the face of transcultural literatures as counter-hegemonic, it does not resolve the problem of a homogenizing reading of urban cultural production. His critical gaze never stops to take in the intertextual processes which can occur between popular cultures and "erudite" literatures, as in Borges' work for example.

Rama's interest in reclaiming the place occupied by popular culture in the development of Latin American literature, is exclusively centered around the rural sphere. As has been stated already, the discourse on transculturation reveals Latin American rural popular cultures' resistance to homogenizing pressures from the modernizing model, and their capacity to articulate counter-hegemonic discourses and to set themselves up as alternatives to modernization. Nevertheless, the a priori denationalization of the city prevents Rama from exploring the possibility of finding discourses that are critical of —or resistant to— domination which may be being articulated within the spaces where modernization has penetrated with greatest force. This position ultimately prevents him from detecting their own transcultural operations. The idea of a single model for national identity undermines the possibilty of articulating a critical discourse which, without reductionism, might be capable of accounting for the totality of literary projects produced in the different socio-cultural formations of the continent. In fact, this bi-polar interpretation of Latin American literature does not favor a perception of the multiplicity of discourses and formulas of identity proposed in the various cultural spaces which still coexist in every Latin American city and which, to great extent, are a consequence of the uneven advance of modernization.

These problems in the Uruguayan critic's discourse, are partly explained in terms of his homologizing of social modernization with literary modernization, which leads on to the supposition that the adoption of the imposed model of material development implies the passive and unmediated adoption of an aesthetic model. This approach ignores the complex operations involved in any process of appropriation and rearticulation of discourses, a complexity which is instead recognized by Rama in his treatment of transcultural literatures.

CHAPTER 3

ALEJANDRO LOSADA: TOWARDS A SOCIAL HISTORY OF LATIN AMERICAN LITERATURES

The epistemological crisis which took place within the immanentist and sociological currents of criticism in the 1970s, along with criticism's incapacity to account for either the specific features of Latin American literature (Losada 1987, 11–13) or the general features of its process of production, provide the background and starting point for Alejandro Losada's discourse. His writings constitute one of the most persistent efforts within Latin American criticism to confer a scientific status on the discipline, and to propose a theoretical model able to act as a foundation for his project of collective construction of a social history of Latin American literature.[1] Losada initially devised and set the project in motion at the Latin American Institute of Berlin University where he was a lecturer of literature from 1978. The project was given further impetus with the foundation of the Association for the Study of Latin American Literatures and Societies (AELSAL) in 1982, which gathers together Latin Americanists from various European countries and coordinates the development of the research (Lienhard et al 1986, 634).[2]

The aim of proposing a conceptual system to support this project runs throughout Losada's work. He conceives of such a system as a tentative formulation which, like his research work, is always open to re-workings and re-definition. His writing is characterized by his disposition for the continual re-working of ideas which he develops further as and when new information arises from advances in research in the field of criticism and other areas of the social sciences. This attitude towards scientific activity, so faithfully reflected in his writing, also demonstrates his conviction that collective and inter-disciplinary work guarantees real advances in the discipline (Losada 1981b, 168–69 and 172–73).

Losada approaches the problem of the specificity of Latin American

---

[1] For an examination of the epistemological discussion which underlies Losada's project, see (1976a). For a systematization of the theoretical principles which control the delimitation and definition of the field and subject of his research, see (1987, 14–46). For a systematization and updating of both his questioning of dominant critical models and theoretical principles which support his proposal since the mid-1970s, see (1981b).

[2] For an account of the origins of AELSAL, see Borel (1987, 200–208).

cultural and literary production from a historical perspective, and examines it in terms of its "dialectical relationship" with the specificity of Latin American societies, a phenomenon which is largely due to their colonial past. For Losada, the understanding of the development of the literary process in Latin America is governed by a central historical conflict which remains unresolved, namely, "...la necesidad de superar la herencia de su pasado colonial...", and to look for a way out of the social and cultural contradictions caused by that past. The Latin American intellectual, in contrast to the European intellectual for example, has had to carry out his cultural production within the tensions created by this context:

> Como un equilibrista, [en Latinoamérica], el intelectual productor de cultura transita por esa parábola que trata de oponer el pasado al futuro, procurando vincular de alguna manera su producción con las alternativas históricas por las que atraviesa su sociedad, haciéndose problema por la destrucción —o permanencia— de las estructuras feudales precapitalistas, de la situación de la masa oprimida, de la necesidad de integrarla transformándola, o de aniquilarla reemplazándola por otro tipo de fuerza de trabajo, o por la constante presencia de potencias imperialistas que frenen el proceso histórico. (180–82)

But Losada also considers the specificity of Latin American literature from another angle: he analyzes it from within the "...contexto global de la difusión, recepción y transformación de los procesos ideológico-culturales internacionales producidos en Europa...", given that, "... los productores de cultura ilustrada de esta región se han identificado con ese horizonte internacionalizado a partir de su posición periférica y dependiente dentro del proceso general de expansión y consolidación del modo de producción capitalista...". But although Latin America is placed in the role of receptor of the discourses produced in the dominant centers of capitalism, the intellectuals of the continent do not limit themselves to a passive adoption of those discourses, but instead transform them, reformulating the functions they had in the societies in which they originated —when adapting them to their own societies— and even proposing counter-discourses. This process of appropriation and reformulation of "...lo que se difunde desde otras situaciones sociales depende de las condiciones concretas en que se encuentra cada formación social latinoamericana en cada etapa de su evolución histórica...", thereby determining the characteristics of the resulting cultural products, specific to the various "sub-regions" of Latin America. This conception of the cultural process in terms of the articulations between each "sub-regional" social formation and the hegemonic centers would later be systematized by Losada in his work in the 1980s. It constitutes a timely questioning of a view of the cultural process in a Latin America conceived of as a dependent unit, according to which the appropriation and rearticulation of the internationalized languages would produce uniform results throughout the region. Losada's emphasis once again rightly falls upon the necessity to break with the homogenizing visions of Latin American literatures and reveal the differences between those literatures (1983b, 7–11).

The purpose of this chapter is to carry out a reconstruction of the Losadian proposal, and to evaluate its key categories in terms of his contribution to the advance of Latin American criticism in its quest for autonomy initiated in the 1970s and its break with the Eurocentric conceptions which were hegemonic within the discipline up until then. In the first section of this chapter, we will discuss the various stages through which Losada's project passes, while in the second, we will set down an inventory of the essential concepts within his theoretical system and attempt to synthesize the successive definitions offered by the Argentinean critic throughout his work. Rather than being an exhaustive description of his conceptual system, the purpose of this synthesis is to illustrate some of the principal uses of Losada's categories in order to orient the reader.

Losada's work, especially in the 1980s, results in a treatment of Latin American literary production which, through the application of his notion of "mode of cultural production" ("modo de producción cultural") to a "(sub-) regional" interpretation rather than a "national" interpretation, lays the foundations for the formulation of an alternative schema of periodization of Latin American literature faithful, this time, to the specific historico-cultural characteristics of the continent.[3] Losada, as is well known, proposes a comparative study between the five "sub-regions" which compose the continent as the point of departure for his social history of Latin American literature. These sub-regions are: the Southern Cone, the Andes, the Caribbean and Central America, Brazil and Mexico, thereby discarding the model of "national" literatures (1980c, 1983b). The recognition that the historico-cultural borders are more pertinent to research than those which separate the national states, is neither the exclusive nor the central Losadian argument against the legitimacy of the concept of national literatures for critical discourse. What is more important is his convincing analysis of the relationship between the *sujeto-productor* ("subject producer") and the various "social actors" ("actores sociales" —local dominant elite, popular sectors and international hegemonic centres) involved in each of the three "modes of cultural

---

[3] For a resumé of his critique of the model of "national" literatures, see especially, Losada (1983b, 23).

production" which dominate the panorama of Latin American letters throughout the nineteenth century ("dependent literatures") and twentieth century ("marginal" and "social-revolutionary literatures").[4] Losada claims that:

> Durante el período de dependencia neo-colonial parece inapropiado el término de literatura "nacional", ya que una literatura producida en función de una élite oligárquica dependiente de los centros metropolitanos dominantes no tiene suficiente legitimidad como para ser referida a la creación de una sociedad y una cultura nacionales, es decir, con independencia política, con un aparato productivo que se dirija a satisfacer las propias necesidades y con una reestructuración social que supere la polarización y explotación coloniales e integre a todos en una unidad solidaria. (1983b, 23)

This approach undoubtedly constitutes one of his most interesting contributions to Latin American literary criticism's endeavor to account for the specific developments of the literary production of the continent.

Another aspect of his proposal, which is equally useful for Latin American criticism, involves his retrieval for modernity of those literatures stigmatized as "traditional" by a criticism which sets up "modernity" as a central criterion of its evaluative exercise, but employs a very narrow understanding of that concept. Losada believes that these literatures ("social revolucionarias") have, in fact, embarked upon an alternative project of modernity which involves a commitment to the eradication of the legacy of colonial conflicts, and the quest for solutions which imply the social and political transformation of society (23–26).

During his time in Lima as lecturer at the Universidad Mayor de San Marcos (1971–1976), following a brief academic experience in Argentina (1967–1968) and an equally brief, though traumatic, incursion into the political life of his country (1968–1970), Losada would dedicate himself to the sociological study of contemporary —and particularly Peruvian— narrative (Lienhard et al 1986, 632–33). Parallel to this research are his reflections on the social character of literary production, that is to say, the way in which literature is articulated to the rest of society and its function within society, the formation of "literary systems" ("conjuntos literarios"), and their links to different social subjects. He would also search for parameters which would make possible the understanding of specific

---

[4] Given the inadequacy and ambiguity of any English translation of *sujeto productor*, henceforth the term will be used in Spanish. For a summary and discussion of definitions of this and other key terms of Losada's conceptual system, see the second section of this chapter.

developments within Latin American writing, with a view to freeing the discipline from the Eurocentric, homogenizing perspectives which traditionally controlled it. Although at this stage his reflections are generally inspired by Peruvian literature, Losada's objective is the projection of his conclusions to the literature of the rest of the continent, since a re-reading of it is a task that Latin American criticism cannot afford to postpone.[5] It is vital to Losada to break with the orientation of a criticism more concerned with finding similarities between "erudite" Latin American literature and European, especially French, literature than with exploring the differences. This explains the continuing absence of a,

> ...horizonte teórico que nos permita comprender los fenómenos literarios específicos que no tienen nada que ver con aquella literatura: esto es, las literaturas gauchescas, la persistencia del realismo social a lo largo de siglo y medio, las literaturas indigenistas, el movimiento de la negritud, la poesía fundacional, para aludir a unos pocos. Tampoco tenemos un modelo, aunque sea primitivo, para periodizar los diversos desarrollos literarios sub-regionales que permitan entender como una unidad latinoamericana, por ejemplo, la literatura de la revolución mexicana en sus dos etapas 1920–40–70; la elaboración de la identidad cultural a través de la novela realista (R. Bastos, J. M. Arguedas, M. A. Asturias, J. Amado); o la nueva literatura testimonial (Barnet, Domitila, G. Martínez); fenómenos sincrónicamente simultáneos a conjuntos tan diferentes como los constituidos por las novelas subjetivistas o experimentales tan impropiamente llamadas "del lenguaje" (J. Cortázar, Lezama Lima, S. Sarduy, Cabrera Infante, J. Donoso). (1981b, 170)

Losada dedicates his critical work to devising a model capable of filling in these gaps in the discipline. His book *Creación y praxis* (1976a), which gathers together most of his research in Peru and synthesizes the intellectual trajectory of his first period, lays the theoretical foundations which, with some modifications and additions, were to form the core of his future writings. This justifies a careful examination of its content.

In the third part of the book, Losada expresses his objections to the dominant conceptual systems within Latin American literary criticism and history (179–89), thus clarifying the context of his intervention in the debate on the continent's literature in order then to make a systematic presentation of his model of interpretation of Latin American "literary systems" ("sistemas literarios") as social institutions.[6] That model, con-

---

[5] For Losada's works published in this period, see (1974, 1975b, 1975c, 1975d).

[6] In this part, Losada includes a text originally published as an article the previous year: "Los sistemas literarios como instituciones sociales en América Latina" (1975b).

ceived by Losada as a first attempt to formalize a sociology of Latin American literatures, would be followed by new proposals arising out of his discovery and incorporation of anthropological perspectives. These would not only refine and broaden the repertoire of categories of the said model, but also enrich its capacity to assist in the understanding both of the literature itself and of the relationship between social and cultural processes.

He criticizes the traditional, positivist model, with its notions of "epoch" and "period" which distort both the nature and significance of literature. While the notion of epoch implies a relationship of homology between literary developments and those taking place within the political and social spheres (pre-colonial, colonial, republican and contemporary epochs), the concept of period, which identifies the various aesthetic movements, assumes the development of Latin American and European literature to be essentially the same, without taking into account the specificity of the former, thus de-historicising it and reducing it to a phenomenon of a "universal" character (1976b, 182–83). In the 1980s, as we shall see later, Losada would dedicate himself to the formulation of a model of periodization of Latin American writing which would break with those Eurocentric perspectives and aim to restore the specific traits of the literatures of the continent (1983b).

The immanentist response to this procedure was also unacceptable to him. Immanentist interpretations attempt to justify their scientific status on the basis of the autonomy of the material being studied and through the historical decontextualization of the texts which, in the first instance, result in being converted into, "...una serie de obras monumentales, inmanentes, intemporales y trascendentales, referidas a cada subjetividad que, a su vez, también es considerada como aislada, interiorizada, ahistórica y autónoma...". Secondly, the texts are conceived of as the heritage of a universal culture, thus effectively losing their social and cultural meaning. Losada sums up his criticism of that perspective as follows: "En estos discursos, que en realidad son los predominantes, se abandona todo modelo que permitiera conceptualizar a esta literatura como un conjunto, entender sus procesos de evolución y articularla de alguna manera a la sociedad hispanoamericana" (1976a, 183–84). Added to this is the resistance within structuralism to any kind of aesthetic or social evaluation and its supposed ideological neutrality and independence regarding any social project —attitudes radically opposed to those of Losada.

On the contrary, his critical discourse explicitly and consciously takes on board his ideological position and his commitment to a concrete social project, and conceives of his intellectual work as a praxis imbued with,

"...una intención liberadora que [apunta] a la totalidad social" (184–85). His work can be considered as sociology of literature, and is specifically affiliated to the project of developing a Marxist aesthetic led by George Lukács, Lucien Goldmann and Arnold Hauser (19–23 and 193–95).[7] Losada's objective is to propose a comparable systematization for Latin American literature, but proposing the reformulations necessary to account for its peculiarities.

Losada believes that apart from the fact that the majority of literary studies in Latin America remain on a monographic level of research and concentrate on individual authors and works, the principal failing rests in the, "...ausencia de la reflexión teórica y epistemológica...[y en el recurso al] discurso ensayístico, la más de las veces simplificador y voluntarista...". In synthesis he pinpoints five problematic areas in the discipline. Firstly, an incapacity to, "...dar razón del diferente desarrollo diacrónico subregional..."; in other words, the differences between the literatures produced in the various regions of the continent have been overlooked when grouping them all under the same heading, as is the case with *modernismo* for example, where the divergences between those authors traditionally homogenized by the term are more pronounced than the characteristics that they share. Secondly, Losada points out the inadequacy of current critical models, "...para dar razón de la simultaneidad de fenómenos que de manera inmediata aparecen como literatureas de cualidad diferente...", that is, the explanation for the coexistence of literary productions as distinct from each other —such as, for example, *indigenismo* and avant-garde literature in the Andean zone during the 1920s. Thirdly, he emphasizes the arbitrariness and inconsistencies of the generational proposals which seek to group together "...autores tan disímiles como Cortázar, Onetti, Ciro Alegría y José María Arguedas..." for the simple reason that they all belong to the same generation. Fourthly, he questions the validity of the "...criterios descriptivos e interpretativos... [que consituyen una mezcla indiscriminada, entre otras, de]...alusiones a la dependencia del desarrollo estilístico con respeto a las literaturas de los paises industriales, con referencia a la sociedad, la nación, las subregiones o la región". Finally, contemporary criticism confuses, according to him, "...la valoración estética de una obra, o un nuevo conjunto literario, y la significación social...", mixing parameters whose orders, furthermore, have not been defined or clarified. As an example he cites the tendency to employ, "...los dos criterios, encomiando...[a la vez]... la autonomía y la

---

[7] For a systematization of the differences between Losada and the dominant tendencies within sociology of literature, see Losada (1983a, 9–10).

madurez artística de la nueva literatura, y su significado social y político..." (179–80).

Losada considers his theoretical model to offer the elements necessary for the discipline to tackle this still unresolved question. The version of that model presented in his first book, far from claiming to be a finished proposal, is conceived only as an initial approach. Nevertheless, it is fair to say that it does already contain the essential notions of his project; as has already been noted, Losada continues constantly to redefine his categories throughout the production of his critical work. This book testifies to such an attitude to intellectual work, since the book is not limited to the presentation of the results of his research, but instead displays the various stages of his investigation and writing, revealing the successive approaches to the subject and the different levels of abstraction through which its composition passes.[8] This questioning of the dominant paradigms within Latin American criticism continues to provide the background for subsequent theoretical proposals, these always being conceived as alternatives both to the limitations of those paradigms and to the distortions of the Latin American literary process resulting from their application (1977a, 7–9).

In the first part of *Creación y praxis* (1976a), he makes an initial attempt to analyze contemporary Peruvian narrative using the concept of "social praxis" ("praxis social") as the basis for his study. However, at this stage he limits himself to putting forward hypotheses on the articulations between the individual works of five representative authors and the groups that make up their society, rather than hypotheses at the level of major literary and social "systems" ("conjuntos o sistemas literarios/sociales"). He does this in compliance with the notion of "perspective" used by Lukács in his work on the historical novel and critical realism, as Losada himself points out (1976a, 119–21).[9] He finds these first results unsatisfactory,

---

[8] On the self-reflexive character of Losada's discourse and its consequences, see Cornejo Polar's illuminating critical review (1977b). This review offers an excellent synthesis and assessment of *Creación y praxis*.

[9] Losada defines his use of the Lukacsian notion of "perspective" as meaning man's form of consciousness of his existence in the world which determines "the form of literary expression". Losada writes: "El autor, guiado y controlado por una emoción particular de su situación en el mundo, seleccionará determinados *materiales*, los presentará técnicamente dándoles una configuración y así, *estructurará* el proceso narrativo. El modo con que un autor es controlado por su emoción significativa para crear una forma expresiva que la objetive, socialice y comunique, es lo que Lukács en términos genéricos llama 'la perspectiva' con la que el autor crea una determinada forma significativa" (1976a, 152; emphasis in the original).

both for their insufficient degree of abstraction and formalization, and also for their lack of methodological and evaluative clarity. Nevertheless, he does not consider them to be totally without merit, since they provide the basis for a model with a greater capacity for abstraction, able to account for the relationship between literary production, the book itself and social praxis in Peru and Spanish America.[10] This is discussed in the final section of *Creación y praxis*, along with the concept of literary system understood as the praxis of a particular *sujeto productor*.

In the second part, and still closely following Lukacs' typology of the literary forms associated with his category of "perspective", Losada systematizes the different tendencies within contemporary Peruvian narrative, articulating them to the different forms of social praxis adopted by both the authors in question and the public which those works of literature generate (160–72). Losada's reservations regarding the advances achieved in the second stage are connected with the incapacity of his model to satisfy the demand for concrete criteria for the social evaluation of literary production, that is, criteria which make possible the articulation of, "...el modelo estilístico-formal con un modelo de praxis de los grupos sociales productores de esas formas..." (175–76). He seeks to resolve this question through the "modelo hipotético-deductivo" of literary system proposed in the third part of the book (241–52). That model should provide the elements necessary for, "...la comprensión de la literatura hispanoamericana posterior a la Independencia como praxis de diversos sujetos sociales..." (179). Perhaps that model does not satisfy Losada's ambitious objective; nevertheless, it synthesizes and systematizes the theoretical foundations derived from his approaches to contemporary Peruvian narrative, and provides the basis for what was to constitute the following stage of his research: the study of the "literary modes of production" which characterize the panorama of Latin American literature of the nineteenth century (244).

Before going any further, it must be added that the emphasis in Losada's proposal is on the interpretation of literature as a social expression rather than as a strictly aesthetic entity, and that his conceptual system ultimately provides sophisticated instruments for its social appraisal rather than for a formal evaluation. This is not to say that the literary

---

[10] The concept of Spanish America is used by Losada to the exclusion of the term "Latin America" in the first two parts of the book, while in the third part, he uses the latter term. In reality, as a field of study, Spanish America dominated his work of the 1970s. From the 1980s onwards, his project would focus on the Latin American area, including Brazil and the Caribbean.

works end up being considered as simple documents in the service of historical or sociological studies, and nor does Losada abandon his stated interest in the formulation of parameters which take both aspects of literary production into account. On the contrary, this preoccupation reappears in various parts of his book. In any case, it must be acknowledged that the Losadian treatment of the texts, especially in his early works, is generally centered —and even more so in his writings previous to the incorporation of an anthropological perspective— on the analysis of content. His treatment of language and form tends to be in terms of their relationship to processes of an ideological order, rather than being based on an interpretation which enables one to establish, among other things, the articulations between those processes and the different cultural formations which are their source (157). In his handling of Arguedas' work (1976a) for example, this kind of limitation in his interpretive parameters is illustrated by the absence of any mention of the complex processes of intertextuality which occur between Western literary traditions and Andean traditions, as demonstrated in the work of Angel Rama, Antonio Cornejo Polar, Martin Lienhard and William Rowe (Cornejo Polar 1989b, Lienhard 1981, Rama 1987, Rowe 1996).

It is interesting to look at Martín Lienhard's comments regarding this. He reminds us that the "...edificio teórico... de Losada [que aquel cataloga como]... una antropología de las prácticas literarias en América Latina...", ends up being questioned by both "orthodox" literary sociology and philology. While from the ranks of the former, he is reproached for breaking with the "...concepción de la literatura (de los textos) como reflejo del devenir histórico-social...", he is criticized by immanentists for his incapacity to sketch "...una poética o...una historia de las formas literarias en América Latina...". Lienhard responds to both positions with this characterization of Losada's project:

> El *status* de los textos concretos, en la teoría losadiana, no es, en efecto, el de objetos últimos de la investigación; basándose, por lo general, en los análisis ya realizados con las técnicas propias de la poética, ella considera los textos como signos de un sistema de comunicación más vasto que los trasciende y llega a constituir el verdadero centro de interés. El enfoque losadiano no niega, en realidad, la necesidad de construir una poética de los discursos literarios latinoamericanos, pero no asume la tarea de fundarla. La realización futura del gran proyecto losadiano de una historia social de las literaturas latinoamericanas exigirá, sin duda, una colaboración más estrecha entre los sociólogos o antropólogos de las prácticas literarias y los "poetólogos" latinoamericanistas. (Lienhard et al 1986, 641–42; emphasis in the original)

For a systematization of his model of interpretation of Latin American literary systems understood as "social institutions" ("instituciones sociales") —in the third part of *Creación y praxis*— Losada's point of departure is the Lukacsian concept "...del fenómeno literario como momento de la totalidad social..." (Losada 1976a, 192). However, he moves away from Lukács as far as his evaluative parameters of literature are concerned, and steers away from the Hungarian's conception of literary forms based on the theory of knowledge as reflection of reality (200 and 274). It is not our intention to enter into the details of Losada's critical consideration of Lukács' work (192–213), but to make a schematic presentation of the fundamental Lukacsian notions used by Losada and his reformulations of the said notions. In this way, we wish to illustrate Losada's endeavor to account for the specific processes of Latin American literature and its socio-historic context.

Lukács considers a literary work to be the result of an "objective situation"; he articulates it to the general social structure and interprets it in terms of the form of "...pertenencia de un sujeto productor a una clase social..." He defines it as, "una forma de conciencia o de conocimiento" which constitutes a reflection of, "...una situación que se desarrolla de manera independiente del sujeto productor...". It is a passive act, without the capacity "...para determinar la existencia concreta del sujeto productor...". Finally, neither literature nor culture can influence, "...la constitución de relaciones fundamentales del sujeto productor con respeto a sí mismo, a los diversos factores de la estructura social y al proceso histórico..." (210).

For Losada, on the other hand, literary production, at least in the Latin American context, is not only understood within a general objective situation, but also in relation to, "...una respuesta subjetiva de un grupo particular, como una toma de posición condicionada por una serie de demandas y requerimientos de esa situación, pero determinada por un proyecto social...". It is not just a "forma de conocimiento", but also a form of "comportamiento" in relation to that situation, and, "...a la naturaleza, función y tareas que ha de cumplir la producción de la cultura...". Nor is it a passive act; on the contrary, "...es producto de una actividad conciente de un sujeto social que, de alguna manera, tiene dominio de sus fines y escoge medios y estrategias para cumplirlos y que, precisamente en el cumplimiento de esa actividad, se constituye en un nuevo sujeto social, sólo posible en esa forma de cultura...". Apart from considering the social subject in terms of language, conscience and culture, he conceives of him, "...en el orden real de la existencia histórica y social, estableciendo especiales relaciones objetivas consigo mismo, con los demás hombres, con la cultura y con la historia, es decir constituyendo una particular realidad histórico-social...". So, adds Losada, if literature is not just "...producto de la estructura social, sino...de la praxis de un sujeto social...", then the only way to attend to its specificity "...es articulando de manera inmediata los conjuntos literarios con la praxis social de los sujetos productores y, mediatamente, con la situación de la estructura social..." (210–11).

Losada's model thus conceives of literature as a "social institution". The understanding of the literary system as a social institution is connected to Losada's critique of both the type of sociological approach described above, and also immanentist perspectives. For him, the analysis of the literary phenomenon cannot be exclusively reduced either "...al nivel inmanente de los textos, ni al nivel trascendente de la totalidad social [ya que] todo conjunto de textos está producido por su sujeto social y sólo en su vida práctica tiene existencia real...". Losada's model thus proposes two stages in the critic's work: firstly, understanding "the new language", and secondly, understanding the fact that, "...allí se constituyen relaciones entre los hombres...". It is precisely this second aspect of literary production that is embraced by the concept of social institution (215), and this involves understanding the "...fenómeno humano como un proceso de autoproducción social...":

> Los resultados...[del proceso de autoproducción social] no son monumentos, ni tampoco efímeros instrumentos, sino el hombre mismo en el momento de instituir su conciencia y su existencia social, fundar el horizonte de su existencia y el modo de sus relaciones sociales, y definir un sentido de sí en el mundo, o para decirlo más exactamente, en el modo en que se da a sí mismo un mundo. De esta manera, las obras literarias son comprendidas como trascendiendo cada subjetividad individual, operando una fundación de la conciencia social más allá de cada existencia privada e instituyendo un mundo. Pero no permanecen ajenas a cada hombre, como "objetos" de contemplación, sino que son la objetivación de su conciencia social. De la misma manera, las obras literarias son comprendidas como directamente vinculadas al proceso de producción y de relaciones sociales en el que se encuentra articulado el grupo social que las produce, pero no son consideradas "productos" efímeros, superestructurales e instrumentales, sino como un momento del proceso de autoproducción social. (220)

Furthermore, although literature is a social institution, its character and function differentiate it from other social institutions. Its peculiarity arises from the fact that it is not related to the totality of society or to a period, but to "...la praxis de pequeños grupos sociales que, en ella, instituyen especiales modos de existencia...". But it also results from the fact that its manner of "establishing social reality" ("fundar la realidad social") differs from that of the State, Technology, Science, and so on, and has more affinity with the way in which Religion, Philosophy, traditions, beliefs, values, etc., "shape social consience" (220–21).

Losada considers the Lukacsian interpretation of the literature of bourgeois societies to be valid for Latin America only on a general level, inasmuch as the evolution of the literature of the continent has been tied to that of the metropoli. However, he implicitly questions the validity of a simple transposition of that interpretation —without modifications or corrections— to Latin American literature whose profile is marked by the terms of dependency which govern its social and cultural articulation to the continent's societies, as well as by the unevenness of their capitalist development and the consequent difference of their "social referents". Thus, Losada's account of Latin American socio-cultural specificity takes its "peripheral" condition as a starting point. This would explain, to a certain extent, the marginality of its entirely urban intellectual elites with respect to national society in general and to the popular sector's demands in particular. Equally, the said condition of dependency also results in the contradictory and conflictive position of the elites in the face of the modernizing projects originating in the metropolitan centers which they intend to reproduce (189 and 195–99). The corrections to Lukács proposed by Losada aim, then, to look at literature,

> como una peculiar institución social no referida a la sociedad en su conjunto ni dependiendo inmediatamente de sus procesos de evolución, sino referida a la constitución de pequeños grupos que, en la producción de tipos diferentes de cultura, han establecido determinadas relaciones con los diversos grupos dominantes y dominados de su sociedad, han tomado diversas opciones frente a las posibilidades del desarrollo histórico y, por todo ello, han constituido de una manera peculiar el ámbito de su realidad. (199)

But before going any further, we would like to call attention to the problematic nature of two of Losada's concepts, namely, his notions of *sujeto productor* and *autoproducción social*. As has already been shown, it is true that both these notions can be understood in the context of his reaction against certain Lukacsian ideas, such as his notion of literature as reflection and his denial of a place for subjectivity within his interpretation. Nevertheless, Losada's attempt to retrieve that subjectivity, as well as an active function for literary production within society which surpasses that of the simple reproduction of the social structure, leads to a certain voluntarist dimension within his discourse which does not consider any mediation between subjectivity and change. This voluntarist dimension is principally suggested by his idea of *autoproducción social*, an idea which appears to suggest that the capacity to transform reality is a matter of pure volition. But this impression of voluntarism is also linked to the vague nature of his concept of *sujeto productor*, whose constitution and concrete socio-cultural articulations are not sufficiently systematized by Losada. The *sujeto productor* is described as being certain "elites" or "small groups", but its identity with regard to its relationship to diverse social or ethnic groups is not presented with sufficient clarity. His discourse on the articulation of that *sujeto productor* to the demands of one or another social sector, is similarly lacking in clarity. Again, these options seem to be explained as being the result of an act of volition on the part of certain individuals, without enabling one to understand the reason for their social coherence as a group, let alone the reason for that choice.

However, Losada believes his model offers a response to the aforementioned problems yet to be resolved by criticism. In other words, in the first instance it would explain the diachronic variations of the literary process at sub-regional level, and the non-simultaneous appearance of each of the three literary systems of the period following the bourgeois revolution, "...según el proceso de urbanización y de transformación de la estructura social tradicional...",[11] as well as the multiplicity of movements until now presented as "...homogéneos en cada sub-región...". Equally, it would account for the coexistence of totally divergent movements in the same region in terms of the existence of, "...proyectos y sujetos productores diferentes frente a la misma situación de la estructura social...". Finally, it would create an alternative to the generational schema by interpreting the differences between the works of contemporary authors, as responses to "diferentes demandas y...[a la identificación de cada uno de ellos] con diferentes proyectos sociales..." (1976a, 212–13). Losada's model, completed and improved through the course of his work, serves as the foundation for his re-reading of the Latin American literary process.

Losada's constant point of departure is the need to provide a conceptual system which would enable the aforementioned failings within criticism and literary history to be overcome. He begins his research project on "erudite" urban Latin American literature ("literatura latinoamericana ilustrada") in 1976 during his stay at Austin University. He continues with this project in West Germany, where he is resident from 1977 working as a lecturer and researcher. Following his contact with the ethnohistorian R. Schaedel in the United States, Losada incorporates into his writing an anthropological dimension which is to remain a constant thread in all his

---

[11] These criteria govern his works on "dependent" and "autonomous" cultures. See (1977b, 1979a, 1983a).

work after 1976, and which, increasingly, facilitates the possibility of integrating his sociological interpretation with a cultural perspective invaluable to his task of clarifying the peculiarities of the Latin American literary process (Lienhard et al 1986, 633–34).

His central objective at this stage is the formulation of "aesthetic/cultural paradigms" ("paradigmas estético-culturales") understood in terms of the "modes of cultural production" which support them. The application of these paradigms would enable him to account for the specific characteristics of the "erudite" urban literature of the continent —Spanish America in particular— and explain its social articulations from "the pre-industrial period of expansion" up until "the metropolitan and internationalist period" (Losada 1977a, 1977b, 1979a, 1979b).[12] "Erudite" urban cultures are understood to be those that began to emerge at the end of the eighteenth century with the collapse of the colonial world, a period in which the still (and even today) unresolved "proceso de crisis social permanente" started. It is within this context —and in a response that has a dialectical character— that intellectuals' production is carried out. So, for Losada, the reconstruction of this historical process and its cultural production is the pre-requisite to understanding the particular characteristics of contemporary Latin American society and culture.[13] In the Argentinean's own words, looking back to the past is indispensable, since, "...los datos del siglo XIX y de los primeros treinta años del siglo XX interesan en cuanto constituyen el horizonte cultural de la sociedad de hoy" (Losada 1976a, 177–79).

In works immediately following on from *Creación y praxis* (1976a), Losada initially proposes two paradigms to classify Latin American modern literary production: that of "dependent" literatures (1780–1920), and that of "autonomous" literatures (1840–1970), and he conceives of them as an alternative to "national" literary models and to the periodization schemes traditionally used in the discipline —schemes which establish a relationship of homology between the evolution of Latin American writing and that of Europe, playing down the particularities of the former. Losada's interpretation reveals the chronological disparity with which each of these aesthetic/cultural projects is articulated in the various regions of

---

[12] For a theoretical systematization of the principles which govern Losada's discourse on the romantic production of Peru and the River Plate region in the second half of the nineteenth century (1983), see Losada (1977a, 1977b). On River Plate "social realism", see (1979a). For a commentary on Losada (1983a) see Ventura (1987, 229–31).

[13] For a description of the break-up of the colonial world and the relationship between this and cultural production, see Losada (1981b, 177–78).

the continent, and associates such disparity with the uneven penetration of the modernizing process into Latin American societies. The said paradigms are understood in terms of their respective modes of production, the distinctive traits of their *sujetos productores*, and the particular social formations to which they are articulated. Dependent literatures, for example, are produced by elites closely associated with, and dependent on, the dominant oligarchical system in their societies and in restricted conditions of modernization, as in Peru between 1780 and 1920, while autonomous literatures make their first appearance when that dependent relationship enters into crisis and when social reconstruction becomes imminent in the River Plate region between 1840 and 1880. Autonomous literatures become consolidated as a dominant phenomenon in the twentieth century, following the First World War, at a time when cities are being transformed into popular, metropolitan and internationalized spaces (1977a, 9).[14]

In his work during the 1980s, Losada concentrates on comparative research into the literary development of the different historico-cultural regions of the continent throughout the twentieth century. He isolates and classifies new modes of cultural production which complement, and to some extent reformulate, the modes of production schema he had worked out towards the end of the previous decade.

Losada continues to refine his interpretation of "dependent" literatures, but he abandons the concept of "autonomous" literatures, and replaces it, as far as the twentieth century is concerned, with two differentiated aesthetic/cultural paradigms which have different social functions and are articulated to two equally differentiated social formations. Firstly, there is the paradigm of the literatures which he defines as "marginal" ("marginales"), produced in the metropolitan spaces with large immigrant populations where a new socio-economic structure has been established. This new structure facilitates an institutional transformation and the incorporation of the "sub-region" into the international market, and in it, "...se trata de reproducir formas de vida y de cultura europeas". Secondly, there is the paradigm of the "social-revolutionary" ("social-revolucionarias") literatures, articulated in periods of crisis and restructuring of traditional society under imperialist domination. In contrast to the previous kind, these are literatures produced in societies characterized by the lack of stabilization of a new socio-economic structure, which bears with it, "...una experiencia histórica de transición irresuelta que determina una tensión prerevolucion-

---

[14] A more detailed examination of these paradigms is offered in the second section of this chapter.

aria o directamente comprometida...". These two social spaces evidently condition the practice of intellectuals and the functions which they conceive for their production (1983b, 8–9).[15]

This reformulation is initially the result of the comparative study of two "sub-regions": the River Plate (1880–1960) and the Caribbean region (1890–1980), extreme exponents of the said modes of production. Losada considers that research effectively shows how all the literary projects of the Southern Cone are produced within a "cosmopolitan metropolis", while the Caribbean region is engaged in a continual struggle to eliminate the colonial legacy between 1880 and 1960. Such a struggle would have occurred in the River Plate region between 1840 and 1880 (1983b, 29–30). Although Losada's work focuses on the study of three "sub-regions" —the Southern Cone, the Andes and the Caribbean— it is possible to extend this methodology of comparative study to the other socio-cultural areas of Latin America where the situation is much more complex since the two formations, their respective problems, and, consequently, both types of literature, co-exist within them.[16] On the basis of this schema, Losada proposes, as the next stage of his project, the design of an alternative system of periodization which, faithful to the specificity and density of the Latin American literary process, makes possible the study of, "...los distintos procesos literarios que se articulan a las diferentes formaciones sociales que co-existen en América Latina a lo largo de los últimos cien años..." (1983b, 9).

Losada would not, however, succeed in completing a new model of periodization for Latin American literary production. He died in an aeroplane accident at the beginning of 1985 when he was on his way to Nicaragua to take part in a literary conference in Managua (Lienhard et al 1986, 635). Nevertheless, based on the results of his elucidation of the dominant modes of cultural production of the nineteenth and twentieth centuries, he would sketch out some concepts in his last writings which support the clarification of the different periods specific to Latin American literatures and provide an alternative to the traditional periodizations. We

---

[15] Losada dedicated several studies to the clarification of these modes of production from 1981 onwards. See in particular (1987, parts II and III), which pulls together the fundamental results of his research during this last period. For a resumé of the general lines of his project, see (176–83). A more complete description of the concepts of "marginal" and "social-revolutionary" literatures is made in the second section of this chapter.

[16] For a comparative study of the conditions of production in the Central American/Caribbean region and Buenos Aires, see Losada (1984a, 1983c).

are essentially referring to his definitions of the *momentos* (*formativos, de superación* or *decisivos*) with which he seeks to give an account of the stages which govern the Latin American social process as opposed to that of Europe, and that would ultimately determine the exact periods of Latin American letters (Losada 1983b, 1986).[17]

Furthermore, Losada's reading does not just constitute a description of two differentiated modes of producing culture, carried out from a supposedly "neutral" ideological position. Losada's discourse is committed to an evaluation of those modes and openly opts for one of them —the "social-revolutionary" literatures. The value of his retrieval of those literatures for Latin American criticism is indisputable, since they represent an alternative formula of modernity. The same is true of his questioning of a criticism which proposes modernity as an aesthetic parameter and which, furthermore, has an extremely narrow notion of modernity: that of internationalized languages, produced in the metropolitan centres, disconnected from the other social spaces which co-exist with them and also from the concerns of the majority of the population (1986, 164). Opting for this perspective leads criticism not only to classify the Latin American literary process in two essentially opposing tendencies, but also to undervalue that production which is linked to social formations still struggling to overcome the colonial legacy, and to stigmatize it as "traditional", or, ultimately, anachronistic (1983b, 23). Losada's opting for "traditional" literatures leads to a retrieval for Latin American criticism of the elements of popular culture which they contain. In this connection, together with Angel Rama's work on transculturation in Latin American narrative and that of Cornejo Polar on the heterogeneity of Peruvian narrative, Losada's work constitutes a fundamental contribution to cultural studies in Latin America.

While not intending to question the general validity of Losada's proposal, it is important to underline the presence of problems of a theoretical and methodological order, such as his disqualifying of "cosmopolitan" literatures on a predominantly ideological basis; these literatures are considered, by Losada, to be condemned to formalize the "capitalist alienation" which governs "human relations" in the metropolitan sphere, to the total exclusion of any other reality within the "national" space. Losada is, to a certain extent, aware of the ideological reductionism suggested in his theoretical proposal; it is a concern which he had already expressed at the beginning of his project in *Creación y praxis* (1976a), and

---

[17] For a reconstruction of the notions on which Losada proposes to found an alternative periodization model, see the second section of this chapter.

which he was to reiterate later on in his article "Bases para un proyecto de una historia social de la literatura en América Latina (1780–1970)" where he recognizes that his delimitation of the modes of production of the literature of the continent provides,

> ...un nivel sistemático de abstracción donde se hace demasiado fácil "clasificar" todos los autores, obras y fenómenos literarios antes de analizarlos...Si deseaba, por ejemplo, llamar la atención sobre la necesidad preliminar de elaborar amplios conjuntos como el de la "novela subjetivista rioplatense" y posteriormente de contrastarlos con conjuntos anteriores (como la "literatura oligárquica") o conjuntos simultáneos (como la "novela indigenista peruana"), para aprender a elaborar otros niveles del fenómeno y ejercitarse en la forma en que se pueden articular a la sociedad y a la historia, me encontraba que en vez de haber estimulado una visión más científica y crítica del fenómeno, los oyentes habían comprendido que se trataba de algo así como de una receta para diferenciar las literaturas reaccionarias de las progresistas. Y se trataba precisamente de superar esas simplificaciones. (1981b, 188)

But despite these expressed good intentions, we wonder whether such simplifications are not present in Losada's treatment of "marginal" literatures, which he sees as being both rootless and confined in subjectivity, and in which he finds no progressive element nor any link whatsoever with realities beyond those which make up metropolitan space. Does this reading stem from the imposition of ideological a-prioris which precondition interpretation? Furthermore, perhaps it is possible to ask whether the said a-prioris originate in the transposition of Dependency Theory schemes onto the cultural sphere? And finally: Beatriz Sarlo's works on the literary modernization process in the Argentina of the early twentieth century would go on to show how all literary production of the time, including that considered to be purely internationalized and non-referential (Borges is a prime example), is immersed in the debate on national identity (Sarlo 1988).

The concept of marginality itself is finally questioned in the collective article which acts as a prologue to Losada's last book: the authors rightly wonder to what extent it is possible to maintain the idea of the intellectual's alienation from society, or whether the "cultural aristocratism" ("aristocratismo cultural") of a Borges or a Macedonio Fernández necessarily constitutes a "marginal" situation within society and, in any case, whether the "marginality" of intellectuals alludes to, "...la posición social del escritor, al tipo de lenguaje producido, o... a ambos?" (Ventura 1987, xviii).

It is equally necessary to consider the critique which has justifiably been made of the very general and indiscriminate Losadian application of the notion of "social-revolutionary" literature. In fact, in the prologue mentioned above, the authors express their disagreement over the lack of attention which Losada's interpretation pays to the political and ideological divergences between the various authors embraced by that term. Their questioning is illustrated by the case of the social novel of North-Eastern Brasil of the 1930s, where "...a partir de una cierta convergencia *temática*, proyectos bastante dispares y contradictorios entre sí..." are grouped (xvi; underlined in the original). In fact, this could be extended to, for example, *indigenista* literatures, whose internal differences have been studied at length by the Peruvian Cornejo Polar (1989b). In the same prologue, another equally valid observation is made about the relationship, widely recognized within criticism, between this deficiency in Losada's discourse, and the notorious "...ausencia de un análisis específico de las formas literarias y de las cuestiones relativas al lenguaje..." (Ventura 1987, xvi). Evidently, this denies the Argentinean critic the opportunity to put his interpretive ideological schemes to the test on concrete literary works and finally to break with this Manichaean tradition within Latin American cultural criticism which prevents him from accounting for the avant-gardes and exploring the complex relationships between the avant-gardes and modernity. Furthermore, an examination of the specific dimensions of literature —language, form— could lead to a revision of the old dominant paradigm within Latin American thought, revitalized by the Cuban Revolution and endorsed by Losada, according to which Latin American literature is only seen to justify itself by making a concrete intervention into social reality. What we are trying to question here is not literature's potential for social transformation, but the lack of any concept of mediation in Losada's discourse when dealing with the articulations between literature and society. It is worth stressing the richness of Mariátegui's critical language in this connection, as pointed out earlier in this study.

In both the above cases, Losada is rightly criticized for the fact that his discourse tends to produce new types of homogenization of the Latin American literary process which, to a certain extent, undermines his project for the elucidation of the plurality of the continent's literary production.

Although Losada's interpretation may be producing new homogenizations, it is also true that the vision of the twentieth century literary panorama that he provides in the final stages of his work enables him to challenge another deeply-engrained perspective within criticism dealing with contemporary literary production: its homogenization of this production through the notion of the "new novel" or "new literature", a notion which dilutes the differences between the various projects that in fact make up not "Latin American literature", but contemporary Latin American *literatures* (Losada 1981b, 180). Apart from the two modes of production defined as dominant throughout the twentieth century, he now presents a new proposal concerning the years 1960–1980. This would be outlined —although never fully developed— in his last works, delineating that new system which relates to the rise of the popular movement and the *rapprochement* between that movement and intellectuals at the time (1987, 172–75). But above all, we must take into account his discourse on the processes of internationalization, his analysis of the "espacio [social] concreto" in which those processes take place, and the social function of the two modes of production that he establishes for Latin American literatures. Losada calls into question a number of the principles on which criticism has constructed the notion of "new literature". In the first place, he rejects the homogenization of "...toda la producción artística de los intelectuales profesionales, eruditos, sofisticados, de élites... en toda la región" under one single literary system. The works of Carpentier or Asturias in no way form part of the same mode of production as those of Borges or Onetti, for example, despite the fact that they all constitute internationalized, metropolitan and professionalized phenomena. On the contrary, they are articulated to different social spaces and fulfill different social functions. The work of Carpentier and Asturias, in contrast to the writers of the River Plate region, is understood by Losada as going through its "internationalization" stage, belonging to the "social-revolutionary" literatures of the Caribbean/Central American region (74–75).

A second perspective rejected by Losada relates to the division made by criticism between "the new literature" and all that production tagged "social realism", a problem we have already discussed. Losada's reading, however, demonstrates how the work of authors classified until then under that heading —and, what is more, undervalued for their "anachronism"— share "un mismo horizonte de expectativas" with the "internationalized" intellectuals of the Caribbean/Central American region, and together form, "un mismo sistema cultural [pero] en un momento anterior a su internacionalización" —that of "social-revolutionary" literatures. For Losada, such a system, in fact, "...se constituye, primero, en un espacio local para, después, sin cambiar de naturaleza, irse ampliando hasta llegar a internacionalizarse y desempeñar las notables funciones que hoy cumple en esta nueva etapa del mundo tanto en Latinoamérica como en la escena mundial" (1987, 75 and 1986, 27–28).

The analysis of the social and intellectual context in which the various Latin American literatures are produced and its notable difference with regard to European societies, would bring Losada to open up a new area of study during the final period of his work. The writings of the last few years gather together his considerations on the general phenomenon of "internationalization" within Latin American letters since their origins and, more specifically, on the diverse processes of internationalization followed by the literatures of the continent during the period between the wars. Through this new approach, Losada offers some of his most interesting contributions to the discipline, enriching the understanding of the particular characteristics of contemporary literary production and the already noted diversity of aesthetic/cultural projects to which that production is articulated (1983c, 1984a).

Losada's point of departure is the unavoidable fact that Latin American literature is by definition an internationalized phenomenon: "[s]u inevitable pertenencia a un...horizonte cultural dominado por actores históricos que estan fuera de la región es un factor constitutivo de sus formas de producción y de su desarrollo" (1984a, 15).

This statement not only underlines a specific characteristic of Latin American letters, but also a problem with which literature of the continent will always be bound up, namely, its articulation —from the periphery— to the cultural developments of the metropoli. Throughout much of their history, the local intellectual elites would be in the position of only being able to receive and reformulate discourses, without ever having the real opportunity to integrate themselves into the arena of the central societies. It is only recently that the chance for active participation "en la configuración de la cultura internacional" has presented itself to Latin American literature. Losada is interested in establishing the theoretical basis which would make it possible to give an account of the processes of cultural production through which the transformation of the role traditionally played by Latin American literature on an international level occurred. To this end, he proposes the examination of differentiated cases and the comparative study of the relations between each of these with both European and Latin American culture, with a view to determining the significance of the processes of internationalization for the literature of the continent. Losada identifies three cases which he considers to be fundamental, in that they figure, "...entre los mayores de [la literatura de la región], son claramente diferentes, y representan procesos y funciones que se articulan a los núcleos constitutivaos de la sociedad y la cultura latinoamericana: espacios tradicionales no occidentales/espacios nacionales autónomos/y espacios europeos de vanguardia". These cases are, firstly, that of Caribbean/Central American literatures, articulated to European metropoli (Carpentier, Asturias, Cesaire); secondly, that of literatures produced in the Latin American metropoli (the "nacional-metropolitano" case) and integrated to "espacios intelectuales autónomos locales" (Borges, M. de Andrade, O. Paz); and finally, that of literatures of traditional urban space integrated "a las culturas nacionales por su articulación con la cultura no-occidental" (Arguedas, Rulfo, Roa Bastos) (20–23).

Losada would only manage to study the first two of these cases. Of the two, the Caribbean/Central American case is perhaps that which offers results most useful to the treatment of contemporary literary production. This is because it discredits, as we have stated, the perspective that reduces its complexity and diversity to the notion of "new literature", which erases any socio-historical articulations, and overlooks the plurality of the aesthetic/cultural projects proposed from the period between the wars onwards. The description and analysis of the circumstances in which the process of internationalization of these literatures occurs enable Losada to establish their existence as an independent literary system, and to highlight the differences of their aesthetic/cultural project with regard to the River Plate avant-gardes with which they have been merged by criticism as a result of a view which sets up an opposition between "modernity" and the "traditional" character of social narrative. As well as making this distinction between two literary systems, Losada restores the links between this narrative and the internationalized literatures of the Caribbean and Central America.

Losada's most interesting contribution here is the attention he gives to the context of double articulation, in both this case and that of the River Plate avant-gardes, in which the processes of internationalization of both literatures occur as well as the attention he gives to the discourses and cultural practices with which each of these literatures identifies in the social spaces from which they originate. The internationalization of Caribbean/Central American literature takes place in the context of the insertion of the *sujeto productor* "...[de una parte] a la sub-región [y de otra]... a los centros hegemónicos ...[desde donde] produce una contra-cultura...". The producer of this literature comes from societies with enormous peasant populations of indigenous or African origin, societies which have yet to eradicate the colonial legacy, societies with urban traditional spaces yet, lacking the institutional networks which would allow for the professionalization of cultural production. Generally, the writer would be, "...un estudiante, que por el sólo hecho de serlo, se separa de su base social y se echa a cuestas un problema de *no-identidad* [underlined in the original] que lo hostigará toda su vida..."; but he would also be an individual incapable of identifying with the dominant elite, be it "...una oligarquía terrateniente que ahoga toda perspectiva intelectual...", or

"...dictadorzuelos que imponen un tipo irracional de relaciones sociales...". The limitations on the work of the intellectual which derive from such a context are at the root of the second social articulation of his work: the central metropoli to which many of them often move as forced exiles as a result of repression. But this second articulation has more precise characteristics: the authors of the Caribbean/Central American case join, specifically, the radical, contestatory, anti-capitalist intellectual sectors within the metropolitan societies. From this particular position, they deal, in their literature, with, "...aquella agenda de cuestiones que se constituyó en su primera experiencia de la propia sociedad...". But, stresses Losada, their vision of the problems of their countries of origin arises from a perspective which is no longer local but global, which calls into question the values which support the hegemonic system: "...la lucha por producir una nueva sociedad en América Latina [es interpretada] como un aspecto de la lucha a que se ve enfrentada toda la humanidad por superar un tipo destructivo de organización social e internacional basada en la explotación capitalista". It is also from their metropolitan experience that intellectuals like Carpentier and Asturias will "discover", re-evaluate and take on as their own, the autochtonous cultures of their societies, and will try to resolve the problem of "...*su no-identidad con su propio pueblo por pertenecer al sector dominante* [underlined in the original] que los rechazaba, y por incorporarse como intelectuales al mundo ideológico e institucional metropolitano que despreciaba su cultura". It is from there that they would formulate and incorporate those "...nuevos lenguajes narrativos que pretenden penetrar la subjetividad colectiva de las antiguas culturas indígenas y negras del Caribe..." into international culture (1987, 62–67).

On the other hand, certain reductionist operations performed on avant-garde languages counterbalance the contributions to criticism offered by the Losadian treatment of the "national-metropolitan" case. This case arises in the metropolitan city, with the development of an autonomous intellectual sphere giving birth, in the 1930s, to its own literary languages —clearly different from the preceding literary systems— articulated and incorporated into international culture; these are those languages generally defined by criticism as "avant-garde" or "cosmopolitan", and evaluated in terms of their modernity. Losada's reading questions the evaluative legitimacy of this criterion of modernity, and calls attention to the insufficiency of simply acknowledging the internationalization of these literatures. Such an approach overlooks, on the one hand, the problematic aspects of the relations between the intellectual sphere of the Latin American cities and the intellectual sphere of the hegemonic centres; on the other hand, it overlooks the fact that "erudite" cultural production in Latin America historically occurs in the context of a no less conflictive relationship with traditional popular cultures which are often not incorporated into "national" society by the capitalist project. The processes of internationalization of Latin American letters are, by definition, of a contradictory nature and have a direct influence on the specificty of their own development. In opposition to criticism's traditional celebratory attitude towards the modernity of the avant-gardes, Losada sets out to elucidate the type of intertextual relationships established between the "erudite" Latin American intellectual sphere, and both the sphere of the metropoli and that of popular culture with which it co-exists in its local environment; in Losada's terms, the official cultures and the popular cultures.

Losada's analysis operates on at least two levels: on the one hand, there is that of the relationship between the avant-garde works and their own intellectual spheres. The "cosmopolitan" writers not only transform themselves as a response to "...los estímulos que...vienen del mundo de la cultura internacional, sino [a]...la articulación a la propia tradición literaria...". Borges can thus be understood, up to a point, as a continuation and rupture in the face of *modernismo*, and Paz may equally be indebted both to the national identity discourses proposed by the Mexican Revolution's cultural policies, and to the weight of avant-garde tendencies. On the other hand, Losada seeks to "...interpretar las transformaciones del sistema literario por la relación entre el espacio intelectual que lo sostiene institucionalmente, con los demás espacios culturales que caracterizan la complejidad metropolitana". Losada's emphasis is focused on the importance of local circumstances in the production of avant-garde languages. The modernization of urban space and its greater socio-cultural complexity accompany the transformations of the "erudite" intellectual sphere; although the latter gains autonomy from the ruling elites, it is also displaced and pushed into marginality and to its disassociation from social developments as a response to the rise of mass culture and the institutionalization of official culture with which it competes:

> *Contra estos dos nuevos espacios culturales* se debe defender, readaptar y desarrollar el antiguo espacio intelectual ilustrado, redefiniendo su propia función y su identidad global. Sus instrumentos serán la creación de un lenguaje de vanguardia que encierra el arte literario en el horizonte simbólico y la herencia cultural de los intelectuales profesionalizados; y para lograr desarrollar ese lenguaje y adquirir una nueva legitimidad, tratarán de establecer nuevas *relaciones literarias* con la tradición cultural popular y con la cultura europea. (25–26; emphasis in the original)

Losada is interested in investigating in what way and to what extent the formulation of avant-garde languages and their new social functions are a result of both their interaction with popular culture and with European culture. But above all —and this is one of his most stimulating contributions to research into cultural specificity— Losada's emphasis is focused on the identification of particular discourses with which avant-garde literatures will establish intertextual relationships, and the light they shed on the nature of the project of the said literatures. Thus Losada underlines the connection between the discourses with which the avant-gardes identify both within the popular framework, and within the European sphere. He also emphasizes the ambiguity with which the works of the time confront the modernization of their society: on the one hand, this literature endorses the national project of capitalist modernization, but, at the same time, it distances itself from the society which results from the advance of that project. Thus Losada calls attention, firstly, to the fact that the "...horizonte de lo popular [que dicha literatura maneja] no es la cultura de masas que transforma rápidamente su antigua ciudad, sino el compadrito orillero (Borges), [o] el gaucho que había despreciado y perseguido pero que ahora está a su servicio incorporado a sus estancias (Güiraldes)..." Secondly, Losada writes, the interest of the avant-garde is not centered on the most progressive European proposals, "...sino [en] los postulados decadentistas de fin de siglo, la fenomenología como una filosofía de la subjetividad, planteos esencialistas, [y] reflexiones sociológicas como aquellas que insisten en una visión racista y discriminatoria de la nueva sociedad o que enfatizan la crisis de lo moderno...". Losada wonders, finally, to what extent the aim of this literature is —through those intertextual processes— to "...reelaborar el mundo contemporáneo a partir de un sentimiento epigonal de la cultura del pasado?" For Losada, this implies "an identity crisis", rather than "...una expansión de la cultura latinoamericana hacia la cultura mundial" (27–29).

The usefulness of this approach is unquestionable in that it directs its attention to historical and cultural processes particular to the Latin American societies which condition the choices ("escogencias") of their authors, leaving behind those ahistorical perspectives which conceive of Latin American literary production as a passive repetition of European models. Without discounting his fruitful point of departure, Losada must be criticized, however, for abandoning half-way his analysis of the processes of intertextuality embarked upon by the avant-garde River Plate writers: it is not enough to specify the discourses and cultural practices with which these authors identify. There should also be an examination —in the texts themselves— both of the transformations which those discourses undergo, and also of the different functions which their new context assigns them. Ultimately, this would involve the displacing of the emphasis on the "sources" to concentrate on the new languages formulated.

Such a procedure would allow us to put to the test the ideological orientation of the circular argument which, in effect, controls Losada's analysis: the "marginal" writers, who are reactionary, select reactionary discourses and so produce reactionary projects. Thus Losada loses sight of his own belief that in every process of cultural production in Latin America there is, "un proceso de selección y transformación" of the materials taken from both the European and the local traditional poles (30). The "social revolutionary" literatures of the Caribbean/Central American region, incorporated into the cultural sphere of the European metropoli, and to which Losada is committed, are conferred a uniformly counter-discursive character; in contrast to the "marginal" literatures, these literatures are considered to be articulated to counter-hegemonic intellectual sectors, and to confront "...la cultura europea tradicional *participando en la producción de una nueva cultura mundial* . Desde Europa logran impugnar la legitimidad de todo el proceso histórico que se desarrolló bajo su dominio, y reinterpretan, con la perspectiva de los pueblos y las culturas dominadas y hasta ahora despreciadas por el centro hegemónico, el sentido del hombre y las posibilidades del desarrollo histórico de la humanidad" (31; emphasis in the original). Losada undoubtedly does justice to this second variety of the processes of internationalization followed by Latin American literature during the period between the wars, whereas his evaluation of the "marginal" writers of the River Plate region is less convincing.

Nevertheless, it is undeniable that his discourse on the processes of internationalization of Latin American cultural production offers a valid new avenue to the discipline. Much can be gained from his proposal for the consideration of those processes from the point of view of the contradictory relationship between erudite Latin American culture, central metropolitan culture and traditional popular cultures, and of the role of this relationship in the formulation of new languages. Furthermore, this approach has the potential to tone down Losada's own ideological reading of the two modes of literary production predominant in the twentieth century ("marginal" and "social-revolutionary"). But it must be reiterated that this would require the analysis of concrete texts and an analysis of its languages and forms, both of which are absent from Losada's work. His discourse again ends in a judgment that, on the one hand, condemns the "marginal" literatures as literatures reduced to a reflection and the copying of the proposals of the central cultures, irredeemably incapable of producing counter-discourses; on the other hand, he considers that the "social-revolutionary" literatures, linked to the European metropoli, monopolize all transforming and counter-cultural potential. While these literatures, "...que se identifican con los oprimidos...", propose to "...configurar la conciencia colectiva y reformular la experiencia histórica de las culturas sometidas por la expansión occidental...", the former, "...que se identifican con Europa...", aim at "...el desarrollo de la conciencia subjetiva marginal, reelaborando la herencia tradicional occidental..." (30–31 and 35).

As we have said, Losada calls into question both the notion of "the nation" associated with the unfinished bourgeois project in Latin America, and the uncritical conception of "the nation" which ignores the fact that Latin American "national identity" is constructed in the context of the tension between metropolitan culture and local popular cultures. Nevertheless, his reading is not expressly trapped in the discourse —linked to the cultural nationalism of the left in the sixties and seventies— which defines the Latin American "national identity" as being articulated to traditional/peasant cultures as opposed to "cosmopolitan" cultures, which are viewed as the antithesis of things national. Although Losada does not resort to language characteristic of nationalism of the left, one nevertheless wonders to what extent his opting for "social-revolutionary" literatures over "marginal" literatures has this perspective as its background, or even, to what extent it constitutes another version of the same dilemma. After all, Losada ends up, in a fatalistic and Manichaean manner, reducing the alternatives by which Latin American culture may define its identity to two options: either a copy of Europe by the internationalized literatures of the Latin American metropoli, or the production of a counter-culture by the literatures linked to traditional cultures. Losada expresses it in the following terms:

> ...se trata de redefinir cuál es la identidad de América Latina sin negar la evidencia constitutiva: su relación con Europa y su pertenencia al mundo hegemónico desde su integración a la historia mundial. Su cultura se ha visto forzada, desde su origen colonial, a desarrollarse como periferia de aquel otro universo que, por la violencia, se constituyó en sujeto de su historia. Si esto es así, hay que preguntarse francamente si este desarrollo cultural no *significa* otra cosa que la internacionalización resignada de esa situación como si ella constituyera su destino definitivo; si sólo es un fenómeno periférico, epigonal y repetitivo de los caminos transitados por la propia Europa; o si además de todo ello, revelando al mundo las vibraciones de un espíritu que quiere ser sujeto y conciencia de su propia historia, no refulge de tanto en tanto un lenguaje cultural que redefine inéditamente su posible identidad, desafiando una y otra vez todas las

evidencias empíricas y todos los discursos culturales que se la niegan. (35–36; emphasis in the original)

Despite his views on the active role of the peripheral cultures in their processes of appropriation and reworking of discourses, this same possibility is denied on principle to the urban modernized spaces, which Losada conceives of as being subjected to an unavoidably dependent relationship with regard to the hegemonic culture, in effect becoming "denationalized" spaces. Throughout his extensive work, Losada reiterates that a modernized urban space is, by definition, irredeemably given over to capitalist "alienation", while all resistance to that domination can only spring from intellectual spaces [with, perhaps, a "*national*" character] —ones which are committed to the traditional popular cultures not integrated with the modernized cities. Is it not also valid to wonder to what extent Losada's perspective actually constitutes just another version of a reading which reduces the understanding of Latin American literary production to a bi-polar schema compared to that discussed in the chapter on Angel Rama's work?

Although his handling of "erudite" literary production in the big modernized cities of the continent is finally problematic, as has been shown, his interpretation of the literatures of the Andean and Caribbean/Central American regions provides a fundamental contribution to Latin American historical/cultural criticism. As in Angel Rama's discourse, in Losada's, the literatures articulated to traditional cultures rightly benefit from a timely vindication and re-evaluation within the spectrum of contemporary literature. His proposal, like that of the Uruguayan critic, simultaneously breaks with homogenizing readings and contributes to the advance of the discipline in terms of the possibility of accounting both for the plurality of projects which make up the corpus of Latin American literature, and for the specificity of those projects with respect to metropolitan literatures.

Losada's Conceptual System: Some Definitions

This seems an appropriate moment to make an inventory of the main analytical categories used by the Argentinean critic throughout his work, and to try to synthesize some of the definitions of those which serve as the basis for his research work:

Social Praxis

The understanding of literary production as "social praxis" ("praxis social") is one of the key conceptual axes which runs through Losada's discourse. The Argentinean critic identifies three levels in his analysis of literature: "...el proceso de producción, el producto y la relación del sujeto productor consigo mismo y con la sociedad". These three levels, which constitute a single process, are embraced in the notion of social praxis which he defines as the social process, "...donde el sujeto productor, precisamente en su forma de producción y a través de su producto, establece un modo concreto de relación consigo mismo y con los hombres de su sociedad" (1976a, 121).

This notion of social praxis, together with the notions of "social institution" ("institution social") (18–19) and "horizon of existence" ("horizonte de existencia"), should be understood, according to Morales Saravia, in the context both of Losada's distancing from that tradition within sociological studies of literature which conceives of the latter as "...un elemento separado al que se tendría que articular [a la sociedad]...", and of his breaking away from "...ciertas formas de la teoría del reflejo..." (Lienhard et al 1986, 635–36).[18]

As Lienhard rightly notes, this notion of literature as praxis —and more precisely, as just another praxis among all the cultural praxes which occur in society— is, in fact, in accordance with, "...un pensamiento antropológico que considera las sociedades como vastos y complejos sistemas de comunicación, cuya segmentación no tiene sino un valor metodológico y didáctico. La práctica literaria, inseparable de las demás prácticas comunicativas, constituye uno de los segmentos aislables para los fines de una investigación científica apoyada en un instrumental específico...". In Lienhard's view, Losada's differentiation between "erudite" literary production and that based on popular culture and oral tradition, together with his work on the processes of intercommunication between both systems in Latin America, represents one of his most important contributions to the discipline (Lienhard et al 1986, 640–41). Nevertheless, as Ventura reminds us, it is fair to note that, in reality, this development is more the work of Lienhard than Losada, since popular literatures were never directly part of his research (Ventura 1987, viii). As Losada himself stresses, in effect, the re-reading of Latin American —and more specifically Spanish American— "erudite" urban literatures constitutes the focus of his writings (Losada 1979a, 9). Secondly, adds Lienhard, Losada's approach leads to, "...el rechazo, compartido hoy por numerosos

---

[18] However, it should be noted with reference to his own reading of modern literature as social praxis in order to account for the existence of literary production as concrete reality, that Losada himself refers us back to the notion of things "concrete" as explained by Lukács in *Historia y conciencia de clase,* Kosik in *Dialéctica de lo concreto,* and Houser in *Introducción a la historia del arte* (Losada 1976a, 215).

investigadores, de una dedicación exclusiva a los géneros literarios canónicos (europeos) y la valoración de los discursos antaño considerados como no literarios (crónicas, testimonios, folletines, etc.)" (Lienhard et al 1986, 640–41).

Literary System

Losada's project seeks to account for general processes and not particular developments. This brings him to formulate the notion of "literary system" ("sistema o conjunto literario"), and to place it at the centre of his research. According to Ventura, this concept originates from "...la distinción propuesta por Antonio Candido entre 'obras literarias' y 'sistema literario' (formado por obras, autores y público)..." (Ventura 1987, ix),[19] and constitutes, for Losada, the praxis of one and only one social group and is explained in terms of a particular "mode of production" ("modo de producción"). If the social group changes, and hence the mode of production varies, then we are in the territory of the formation of a new system (Losada 1976a, 276–77).

Now, within one system there can be different "tendencies" or "variations" ("tendencias" o "variaciones"), as is the case with the system of contemporary Peruvian narrative. The variations are a consequence of various types of "individual praxis" ("praxis individual") within the same collective subject in response, for example, to changes in the social context or to a transition in the socio-historic process (279). Contemporary Peruvian narrative is interpreted by Losada:

> ...como un sistema simbólico donde predominan los rasgos escépticos, negativos y nihilistas, la protesta y la falta de un sentido positivo de la existencia, como el quehacer cultural de un grupo marginal, como el hecho social de un sector de intelectuales que no ha podido hacer otra cosa que elaborar su propia frustración, atendiendo a las certidumbres que nacían en lo más auténtico de su subjetividad, y que se vieron condicionados por una situación de estrecha dependencia a una clase social y a una época histórica que los ha determinado y de la que nunca pudieron evadirse. (271)

But if, on the one hand, it is true that Vargas Llosa, Arguedas, Ribeyro, Scorza or Brice are read by Losada as members of the same "social subject" and that their cultural practice is characterized as marginal, it is also true that each one of them has interrogated his social reality from different angles, attempted to find answers following different paths and analyzed his relationship to society in diverse ways. This multiplicity of

---

[19] Ventura refers the reader to Candido (1975).

quests takes place even within each of these authors' work (140–71).

Faithful to his definition of literary system as the praxis of a *sujeto productor* in certain conditions of production, in later works Losada devises typologies of the dominant tendencies within the two literary systems associated with his "aesthetic/cultural paradigms" ("paradigmas estético-culturales"), "dependent cultures" ("culturas dependientes", 1780–1920), and "autonomous cultures" ("culturas autónomas", 1840–1970). Those paradigms lay the foundations for the reformulation of the Eurocentric system of periodization which governs Latin American literary histories. The former embraces those literatures traditionally grouped by criticism under the headings *clasicismo, romanticismo* and *modernismo*, or, more precisely, "...ilustración borbónica colonial, romanticismo peruano-mexicano, modernismo peruano-mexicano-chileno-argentino...", as for Losada, all of them "...pueden ser interpretados como distintas variaciones de un mismo fenómeno cultural..." (1977b, 3). The second, on the other hand, refers to the *romanticismo* of the River Plate region, a movement which would, in fact, inaugurate a new mode of cultural production which was to occupy a dominant place throughout the twentieth century (1979a, 23). Although it is not appropriate to comment now on the tendencies Losada identifies within each paradigm, we wish to take this opportunity to note them here; within the first paradigm, Losada identifies three tendencies: *populismo ilustrado, radicalismo abstracto* and *aristocratismo intimista*, while within the second he recognizes three projects: *realismo revolucionario (o social), subjetivismo marginal* and *naturalismo populista (o tremendista)*.[20]

The interpretation of the evolution of Latin American literature in terms of literary systems, rather than the traditional classification by "period", allows Losada to show the a-synchronicity of the literary process among the various regions of the continent. It also allows him to demonstrate the persistence of certain modes of production and certain aesthetic/cultural paradigms in particular regions, throughout periods which are longer than criticism is willing to accept and despite the fact that, in other cultural areas, new literary systems —linked to new *sujetos productores-receptores* and new social circumstances— may already have been articulated. Losada understands the changes in these circumstances to be largely the consequence of the varying pace at which the modernizing process penetrates Latin American societies and transforms their social structure —changes

---

[20] For a characterization of the tendencies within the first paradigm, see Losada (1977b, 11–23). The tendencies within the second paradigm are described in Losada (1977a, 30).

which are correlative to the variations on the cultural production level. This is the case with, for example, "dependent" literatures (*romanticismo peruano*) and "autonomous" literatures (*romanticismo del Río de la Plata*) which are projects which have essentially divergent literary and social meanings despite their chronological coincidence (1977a, 1977b).

Finally, the literary systems do not necessarily appear in succession one after the other, as traditional critical models would have it. In fact, they can even exist simultaneously, so that in any given historical period it is possible to find various systems in coexistence. Thus, while, for example, contemporary Peruvian literature is categorized as forming one single literary system, in other Latin American countries the predominant feature is instead,

> ...la coexistencia de tres sistemas literarios ampliamente diferenciados, contando cada uno de ellos con una evolución relativamente autónoma e independiente, siendo así que...la peruana no ha podido desplegar ni un sistema populista, vinculado a los *mass media* que atienda a la necesidad de consumo, distracción y consentimiento pasivo, aproblemático, de sectores medios que constituyen un mercado constante y determinan un modo de vivir cultural; ni tampoco un sistema aristocrático esteticista, autónomo, con voluntad de realizar una creación lingüistica que tenga el efecto de constituir a la propia subjetividad como una realidad "superior" de sus condicionamientos sociales (Borges, Cortázar, Lezama Lima, con una vida literaria aparentemente libre de toda coacción y toda referencia a la vida práctica política, económica y social como lo habían comenzado a esbozar el primer Vallejo, Eguren o Martín Adán). (1976a, 270; emphasis in the original)

Losada explains this characteristic of Latin American literary systems in terms of the peripheral condition of the societies of the continent and their economic and cultural dependency (195–200).

Ventura rightly identifies the principal virtue of the Losadian application of the notion of literary system to be his challenging both of the "homogeneous" and "unitary" vision of Latin American literature, and of the disregard for literary variations as a result of the use of criteria of "cultural synthesis". Certainly the legitimacy of the idea of *mestizaje* as an interpretive principle and supposed definition of Latin American literature is questioned by the Argentinean critic, insofar as the notion of *mestizaje* actually obscures the specific features of Latin American society, literature and history:

> En Latinoamérica, la idea del mestizaje olvida la de la dominación y dependencia, la articulación de la sociedad latinoamericana al proceso de desarrollo histórico desatada por la Edad Moderna y, posteriormente, por la revolución burguesa como entidad subordinada y subdesarrollada,

excepto ciertos enclaves productivos y ciertos grupos sociales que se desarrollan bajo su dominio. (187-88)

Just as the concept of *mestizaje* illegitimately homogenizes literatures which are essentially different, it also conceals the conflictive character of Latin American societies by diluting the plurality of socio-cultural projects to which the various proposals within the Latin American literary process are articulated (187-88).[21] This perspective was to bring Losada in later works, to the study of the "...literaturas latinoamericanas consideradas como formas diferenciadas de producción (y recepción) de textos literarios en diferentes espacios sociales y geográficos, constituidos en una situación colonial común...", and to his proposal of division of the continent by cultural regions as a basis for research into the various literary systems produced within them (Ventura 1987, ix).

Up until the 1980s, the notion of "literary system" plays a central role in Losada's work. After that time, however, the concept of "mode of cultural production" takes over as the key concept of his research. His rereading, redefinition and reclassification of the continent's literary process, which was to serve as the foundation for his alternative proposal of periodization of the said process, centers on this latter notion rather than that of "literary system" which dominates his discourse until the end of the 1970s.

Losada's *sujeto productor*

The *sujeto productor* no longer refers to the individual author, but to the social group to which the author is articulated. The work is not the product of an individual, but of a collective subject which also embraces the notion of public: that social subject not only produces the works, but also identifies with them and appropriates them (Losada 1976a, vii). This notion, which Losada initially links to Goldmann and Hauser's studies, is identified by Martin Lienhard as one of the Losadian perspectives which originates in modern anthropology (19). Thus, Lienhard comments on Losada's views on the collective character of all processes of cultural production and dissemination:

> En vez de considerar los textos como objetos de investigación autosuficientes, Losada subraya el carácter de práctica social que suponen las operaciones constitutivas —producción, recepción, transformación— del "fenómeno literario". El concepto de "grupo productor", llamado a sustituir al de "autor", vincula la concepción antropológica de una práctica

---

[21] See also Losada (1977a, 8).

colectiva con la definición sociológica del lugar de los intelectuales en las formulaciones sociales modernas de América Latina. (Lienhard et al 1986, 640)

The literary systems, "...como [conjuntos] con cierta unidad intrínseca y con referencia esencial a su sociedad..." (Losada 1976a, vii), and not the individual works constitute the subject of Losada's critical practice. Although it is not our intention to enter into this discussion here, we would ask to what extent it is necessary to set up this opposition between the collective and the individual, and whether an analysis which combined the two dimensions would not be more fruitful for the discipline.

The notion of *sujeto productor*, on the other hand, represents an indispensable conceptual tool within his project of interpretation of the process of formation of the various Latin American literary systems, the social significance and the understanding of the particularities of the said systems in relation to the literary production of the central societies (255). Furthermore, the identification of the various *sujetos productores* and their articulation to the corresponding literary systems, enable Losada to isolate a central concept in his discourse —the fact that the literary systems that criticism had traditionally labeled "Spanish American literature" are, in reality, the "praxis de ciertas élites sociales" and not the totality of its corpus (181).

So this *sujeto productor*, composed of a minority elite which, at a given moment, articulates itself to the demands of the dominant sectors, and, at another moment, to those of the popular sectors, serves as the foundation for Losada's questioning of the notion of "national" literatures, since there has never been a project in Latin America in which all the social actors could "reconocerse y reconciliarse" in a way which would justify calling it "national" (1981b).

Mode of Literary/Cultural Production

Although Losada repeatedly resorts to the concept of "mode of literary production" in *Creación y praxis* (1976a) —where, at least in the first section (12), the notion of "mode of *creation*" is still interchangeable with the former—, he does not attempt there to give a concrete definition of the term; a definition of it must be drawn from his examination of contemporary Peruvian literature and from the various uses he makes of this notion when referring to that literature. Firstly, it must be pointed out that in that study, the said notion provides an alternative perspective to both generational and aesthetic/formal approaches to the literary process, as well as offering an interpretive strategy which makes possible an account of the emergence of new literary systems (14 and 172–213). Losada uses this category here to analyze various aspects of literature: it enables him to examine how the *sujeto productor* and the works are articulated into society, and what their functions are with respect to society. Equally, through the application of that notion, he analyses the interpretations that these works make of reality, or, rather, the reality that these works generate, and explores the relationship between such interpretations and the forms in which they are embodied. He also uses it to evaluate the social and historical meaning of the said forms (3-35).

Evidently, this notion is associated to post-Althusserian developments within criticism which question the vision of literature as an act of "creation" *ex-nihil*, and reformulate it in terms of the concept of literary production. The author ceases to be a "creator" and comes to be understood as a "producer" of texts, thus restoring the socio-historic articulations of the process of writing (Macherey 1966).[22]

The concept of mode of literary production would be extended to the sphere of cultural production in Losada's article, "Rasgos específicos de la producción literaria ilustrada en América Latina" (1977a): Losada calls it "mode of cultural production'" on some occasions, and "social mode of cultural production'" on others, and stresses how recent the use of that notion is within literary studies (1977a, 19 and 22).[23] Although Losada does not offer a systematic definition of that concept, he does specify the functions it fulfills within critical discourse. According to the Argentinean critic, without this category, it would be impossible for the discipline to account for the stylistic, cultural and socio-historic differences between movements, up to then presented by criticism as uniform and homogenous, as is the case with, for example, *romanticismo peruano* and the River Plate literature also labeled *romanticismo* :

> Sólo el concepto de *modo social de producción* respeta la complejidad de los hechos y reproduce conceptualmente la diversidad radical de los lenguajes que produjeron [ambos fenómenos literarios]; de los diversos paradigmas de lengua y expresión que utilizaron; de los distintos sentimientos y géneros que prefirieron; de las distintas funciones que

---

[22] The term "literary mode of production" also forms part of Terry Eagleton's conceptual system (1976). However, there is no reference in Losada to suggest any link whatsoever with the British critic.

[23] Morales Saravia believes that the concept of "mode of production" is formulated by Losada in his works on "dependent" and "autonomous" literatures (Losada 1987, 229-30). Despite the emphasis that Losada places on the recent introduction of that concept in those works, he had already been using that category in his discourse since *Creación y praxis* (1976a).

cumplió esa producción y, sobre todo, de los diferentes horizontes existenciales que instituyeron y de las distintas relaciones que establecieron —en ese nuevo lenguaje— consigo mismos, con su sociedad y con la cultura. (22; emphasis in the original)

The notion of "mode of production" facilitates not just the characterization and differentiation of the various aesthetic/cultural paradigms, but also their articulation to the various types of social formation detected within the different historico-cultural "sub-regions" of the continent —rather than within the diverse national states as traditional criticism up to then would have had it.

From the beginning of the 1980s, this category, now sometimes interchangeable with "form of production" (1984a, 33), would play an increasingly central role within Losada's theoretical model. In his opinion, it is the key instrument for the systematization of the specificity of the historical development of Latin American literature. In that period, Losada elucidates the dominant modes of production in the Latin American literary process during the nineteenth and twentieth centuries —"dependent", "marginal" and "social-revolutionary" literatures. In effect, this allows Losada to offer an alternative to the system of periodization which had traditionally been modeled on European literary histories. Losada's interpretation breaks with a vision of the Latin American literary process as a passive, often anachronistic and impoverished imitation of the metropolitan "model", thus restoring its specificity, and also demonstrating that the socio-cultural changes in the peripheral societies are not only in response to external motivations (changes in the dominant centres), but also relate to the influences that the local context has on the ways in which the central discourses are appropriated and rearticulated, frequently resulting in counter-cultural projects.

Losada's work during the 1980s is centered on the literary production of the twentieth century; as we have already said, this work is based on a "regional" rather than "national" conception of Latin America. Results from his research show the co-existence of two clearly differentiated social formations and modes of cultural production in the twentieth century in the continent, and often within one "national" space. These are the "marginal" literatures, produced in an internationalized metropolitan space, and the "social-revolutionary" literatures, produced in societies which are still struggling against the conflicts dating from the period of colonial domination.

The "marginal" literatures, which embrace the movements traditionally identified as "*modernismo*" and "*vanguardismo*", constitute those projects articulated,

...como una respuesta de la élite intelectual aristocrática frente a la incorporación acelerada de la masa de población inmigrante [primordialmente proveniente de las áreas deprimidas mediterráneas] que abruptamente se apodera de las instituciones, domina la vida política, presiona y obtiene una mayor participación del excedente productivo, se organiza y, finalmente, transforma las pautas culturales dominantes y desplaza a la antigua élite artística del lugar de privilegio que pensaban les correspondía... (1983b, 21)

In addition to this process of immigration, which occurs above all in the Southern Cone region, there is also a process of internal, peasant immigration which radically transforms the cultural profile of many cities (Lima, Mexico), and which would lead the internationalized elites to seek to identify with the hegemonic culture. This immigration engenders a divorce between elite cultural production and that of the popular sectors, and even results in the denial of any connection with the latter and their social reality. Losada sums up this process thus: "...desde que esas masas mayoritarias se constituyen en dominantes en cada espacio urbano nacional, la producción literaria internacionalizada de la propia región tiene un sentido, no sólo de identificación con los procesos que se desarrollan en las ciudades europeas o norteamericanas, sino de negación de la pertenencia a la propia sociedad". Losada adds that in situations of extreme political agitation among the popular sectors, those literatures pass from their situation of marginality and rootlessness ("desarraigo") to one of even reactionary significance. Those conditions of production continue until the 1970s, when a *rapprochement* between the intellectuals and the popular sectors is attempted; this leads to, "...una transformación de los géneros tradicionales y [al] surgimiento de nuevas expresiones artístico-literarias directamente articuladas a la movilización popular a lo largo de todas las metrópolis de América Latina..." (20–22).[24]

"Social-revolutionary" literatures, produced since the Mexican Revolution and throughout the twentieth century, especially in Central America, the Caribbean, the Andean region, Paraguay and certain regions of Brazil, constitute a mode of production which is different from "marginal" and "dependent" modes. They are considered to be the founders of a new tradition which would lead right up to García Márquez, Asturias and Rulfo: in effect, Caribbean negritude, Andean *indigenismo*, the literature of the Mexican Revolution, the West Indian, Paraguayan, Ecuadorean or North-East Brazilian social narrative are: "...un fenómeno específico que no puede ser conceptualizado a partir de los modos de producción urbanos

---

[24] For a more detailed examination of this hypothesis, see (Losada 1987, 148–75).

dependientes de la estabilización capitalista en el período neo-colonial ni en el período metropolitano" (1983b, 24).

These literatures fulfill a social function different to that of either the "dependent" or "marginal" literatures, since they are articulated to movements which aspire to transform the social conditions of their sphere, and which are produced, "...con la perspectiva de realizar una revolución social que logre liquidar la herencia colonial, enfrentar al imperialismo y reestructurar la sociedad de una manera alternativa, no capitalista, y en función de las demandas y de la identidad de la masa popular". The *sujetos productores* of this type of literature emerge in societies described by Losada in the following terms:

> ...estas sociedades están dominadas por una situación de *transición* prerrevolucionaria que permanece irresuelta. No son sociedades que se reestructuran globalmente bajo un nuevo período de avance del capitalismo... sino que se encuentran en un momento histórico cuando entra en crisis el sistema neo-colonial dependiente; y por otro lado, no logra imponerse el sistema capitalista a la sociedad global y reestructurar las relaciones sociales bajo una nueva forma de producción. (25; emphasis in the original)

Losada emphasizes another difference with respect to the other two modes of production of Latin American literature, which is the fact that this literature is, in reality, the first in the continent to articulate itself to the "...sociedad presente como totalidad...", in other words, to the popular masses and the oligarchic elite and the hegemonic centers. It is the first literature which has both "national" content and continental and internationalist projections.

Finally, Losada refutes those critical discourses which disqualify these literatures as "non-modern" or "traditional", in contrast to the internationalized avant-gardes which they are committed to. Losada retrieves their modernity in terms of the alternative notion of modernity proposed by social-revolutionary literatures which is "...un concepto histórico y social, revolucionario, de qué es la modernidad... (26–28). This retrieval of "traditional" literatures, which involves the retrieval of their popular component, is undoubtedly one of his most enriching contributions to Latin American criticism.

Literary Forms

Literary forms express the way in which the author becomes aware of reality, or, more precisely, of how he/she exists in and relates to the world. They are the "...expresión de las formas de conciencia que tiene el hombre de sus formas de existencia en el mundo". Furthermore, Losada states that these literary forms are also forms of consciousness and forms of social praxis of the *sujeto productor* (1976a, 134–39). In his analysis of Peruvian narrative, Losada makes use of the typology of forms of the epic genre —to which the novel belongs— proposed by Lukács. The epic, according to Lukács, poses questions on the meaning of man's existence on earth and responds to that question through three forms: realist, naturalist, and subjectivist (140). Losada sums up the Lukacsian conception of those three forms in the following manner:

> ... el realismo trata de crear una forma que muestre el sentido de la totalidad del mundo; el subjetivismo, en cambio, de crear una forma que sea la imagen del caos. El punto de partida del naturalismo no es ni uno ni otro pues ignora el problema de la significación. Trata de "mostrar" la totalidad tal como aparece a los ojos o como es sentida en el interior del hombre, de modo que el lector mismo le dé significación" tal como actúa en la vida misma". (142)

Realism, adds Losada, sets out to create a form which expresses a "...realidad como tendencia objetiva y coherente..."; subjectivism creates a form which is an expression of "...la experiencia del interior..."; naturalism, on the other hand, expresses "...la realidad como es experimentada en la inmediatez de la vida cotidiana tal como se presenta al alcance de los sentidos..." (142–43).

Horizon of Existence

The notion of "horizon of existence" ("horizonte de existencia") plays an important role in Losada's discourse in his examination of the meaning of the aesthetic/cultural projects constituting the different literary systems which characterize Latin American literature. Losada understands that notion as, "...todo aquello que determina en una sociedad la idea de su destino, de lo que está concedido y le está negado por la vida, lo que puede y debe cumplir, lo que le está mandado evitar, sus modos de comportamiento, de sentimientos y de comprensión de sí en el mundo...". This Heideggerian concept, Losada points out, refers back to the debate on the "subjectivization" of meaning in the modern age: if, in the Classical world and in the Middle Ages, it could be said that a totality of meaning which transcended individuals' subjectivity reigned, then in the modern age, this meaning has broken down, obliging those individuals to "...construir el mundo a partir de la interioridad...". This act of construction of a world would be conceived of by Heidegger as the projection of a "horizon of existence". For Losada, human beings give their existence and their relationship to the world meaning through literature, thus generating a "horizon of existence" (19–20).

Aesthetic/Cultural Paradigm

The interpretation of every "...movimento cultural como proceso histórico dentro de una determinada matriz estructural..." (1977b, 35), leads to the formulation, towards the end of the 1970s, of the notion of "aesthetic/cultural paradigm" ("paradigma estético-cultural") within Losada's critical model. This category makes possible the reconstruction and characterization of the languages, genres and expressive forms which, articulated by a new *sujeto productor* dominant in a particular period and in accordance with a certain mode of production, can be associated with a particular literary system. Losada defines this category on the basis of the conception of cultural production which the corresponding social subjects have, in terms of its social function and the aesthetic principles that support it. So it is through that aesthetic/cultural project and the languages that it formulates that the *sujeto productor* generates his horizon of existence and, also, "...diferentes relaciones consigo mismo, con su sociedad y con la cultura europea..." which, in effect, confers on the said project its particular profile (12–13, 16, 22).

Losada proposes that, ultimately, a paradigm persists as long as the same historical conditions of production (which he also calls "matriz cultural") endure. In the case of "dependent cultures", for example, its aesthetic/cultural project, obviously including existing variations or tendencies, will persist as long as the urban sphere of limited modernization remains virtually untouched, and as long as the relationship of dependence between the intellectuals and the traditional oligarchy also remains. This had in effect been the context for the production of the literature which followed the court culture of the colonial elites and preceded the crisis of the system of oligarchic domination and the appearance of the "autonomous cultures of the middle classes". This paradigm of autonomous literatures would be modified by Losada in his writings during the 1980s; towards the end of the 1970s, however, Losada understood autonomous literatures to be those produced as a development of the romanticism of the River Plate region, hegemonic during most of the twentieth century and particularly since the First World War. Some examples are: Vallejo, Martí, Mariátegui, Arguedas, García Márquez, Borges, Neruda, Octavio Paz, etc.. Those literatures are produced in a "...situación de reestructuración social, que posibilita la perspectiva de un horizonte abierto que ha de ser definido por la propia subjetividad...". That restructuring involves the deepening of the modernization of urban space and its transformation into metropolis, as well as the formation of secondary and tertiary sectors not rigidly dependent on the oligarchies. It is a literature of, "...un grupo problematizado de intelectuales desarraigados, que intentan una producción autónoma de las élites oligárquicas, de su sociedad concreta, y aún, de la identidad social que habían recibido...". This literature raises the problem of social and even national or continental identity and seeks to define it; it equally pursues the rearticulation of its producers to their society and to a world which they must reinterpret along with their history. Through the writing and the languages which they formulate, "...instituyen *su* realidad [una realidad literaria], se dan a sí mismos una nueva función social y se crean una identidad..." (1977a).

It is worth reiterating here, that behind this is one of Losada's most interesting contributions to Latin American criticism's quest for autonomy: his emphasis on the fact that the structural changes cited above —which accompany the transformations in the sphere of cultural production— occur at different paces in the various regions of the continent, allowing him to break with the "national" models and the myths of "unity" and the homogeneity of the Latin American literary process which supported previous criticism.

So, although the 1980s would see Losada continuing the line of research initiated with his notion of aesthetic/cultural paradigms, as well as his attempt to elucidate the literary projects formulated throughout the twentieth century and their articulations to the different social formations established in the same period, the emphasis of his research shifted from the concept of "paradigm" to that of "mode of production". In those years, the concept of "autonomous" literatures would disappear from his conceptual system and would be replaced by two modes of cultural production considered dominant within Latin American literature in the twentieth century. These are the "marginal" literatures of the metropolitan areas, and the "social-revolutionary" literatures from the areas in which the conflicts brought about by the colonial legacy were still unresolved. The latter type of literature would have first been articulated in the River Plate region between 1840 and 1880 through the romantic movement. In order to be consistent with the shifts in emphasis within Losada's discourse, these two literary projects will be described in the section dealing with modes of production.

Periodization

Losada finds the characterization of the "Latin American urban space" to be too general; in order to make it more precise and with a view to formulating a system of periodization which reflects the specificity of that space, in his last works he suggests some temporal concepts ("momentos") which he believes allow an approach to the historical and cultural process of Latin America independent from the changes operating in the hegemonic centers. After all, the transformations in the metropoli have traditionally been considered the independent and determinant variable of the changes in Latin America.[25]

In his article "La historia social de la literatura Latinoamericana", Losada proposes three categories which he calls *evidencias* which serve to explain the, "...contradicciones generales que definen el espacio social latinoamericano a partir de procesos concretos...", differentiating the relationship between the social and literary processes in each "sub-region".

The *momento formativo,* or, *fundacional,* refers to the constitution of Latin American societies as a consequence of the trauma of Conquest, which would give rise to their specificity both with regard to Europe and between the distinct "sub-regions". The differences between these "sub-regions" are due to both the epoch in which the *momento formativo* took place, and the diverse cultural interaction which occurred within each one. That *momento* inaugurates an epoch which lasts until the present day, and which exerts a determining influence on literary production in the "sub-regions":

> El mundo andino y mesoamericano debe elaborar todavía el hecho de la conquista colonial de sociedades con un grado significativo de acumulación e identidad cultural. El espacio caribe adquiere su especificidad de la emigración esclavista y de la economía de plantación colonial, con su enorme diferenciación social y sus estrategias de aniquilación de la identidad cultural de la fuerza esclava de trabajo. El Cono Sur, junto con otros bolsones urbanos, adquieren su fisonomía a partir del proceso de colonización reciente de extensiones enormes de tierras fértiles, en base a la aniquilación de la población local y a la emigración europea. (23–24)

That *momento* had already been discussed in comparable terms in "Articulación, periodización y diferenciación de los procesos literarios latinoamericanos" (1983b). In that study, Losada proposes a second *momento de superación* which does not reappear in his last formulation. Losada understands that *momento* to mean the surpassing of the way in which Latin American societies had, until then, been structured, founding a new phase in their development, a period which opened at the beginning of this century (14).

In "La historia social de la literatura latinoamericana" (1986), Losada

---

[25] Losada (1983b) provides an inital sketch which, however, would later be redefined in (1986). This proposal of periodization is applied to the analysis of the three modes of cultural production established by Losada for the nineteenth and twentieth centuries in Latin America ("dependent", "marginal" and "social-revolutionary"), as well as to the process of internationalization of the continent's literature in (1987, 47–109).

puts forward two more *evidencias:* the *momentos decisivos* (Antonio Candido's term) allow the particular development process of each "sub-region" to be accounted for, and ultimately aim to "...dar razón del horizonte de problemas contemporáneos". They are "momentos traumáticos... que reorganizan la comprensión del proceso global de desarrollo de cada unidad sub-regional y lo articulan en un centro de conflictos". The *momentos decisivos* determine a "before" and "after" in the historical process of each "sub-region". The articulation of the literary processes to these *momentos* makes possible the understanding of those processes.

The interpretive framework that regions such as Paraguay, the Andes and the Caribbean, for example, propose for themselves, is that of a "problematic nature", or that of a "...serie de crisis irresueltas que se repiten desde la desestructuración social que trajo consigo la crisis colonial". Their literatures are articulated to, "...un único momento decisivo: la lucha por liquidar la herencia colonial y por constituir una nueva sociedad". Other regions, on the other hand, (Mexico, Brazil, River Plate), propose an interpretive framework of their history and identity which has an "affirmative" and even "triumphalist" nature. They view their *momentos decisivos*, como una progresiva superación del pasado colonial y una mayor constitución de la identidad nacional": "reestructuración oligárquica, liquidación de la herencia colonial y surgimiento de una sociedad integrada y moderna, sobre todo en sus espacios industrializados y urbanos". Their literatures are articulated "...a estos movimientos sociales y... los tres, puestos en relación con el momento fundacional, toman un significado diferente del que se proponen las ideologías dominantes" (24–25).

The third "*evidencia*" has to do with the present time and "combines" *momentos formativos* and *decisivos*. This involves the examination of, "los resultados [del] proceso fundacional y formativo", or in other words, "la evaluación de la situación de la sociedad y la cultura a la que se pertenece" (26).

Social Space

Losada's theoretical model seeks to articulate literary process to social process, and does this through the analysis of the relationship that the *sujeto productor* establishes between them through a specific project.

The notion of "espacio social" refers to the historical process of which it is a result: "Latin American social space" is a contradictory space which originated in the trauma caused by Conquest. It forms, "...una totalidad social constituida por las relaciones contradictorias entre tres sociedades articuladas: Europa/USA como centros hegemónicos, las sociedades tradicionales 'interiores' en la región latinoamericana, y las ciudades en proceso de modernización". The interior of each of the components of this totality is strained by the "general contradiction". Losada's work method proposes, "...la descripción de la manera en que un proyecto literario se vincula (o trata de desvincularse) con este espacio cargado de contradicciones", as the objective of "...la observación de los procesos de producción literaria" (22).[26]

---

[26] For an application of the concept to the study of the social spaces of the three modes of production which characterize Latin American literature of the nineteenth and twentieth centuries, see Losada (1987, 47–109).

CHAPTER 4

ANTONIO CORNEJO POLAR: ON CULTURAL AND LITERARY HETEROGENEITY IN LATIN AMERICA

Antonio Cornejo Polar's critical work constitutes, along with the works of Angel Rama and Alejandro Losada, a third and crucial contribution to the collective enterprise within Latin American criticism of the last decades to endow the discipline with theoretical and methodological perspectives which enable it to account for the specificity of the literatures of the continent and reveal the articulations of the latter to the particular historical and cultural processes of Latin American societies.

Cornejo Polar's discourse forms part of the rich tradition of debate of socio-cultural issues which began in Peru in the 1920s. This debate was to be reopened in the 1970s and, as we have indicated, was primarily connected to Mariateguian thought, to which Cornejo continually reiterates his indebtedness. We shall examine the Mariateguian proposals which Cornejo develops and which open up a fertile area of discussion on cultural and literary production in Latin America.

Of course, this is not an exhaustive account of Cornejo's affiliations. The aim here is only to highlight the relevance which the Peruvian debates of the 1920s, and especially Mariátegui's works, have for the formulation of his critical proposal, which, in any case, was to enter into a fruitful dialogue with the works within Latin Americanist criticism of recent decades which emphasize the region's cultural plurality —in particular Rama's writings on transculturation and García Canclini's on the region's processes of cultural hybridization (Rama 1987 and García Canclini 1990).[1]

Cornejo synthesizes the debate on the structure of Peruvian society, basically focusing on two lines of argument: firstly, that which supports unification through the capitalist system, and secondly, that which favors, "...su dualidad sustancial por acción de dos órdenes diversos, uno capitalista y otro feudal o simplememte precapitalista" (1980b, 5). However, Cornejo adds that:

---

[1] Cornejo incorporates the categories of "transculturation" and "hibridity" into his critical discourse. For a problematicization of the use of these categories, the first of them in particular, see Cornejo Polar (1994a).

> Un análisis de las más importantes caracterizaciones permite observar... una estrecha franja de convergencia. En efecto, inclusive dentro de la tesis unitaria, se reconoce la coexistencia de niveles sociales en distinto grado de desarrollo, o por lo menos la acción de un polo hegemónico y otro dependiente —al margen de que ambos, por cierto, están sometidos a los intereses del imperialismo. (1980b, 5)

The Peruvian critic's participation in the said polemic is articulated to the thesis that supports the essential plurality not only of the social configuration of his country, but, more importantly, of its cultural make-up as well. And this latter conception, Cornejo reminds us, corresponds to, "la conciencia empírica del Perú" (8). These socio-cultural differences are glaringly obvious: while the indigenous culture operates within the underdeveloped space, Western culture ("westernized" as Cornejo prefers to call it), functions in the more developed space (7). Thus he tells us that, although,

> ...cada vez con menos claridad, en razón del creciente proceso transcultural, sigue siendo [en todo caso] relativamente fácil distinguir entre un sistema históricamente dependiente de la cultura impuesta a partir de la Conquista y otro que responde, en consonancia con su propio desarrollo histórico, a las culturas nativas. No se trata... del mitológico deslinde entre una cultura "occidental y cristiana" y otra "incaica" ... [sino de la] convivencia en un solo espacio nacional de por lo menos dos culturas que se interpretan *sin llegarse a fusionar*. (6; my italics)

This idea of a society that is fractured by differences and conflicts of a socio-cultural nature forms an axis that runs throughout Cornejo's work. For him, criticism must demythify those interpretations —such as theories of *mestizaje*— which favor processes of conciliatory synthesis. In his re-examination of the process of development of Peruvian literature, in his latest book, *Escribir en el aire: ensayo sobre la heterogeneidad socio-cultural en las literaturas andinas* (1994b), for example, Cornejo demonstrates how a reading against the grain both of the Inca Garcilaso's attempt to, "configura[r] un espacio de convergencias y armonías", and the construction of the "imagen simbólica de una nación integrada", attained through the emancipation movement in the nineteenth century, clearly reveals the contradictions and fissures that exist amongst the different ethnic and socio-cultural spaces that make up Peru (92–93). Likewise, in his latest works he emphasizes the conflictive nature of this "red articulatoria multicultural" through the use of a new and not yet fully formulated category in his discourse, that of the "migrant" (who moves across both geographic and cultural spaces), a category that is contrasted with that of the *mestizo* (a metaphor for fusion and synthesis).[2] Through use of this category, he attempts to explore alternative approaches to those readings which propose harmonizing fusions of inter-cultural relationships, and instead highlights the sense of uprooting, discontinuity, fragmentation, and fluidity in the formulation of identities. Thus he offers a radicalization of his own reading of the break-up and heterogeneity (a key category within his discourse) of Peruvian society and culture (1995, 1997). To sum up, Cornejo understands the fundamental objective of Latin American criticism to be the forging of a conceptual framework that makes it possible to account for the plurality of the region's "situaciones socio-culturales y de discursos en los que las dinámicas de los entrecruzamientos múltiples *no* operan en función sincrética sino, al revés, enfatizan conflictos y alteridades" (1994a, 369; emphasis in the original).

For a Historical and Cultural Reading of Latin American Literature

One of the central objectives of Cornejo's proposal lies in the retrieval of the social and historical dimensions of literary and cultural processes for criticism. These had been dismissed by the immanentist methodologies of stylistics and structuralism which dominated the discipline until the early 1970s in Latin America. For Cornejo, it is an unavoidable fact that,

> ...las obras literarias y sus sistemas de pluralidades son signos y remiten sin excepción posible a categorías supraestéticas: el hombre, la sociedad, la historia. (1981b, 118)

Furthermore, Cornejo reminds us that immanentism is as much the result of the influence of the Saussurean linguistic model, as of the illegitimate universalization of a theory built on the principles of a particular poetics —that of symbolism and the avant-gardes (118). These movements propose "la radical autonomía del fenómeno literario" and the self-referentiality of language, aesthetic premises which found their "...razón de ser en la dialéctica de un proceso histórico concreto..." (1982, 10).[3]

Cornejo points at the epistemological crisis experienced by European and North American criticism during the 1970s, and questions "la validez del conocimiento que [tal crítica] propone", and even "la legitimidad de su existencia misma". But he stresses that the same crisis within Latin

---

[2] Trigo explores the critical potential of the category of migrancy (developed from Cornejo's notion of the migrant) for the study of processes of transculturation in a transnational context in Moraña (1997, 163–66).

[3] See also Cornejo Polar (1982, 13–14 and 1986, 118).

American criticism is even more serious, since it includes a specific problem:

> ...la necesidad de articular coherentemente las cuestiones propiamente científicas de la crítica, ya de por sí inquietantes, con una realidad social que no admite la neutralidad de ninguna actividad humana —y menos de aquellas que, como la crítica, suponen una predicación sobre los problemas fundamentales del hombre. (1982, 9)

His radical questioning of the principles of immanentist criticism stems from this. Cornejo's position accounts for his interest, apart from Mariátegui, in pre- and post-Althusserian Marxist contributions to the sociology of literature.[4] It also explains the affinity with certain Gramscian perspectives which can be detected in his discourse, such as his concern for the retrieval of popular culture for art, and his consequent mistrust of an art which is confined to the sphere of a narrow intellectual elite and disconnected from the rest of society (Gramsci 1976, 31 and 125). In short, we are referring to Cornejo's preoccupation with the problems involved in the shaping of a popular-national literature in a country where the process of national unification was never completed (100–102 and 123–24). It must not be forgotten, however, that these are also central themes in Mariátegui's work, as we have already seen. Cornejo refers back to these themes and adopts them as key issues within his own discourse. In any case, we would suggest that a more or less indirect presence of Gramsci in Cornejo's thought may be deduced from Cornejo's radical reading of Mariátegui.

Cornejo considers that it is particularly necessary for Latin American criticism to employ a historical and social perspective in dealing with the continent's literature. Firstly because, "...está sustantivamente ligada desde sus orígenes a una reflexión sobre una realidad que unánimemente se considera deficitaria...", and secondly, "...porque las imágenes que [tal literatura] instaura contienen con frecuencia postulaciones proyectivas: hay en la literatura latinomaericana...una suerte de modulación propiciatoria que parece ensayar desiderativamente un mundo todavía no realizado" (1982, 10–11).

His defense of the approach to literature as social production is also

---

[4] Worthy of note amongst the former is his conformity with the characterization of the novel as proposed by the theoretical tradition that stems from Georg Lukács, continues with Lucien Goldmann, and culminates with Jacques Leenhardt. Amongst the latter, Alejandro Losada deserves special mention. His categories of "sistema literario" and "modos de producción" —defined in the chapter devoted to the Argentine critic— are incorporated into Cornejo's critical discourse.

based upon the peculiar nature of the insertion of Latin American literature into, "...una sociedad igualmente peculiar, distinta, al menos si el término de comparación es [sic] la literatura y la sociedad occidentales". Such particularity has its roots in the problems arising from the heterogeneous cultural composition of the various Latin American countries, as well as from the consequences of their subjection to a history of "...conquista y dominación colonial y neocolonial..." (15). Thus, Cornejo believes it is imperative that criticism take on the urgent task of clarifying,

> ...el modo específico de la articulación de *esta* literatura con *esta* sociedad, lo que importa definir en términos históricos el funcionamiento de la institución literaria, los modos de producción que emplea, el sistema de comunicación en que se inscribe. (15; emphasis in the original)

And he concludes by saying that, until we understand the social functioning of our literature, "...será imposible comprender con rigor el sentido de su desarrollo histórico y hasta sus manifestaciones textuales concretas (15).

It must be stressed, however, that this option for perspectives which favor the socio-historical and cultural components of the literary phenomenon and which declare their "ininteligiblidad... como categoría autónoma", does not imply a total disregard for the achievements and sophistication of essentially structuralist methodologies. Particularly in his early works, Cornejo resorts to structuralist categories in his description of the texts under analysis.[5] On the other hand, we should not overlook the Peruvian critic's skepticism regarding, "...la conveniencia de emplear [tales] métodos dentro de otro proyecto crítico..." (1982, 14).[6] However, the fact is that, without falling into the eclecticism he fears, Cornejo uses structuralist descriptive methods which, with increasing clarity, will come to form part of a hypothesis of work which transcends the limits of textuality. This places the interpretation of the texts into broader explanatory frameworks, such as the specificities of the functioning of the literary institution and its articulations to social and cultural processes in Peru. In effect, the Peruvian's work follows less clearly from his stated refusal to use structuralist methods, than from the strategy he defended earlier in his article, "Problemas y perspectivas de la crítica literaria latinoamericana" (1982).[7] In that article, he emphasized the need within an autonomous

---

[5] Todorov in particular. See, for example, Cornejo Polar (1989b).

[6] Originally published in 1977.

[7] Originally presented as a paper at Universidad de San Marcos in 1974 and first published in 1975.

Latin American criticism project, to appropriate these methodologies while at the same time freeing them from the socio-cultural determinants under which they had been produced, thus adapting them to this project:

> Hay que reconocer que la crítica inmanentista viene desarrollando métodos cada vez más precisos en orden a la descripción de [las] categorías formales, y es posible que instrumentalizados dentro de la perspectiva [histórico-social] propuesta, puedan resultar efectivamente esclarecedoras. En todo caso, puestos en contacto de servicio con la tarea de revelar el sentido de las imágines del mundo que provienen de la peculiaridad latinoamericana, estos métodos tendrán que perder el peligroso mimetismo que suele vincularlos irrestrictamente, a modelos concebidos bajo el imperio de otras urgencias sociales y culturales. (11–12)

In 1977, Cornejo Polar first published *La novela peruana: siete estudios*, a compilation of seven monographic studies written between 1967 and 1975. All but one were dedicated to *indigenista* novels.[8] Cornejo conceives of the studies brought together in this book as the initial stage of an investigative process oriented towards the future theoretical elaboration of the historical development of Peruvian literature and its social meaning.[9]

Through this procedure, through the defining of the cosmovision which gives account of the texts, and through his determining of the relationship between these texts and the literary system of which they are a part and the society in which they are produced, Cornejo hopes to, "llegar a la comprensión de la literatura como hecho social". This was to constitute the next phase of his project (1989b, 9–10).

This sociological approach is especially characteristic of the last six essays in the book which were written between 1972 and 1975. In the first of these, "La estructura del acontecimiento de *Los perros hambrientos*", which dates from 1967, however, he still applies a structuralist model to

---

[8] In chronological order, these articles are: "La estructura del acontecimiento de *Los perros hambrientos*" (1967); "La obra de José María Arguedas: Elementos para una interpretación" (1970); "Los ríos profundos: un universo compacto y quebrado" (1973); "El zorro de arriba y el zorro de abajo: función y riesgo del realismo" (1974); "Aves sin nido. Indios, 'notables' y forasteros" (1974); "La imagen del mundo en La serpiente de oro" (1975); and "Los geniecillos dominicales: sus fortunas y diversidades" (1975).

[9] A little over a decade later, Cornejo tackles this project of producing a global account of the Peruvian literary process in his book, *La formación de la tradición literaria en el Perú* (1989c) in which he examines the historical process of the formation of Peruvian literary traditions and the articulations of the latter to the various national projects formulated after the Republican period, in some ways developing the initial model sketched out by Mariátegui in "El proceso de la literatura".

his description of Ciro Alegría's novel. It is only fair to point out, however, that it is possible to detect certain aspects that would later acquire an extra-textual significance when read in the light of Cornejo's culturalist theories. In the following five essays, Cornejo puts structuralist methodology at the service of a sociological reading of the *indigenista* novel whereby he continues this process of revealing elements peculiar to both *indigenista* narrative and Peruvian society. He later develops these elements into the theoretical foundation of his critical discourse. The seventh essay deals with Julio Ramón Ribeyro and the question of the "urban" Peruvian novel. To a certain extent, Cornejo sets this kind of narrative against the literatures he classifies as "heterogeneous", which form the core of his critical proposal.

A second and fundamental point of departure in Cornejo's critical project is the retrieval of the moment, function and significance of *indigenista* narrative, and the meaning which that narrative may have for the present-day reader. Both objectives involve the task for criticism of clarifying the socio-cultural elements which that narrative brings into play (1989b, 53). Apart from the monographic essays on Peruvian *indigenista* narrative we have mentioned, Cornejo dedicates a series of studies to this material through which he pursues an overall tracing of the movement and a systematization, on a theoretical and methodological level, of the conclusions arrived at in the earlier essays. All this was to be brought together and synthesized in his book *Literatura y sociedad en el Perú: la novela indigenista* (1980). This book also incorporates material already dealt with in his articles, "Para una interpretación de la novela indigenista" (1977), and "El indigenismo y las literaturas heterogéneas: su doble estatuto socio-cultural" (1978).[10] In his latest book, *Escribir en el aire*, the national space as the subject matter of his theorization is extended to a trans-national Andean space that includes Bolivia and Ecuador. In the book, Cornejo characterizes the *indigenista* novel using, as a starting point, the conflictive relationship between tradition and modernity that gives rise to it. He explores the tensions which this relationship produces in the novel and evaluates the novel's capacity to process the socio-cultural juncture that generates it (1994b, 194–207).

Cornejo brings to the fore the fundamental contribution which *indigenismo* has made to Latin American narrative's exploration of the

---

[10] In his enlightening work, "La novela indigenista: una desgarrada conciencia de la historia", originally published in 1980, he makes a detailed analysis of the Peruvian *indigenista* novel of the 1930s and the "conciencias de la historia que la atraviesan" (1982). For a study of Manuel Scorza's work and *neo-indigenismo*, see (1989b).

cultural reality of the region. He highlights Ciro Alegría's, work and in particular his reformulation of Sarmiento's dichotomy, through his, "...afirmación de la superioridad de la comunidad indígena...", and his "...inversión de los valores tradicionalmente subyacentes en los términos civilización y barbarie...". Cornejo concludes that that contribution, paradoxically originating from that "civilizing" world but now unmasked as truly "barbaric" as a result of its historical role as oppressor, nevertheless constitutes, "...la construcción de un sólido sustrato ideológico para el desarrollo de una novelística campesina..." (1982, 68–69).[11]

Cornejo's discourse, in turn, echoes this challenge to the Sarmentian terms found in Alegría's narrative. Cornejo provides Latin American criticism with theoretical and methodological elements for the re-evaluation of a literature articulated to a peasant culture and problems related to it. Cornejo also retrieves this literature rooted in indigenous culture as part of the Latin American literary corpus. Until then, such literature had not been recognized or valued by a criticism which was grounded in ethnocentric premises, and which had taken the literary forms originating from the Western world as universal aesthetic models.

Cornejo notes that this is precisely how it is that *indigenismo*, read from the perspective of the new novel, is discounted as a deficient and imperfect narrative form. Cornejo questions a criticism which approaches this narrative using parameters established by a particular poetics: that of the "new Spanish-American novel", which Mario Vargas Llosa called the "novela de creación", in contrast to earlier narrative production or the "novela primitiva". Cornejo deems this opposition to be inaccurate, and sees the procedures of a criticism based on such criteria to be illegitimate. He discusses this in his article on Ciro Alegría, "La imagen del mundo en *La serpiente de oro*". Here, he proposes to restore Alegría's own aesthetic parameters and his rightful place within the Peruvian literary process:

> Algunos enjuiciamientos últimos, que comienzan y concluyen asimilando la obra de Alegría a la "novela regional", casi siempre en condición de único y anacrónico eslabón, no hacen más que repetir la imagen formada desde la perspectiva de la nueva novela hispanoamericana de toda la narrativa anterior; de esta manera, a través de una interpolación ilegítima, la crítica ha asumido lo que en realidad es el arte poética de un movimiento literario, su justificación dentro de un proceso que pretende alterar sustantivamente. (1989b, 83–84)

---

[11] On the narrative strategy through which Alegría attempts to solve the tensions between tradition and modernity in his novel *El mundo es ancho y ajeno*, see Cornejo Polar (1994b, 200–207).

Cornejo restores the historical dimension to Alegría's novel and clarifies its structural and technical "problems" within the framework of a sociocultural reading. He is not interested in whether it meets the aesthetic criteria of the "new novel", as understood by Vargas Llosa, but instead focuses on understanding the peculiarities of this narrative, and on how it treats the specificities of Peruvian culture and society. Cornejo illustrates how the basic linguistic contradiction in the construction of the novel —a duality of norm used by a single "narrador representado"— actually,

> reproduce una de las contradicciones básicas de la sociedad y cultura peruanas, su heteróclita pluralidad, y expresa al mismo tiempo el doloroso desencuentro del escritor que, sin posibilidades efectivas de modificar la estructura social que condiciona su actividad, intenta revelar positivamente algunas dimensiones del mundo que esa misma estructura desprecia y margina. En el fondo la persona misma del escritor se compromete en el conflicto: él también es ajeno a ese mundo que pretende representar con autenticidad; por eso, para hacerlo, no le queda otro camino que fundar — paradójicamente —un artificio... Su legítima intención de interioridad hace evidente su inevitable exterioridad. La contradictoria y disgregada realidad peruana —en términos generales, hispanoamericana— deja aquí su marca definitiva. (86–89)

Echoing the Marxist notion of literature as a super-structural phenomenon, Cornejo defines literary production as, "...un proceso...que *reproduce* la estructura de los procesos sociales..." (1982, 17; my emphasis).[12] This perception of literature as a mimetic reproduction of reality —obviously indebted to the principle of reflection as utilized in Marxist aesthetics— distorts its functioning by overlooking the ways in which it prefigures social changes and its capacity to imagine new worlds.

To do justice to Cornejo, it should be said that while this notion of novelistic construction as reflection underlies his discourse, other conceptions —even if in a context of tension— also coexist with it. His interpretation of the dual narrative structure of Alegría's novel implies that such a structure does not simply reproduce the structure of society, but that the very narrative structure, the very composition of the novel, stands as a questioning of that social order, an order which marks the writing with the unresolved conflicts of its own heterogeneous socio-cultural identity. Besides, Cornejo also introduces (although unfortunately does not develop) a much more enriching view of the nature of literature which stresses its anticipatory and prefiguring character ("Problemas y perspectivas de la crítica literaria latinoamericana" (11). In another piece on the *indigenista*

---

[12] See also (1983, 49–50).

novel, something similar occurs: without further elaborating on his statement, he emphasizes his refusal to consider the genre as, "...reflejo inmediato de una realidad determinada ni tampoco como traducción a términos literarios de una problemática ideológica preexistente...", and he concludes that, "...se trata, más bien, de la convergencia sobre un núcleo conflictivo de diversos modos de ejercicio de la conciencia social —lo que supone, a su vez, un complejo juego de autonomías y dependencias entre cada uno de ellos y en relación con su fuente de realidad" (97–98).

Returning to Cornejo's objective, that of achieving a level of analysis which transcends the limits of individual texts —the aim of his initial monographic research— this study of Alegría's novel represents a significant step forward. It systematizes the conclusions already drawn in earlier works, and offers the first general theories on the heterogeneity of the *indigenista* novel and the society in which it is produced, and on the need for criticism to approach the literary process in terms of its specificity, restoring its historical and cultural articulations.

The reappraisal of the *indigenista* novel effected by Cornejo is an undeniable contribution not just to Peruvian criticism, but to Latin American criticism in general inasmuch as it points out the importance of a reconciliation between criticism and history, and calls attention to the need to rethink the legitimacy of the institutionalization of judgments based on the idea of "impurity", "anachronism" or the aesthetic ineffectiveness of Latin American regional literatures.[13] In any case, Cornejo writes two years later (1977), these latter judgments focus on those literatures' "deviations" from Western "models", neglecting that which is most important from a historical and cultural point of view —the very existence of heterodox forms and their meaning, which for Cornejo, is, "...el resultado del vigor del referente entregado a un proceso exógeno de enunciación, o si se quiere la transformación del producto a partir de la naturaleza contradictoria de su modo de producción, cuanto, al mismo tiempo, la consecuencia formal de la estructura de base que expresa homológicamente en el texto" (1989b, 79).[14] And, ultimately, Cornejo's discourse underlines the unsatisfactory results of a criticism which constructs an aesthetic model against which all other proposals should be measured, or, as Cornejo already noted in 1975 paraphrasing Néstor García

---

[13] For a detailed re-reading of the problematic aspects of Alegría's narrative, traditionally perceived by criticism in terms of "errores de construcción", see Cornejo Polar (1989b, 58–60).

[14] For Cornejo's re-reading of the heterodoxy of pre-boom narrative see also (1980b, 68–76).

Canclini, which confuses "dos órdenes discursivos distintos, el arte poética con la crítica literaria" (83–84). Thus Cornejo lucidly synthesizes his rejection of the prevailing reading of the regional novel in his 1977 article "Problemas de la crítica, hoy":

> A partir de un cierto concepto de novela... [el de la] "novela de lenguaje", se establece la defectividad de estas formas heterogéneas y se postula la necesidad de liberar a la nueva novela de esas impurezas. No se sospecha siquiera que tal heterogeneidad, al margen de producir un sesgo peculiar en la constitución del género, representa la formalización del conflicto básico de una literatura que quiere revelar la índole de un universo agrario, semifeudal, con recursos y desde perspectivas que inevitablemente están señalados por su presencia citadina y burguesa. La tensión que subyace en este proyecto... determina la apertura de la forma novela para dar cabida a otras formas que provienen, no de la instancia productiva, sino, más bien, del mundo referido. Este hecho específicamente literario pues consiste en la modificación de la estructura del género, incluso en sus aspectos formales, resulta inexplicable al margen de su peculiar correlato social; o sea, al margen de la heterogeneidad básica de la sociedad y la cultura latinoamericanas. (1982, 16)

Cornejo concludes that the type of critical exercise he questions involves a tacit recourse to aesthetic parameters originating from other social contexts (Europe, the United States). Such critical practice ends up establishing these as universal models which are then used to measure the formal "achievements" or "deficiencies" of Latin American literature (16).

Although it is true that Cornejo does not dedicate much space to it in his writings, this issue takes us back to a question we have already discussed in this study —the difficulties criticism faces in handling the problem of modernization in the artistic and cultural field. This problem frequently overlaps with the apparent dilemma between local cultural traditions and insertion into an internationalized cultural space. It is worth reiterating the fact that, to a great extent, this issue articulates the cultural debate taking place in the continent from the late 1960s and throughout the 1970s, and that it constitutes one of the most controversial aspects of the projects towards a Latin American criticism that were formulated in that period.

Cornejo explores the question of modernization, in particular where it concerns the Peruvian literary process from the 1950s onwards, in his 1979 article, "Hipótesis sobre la narrativa peruana última", published as an appendix to his book *La novela peruana* (1989b). In his opinion, the process was initiated at about the time when the monopoly of traditional *indigenismo* started to give way to a diverse range of literary experiences which shared a commitment to technical and formal innovation. Although, for Cornejo, the narrative of the 1950s in no way constitutes the Peruvian correlative of the "nueva novela hispanoamericana", his analysis of it throws light upon both his general conception of the modernizing phenomenon and the "nueva novela" itself, as well as on the relationship he perceives between social modernization and literary modernization (1989b, 257–58); these aspects should be examined in the context of the ideological and theoretical framework of the Latin American criticism of the last few decades.

In short, writes Cornejo, after an energetic take-off, the majority of the writers of that generation reached a plateau in their work. According to Cornejo, this first modernizing project within Peruvian letters failed because it was carried out in adverse circumstances: the whole process of literary production was precarious, and a limited public was incapable of keeping pace with the changes in aesthetic proposals: "...los narradores 'del 50' [notes the Peruvian] pretendieron producir artesanalmente, pues este era el signo del sistema editorial que los acogía, una literatura moderna" (260). Cornejo's interesting approach becomes problematic, however, at the moment it establishes a relationship of homology between literary modernization and the equally unsuccessful general process of material modernization taking place in Peruvian society at the time. The most questionable aspect of Cornejo's discourse is this very leap from his analysis of literary form and the communication system which frames writing's circuit of production and reception (an analysis which characterizes his reading of *indigenismo*), to the imposition of an ideological schema onto the texts:

> Existe una cierta relación homológica entre este proceso social de falsa modernización (en el fondo imposible: el orden oligárquico es inmodernizable) y los conflictos de la narrativa "del 50". También aquí las categorías novedosas, las nuevas formas del relato, se artificializan y pierden consistencia al adelantarse a un sistema productivo que repite sin mayores modificaciones su arcaismo. (261)

Ultimately, in appealing to the notion of homology between the social phenomenon and the literary phenomenon, Cornejo is stating that literary modernization is impossible without social modernization. This vision of literary production as reproduction of social processes involves condemning urban literature —to which he refers exclusively here— to the imitation of models supposedly on a par with the historical development of society. This is inferred in his commentary on the work of Ribeyro —one of the writers of the "generación del 50" whose production, unlike the rest, was never interrupted: "...es sintomático que uno de los escrtiores de este grupo que matiene una actividad narrativa constante, Julio Ramón Ribeyro, se caracterice por su apego a los cánones del relato tradicional" (261).

In keeping with his conception of literature as reflection of the social structure, the only route to literary innovation which Cornejo appears able to recognize is that taken by *indigenista* literature —particularly that of José María Arguedas or Manuel Scorza— because of its articulation to peasant culture and to the heterogeneous character of Peruvian society (1989b, 266–69 and 209–216).

This procedure bears the ideological mark of Dependency Theory, and it is this which leads to the mid-course abandonment of any specifically literary approach to literary material. Thus, Cornejo reduces the plurality of quests within his country's literature by presenting heterogeneous literatures as the only legitimate model of literary modernization. Although Cornejo does not make it explicit in his work, one can detect behind this thinking an idea present throughout the projects of autonomous Latin American criticism of the time, which is the belief that the only truly national literary model is that articulated to local traditional cultures. Consequently, the city is seen to be incompatible with "lo nacional", as it is stigmatized as the prime space of capitalist penetration within the circuit of international culture. Such stigmatization impedes an unprejudiced approach to the rich cultural and literary production of the cities of the continent. It prevents the exploration of the alternatives formulated there, and ignores the actual transculturation processes that take place between the various socio-cultural groups in urban areas, as well as between the urban and rural spheres.

It could also be argued that this condemnatory reading of city culture arises from the attempt, within Latin American leftist nationalist criticism of the 1970s, to invert Sarmiento's opposition between civilization and barbarism through the vindication of peasant and autochtonous cultures. Unfortunately, however, although the rural sphere is justly re-evaluated, the urban sphere is, in effect, unmodified. If the valuation of the Latin American cities put forward by Sarmiento in *Facundo* is inverted, the definition itself is not questioned: the cities continue to be perceived as an extension of the metropoli, only now this is viewed negatively.

Cornejo's handling of urban production leads to reductionist notions being imposed on Peruvian literature. However, to do justice to the Peruvian, it must be recognized that his project also constitutes an ambitious theoretical and methodological quest which aims to overcome unitary readings of his country's literature, and to account for the multiplicty of systems which form the corpus of Peruvian literature. Furthermore, as we shall see, one of the objectives of his work on heterogeneous literatures is the study of the zones of intercommunication between the cultural spaces which coexist in Andean societies, Peru in particular, and the aesthetic proposals that the said literatures will put forward.[15]

Towards a Redefinition of the Latin American Literary Corpus

Cornejo's critical project is guided by a third and vital objective: the redefinition of the Peruvian —and by extension Latin American— literary corpus with a view to incorporating the literary systems articulated to popular cultures.[16] In effect, the retrieval of the specificity of the cultural and literary process of the region and the dismantling of universalist and ethnocentric perspectives which dominate criticism up to this point, enable Cornejo to bring to light the narrowing and distortion inflicted by such criticism on Peruvian and continental literature in the name of an "erudite" conception of literature. The dilution of the particularities of our literature in a universalist and hierarchical vision of literary production, leads criticism,

> ...a privilegiar en términos absolutos la literatura "culta" y a remitir hacia el folclore la literatura de los estratos más deprimidos de la sociedad latinoamericana. Se cancela así un riquísimo horizonte de creación y en algunos casos se asume como único espacio lingüístico el de las lenguas "modernas", prescindiendo por completo de las literaturas en lenguas "nativas", o considerándolas sólo a la manera de estrato arqueológico, como si efectivamente hubieran dejado de producirse a partir de la conquista. (1982, 15–16)[17]

Cornejo rightly believes that this misrepresentation and impoverishing of the complex body of Latin American, and particularly Andean, literatures, creates methodological difficulties in accounting for the multiplicity of literary systems produced. It also reflects, at the level of criticism, an "oligarchical-bourgeois" conception of criticism that implies the validation of the structure of those societies and the illegitimate universalization of the dominant cultural canon. Cornejo adds that the unifying mechanisms

---

[15] An example of this transculturation process in heterogeneous literatures can be found in Cornejo's reading of Arguedas' project, amongst other works, in his article "Hipótesis sobre la narrativa peruana última" (1989b, 268–269).

[16] For an alternative outline of the corpus of Latin American literature and a systematization of its theoretical foundation, see "Unidad, pluridad, totalidad: el corpus de la literatura latinoamericana" (1982, 43–50). This article constitutes a revised, improved and combined version of, "El problema nacional en la literatura peruana" and, "Para una agenda problemática de la crítica literaria latinoamericana: diseño preliminar" (1982, 19–31 and 33–41).

[17] See also Cornejo Polar (1982, 43 and 120–21).

used by this critical perspective lead not only to the ignoring of popular and native manifestations, but also to the distorting of "erudite" manifestations when they do not coincide with the "consecrated paradigms" or the "model provided at a given moment". A prime example in contemporary criticism is the disqualifying of the regional novel in the face of the imposition of the single model dictated by the "new novel" (43–46).

Cornejo correctly states that another narrowing inflicted by criticism upon the corpus of Latin American literature is a result of, "...la fijación de secuencias unilineales en el proceso de la literatura latinoamericana..." which leaves out, "...todos los desarrollos que, por uno u otro motivo, no se integran en esa secuencia de realización sucesiva de modelos únicos". This procedure is illustrated within Latin American literary historiography by the readings made of *pre-modernismo, modernismo* and *post-modernismo,* the literary production "...que va hacia Darío, Darío mismo y su escuela, y luego 'el abandono del modernismo' forman un proceso que cubre un extenso período dentro del cual se desapercibe todo lo que escapa a esa dinámica, o se le asigna carácter de excepción no significativa" (45).

Cornejo considers that any broadening of the Peruvian literary corpus would require the study of the zones of convergence between the various literary systems in order to trace the circuits of communication which may have been established between them, and to examine the nature and significance of that communication. Cornejo states that it is generally, "...inestable, ambigua y contradictoria, sin duda, pero suficientemente significativa" (1982, 25–26).[18] In his article, "El problema nacional en la literatura peruana", Cornejo explores this communication processes in the case of *criollismo* and *indigenismo,* while in "Literatura peruana: totalidad contradictoria", he examines these processes with reference to the literature of the Conquest, and linguistic loans between "erudite" and popular literary systems (27–31).[19] In *Escribir en el aire* (1994b), Cornejo follows the intricate history of the clashes between the oral and the written in Andean (and not just Peruvian) literatures, from the *degree zero* —the dialogue between Atahuallpa and Valverde in Cajamarca in 1532— to the region's testimonial literature of the 1970s. This attempt to trace the flow of cultural and literary information between the systems articulated either to the indigenous world or the Western sphere within Peruvian society, constitutes a key issue in his work on heterogeneous literatures and on *indigenismo.* As we shall see, this functions as one of his evaluative

---

[18] See also (46–47).

[19] See also (1983, 46–49).

criteria when looking at the different variants in the *indigenista* movement.

The Category of Heterogeneity: An Approach to Cultural Plurality in Latin America

On the basis of his research on regional narrative, and especially *indigenismo*, Cornejo begins, in 1977, a period of theorizing on Heterogeneous Literaturas, or, "literaturas sujetas a un doble estatuto socio-cultural" (1978, 7). He fully recognizes how much his project owes to Mariátegui's reflections on the literatures produced in societies fragmented as a result of Conquest. The aim of Cornejo's theorizing is a comprehensive re-reading of the Peruvian literary process which can be extended to the whole of Latin America, since the concept of heterogeneous literatures refers to all those "...literaturas situadas en el conflictivo cruce de dos sociedades y dos culturas" (8).[20] Furthermore, his project responds to the challenge proposed by contemporary cultural debate, namely, to search for formulas which enable literary criticism and history to give account of the literary process in its plurality. This requires the overcoming of the simplifications imposed by the discipline's traditional recourse to unifying perspectives, very possibly derived from the unitary model which governed Europe's own literary histories, which, from the very beginning, inspired their Latin American counterparts (1982, 43).[21] As far as the "plurinational" nature of Peruvian literature and society are concerned, Cornejo stresses the need to retrieve the richness implicit in that diversity, even if that very diversity is itself a consequence of the historical failure to achieve a democratic project of national integration. This task of retrieval involves a political conception of criticism:

> ...la imagen desiderativa de la literatura peruana no tiene por qué seguir dependiendo de una idea de unidad abstracta, que en el fondo sería sólo la universalización del patrón dominante; al contrario, puede y debe postularse la preservación de su multiplicidad, siempre que pueda desligarse de su actual significado opresivo. Sólo desde esta perpsectiva la pluralidad se convierte en plenitud. La realización de esta alternativa, que Arguedas expresó como la opción de "vivir feliz todas las patrias", no es ya tarea literaria: es obra política. (1982, 30–31)

Moreover, Cornejo sees this quest as criticism's contribution to the general process of "liberación de nuestros pueblos" taking place in the

---

[20] See also (42–43).

[21] For a resumé of the various unitary readings of Peruvian literature, and an illustration of the inadequacy of the category of unity, see also Cornejo Polar (1983, 38–42).

continent in the 1970s. In his opinion, this not only corresponds to the ideological component of critical practice —criticism also has a part to play in the "esclarecimiento de la realidad"— but also, "...porque al proponerse un desarrollo en consulta con los requerimientos específicos de su objeto está cumpliendo, en el orden que le corresponde, una importante tarea de descolonización" (17).

Cornejo's notion of the relationship between politics and the critical discipline is very useful for Latin American criticism. He does not deny the articulations which operate between the ideological sphere, the critic's political conception and his/her reflections on culture, but, instead of subjecting the logic of the latter to that of the first two, he seeks to resolve their interaction at the level of the cultural processes themselves. While at the same time clarifying the historical reasons which account for the cultural and literary plurality and the conditions of oppression and social marginalization evident within Latin American countries, Cornejo's discourse identifies its political function as the retrieval of heterogeneous literatures and its capacity to generate forms and identities with counter-hegemonic potential.

Cornejo's discourse on heterogeneous literatures is at the core of his most important contribution to the development of a Latin American criticism which, breaking with the principle of universality which dominated the discipline until the early 1970s, would endeavor to formulate parameters appropriate to the reading of the continent's literary production.

Cornejo's proposal forms part of a more general tendency within criticism, not necessarily connected to Mariateguian thought, which also includes Angel Rama's work on narrative transculturation (1976), Noé Jitrik's study of Alejo Carpentier (1975), and Agustín Cueva on García Márquez (1974). These studies offer a stepping stone for the formulation of his theoretical schema (from 1977 onwards). This tendency, which spreads throughout the continent over that period, is committed to the exploration of, "...la heterogeneidad socio-cultural de algunos sectores básicos de nuestra literatura...", and to overcoming the homogenizing and unifying versions of that literature which had hegemonized the discipline until then (1978, 8 and 12–13).

Cornejo questions the legitimacy of the notion of "national literature" then prevalent within Latin American criticism and historiography. He seeks to reformulate both the contents of such a notion and its theoretical foundations, as well as the periodizations of that so-called "national literature". Thus, he restores the density of the socio-cultural processes involved in the production of Latin American literature (1983, 38). On the one hand, Cornejo writes, the category "national", when applied to literature, presents difficulties, not just for the delimitation between "erudite literature" and "popular literature" (1982,10) but also because of its apparent inability to account for the intranational variants, ignoring the coexistence of productions articulated to different strata. This is the case, for example, with the literatures of the Andean countries, where the notion of national literature, "...alude...exclusivamente a la literatura culta en español que se escribe en [ellos]...", completely bypassing the literatures in native languages (1981b, 119). On the other hand, the recourse to the label "national literature" means that movements which transcend national borders and find correlatives in other regions of the continent are also overlooked: the areas of confluence and the moments of communication between the literary productions of the various countries and regions of the continent escape criticism (1978, 10).

Since the concept of national literature is particularly problematic as far as the literature of the continent is concerned, Cornejo proposes an alternative system: that of "Latin American literature" as the, "...categoría idónea para la captación de las unidades menores" (10). Furthermore, as we have seen in the chapter on Angel Rama, in accordance with a generalized vision within 1970s criticism, the minor systems and the major system need not be seen as contradictory. He insists that the key lies in a dialectical approach:

> Las categorías puestas de manifiesto hasta aquí: el sistema nacional, su disolución en una estructura mayor y su fragmentación en sectores menos amplios no tienen por qué ser contradictorias. Un buen tratamiento dialéctico podría dar razón de la coherencia de su funcionamiento en el proceso real de nuestras literaturas. Es importante advertir que en todas ellas se busca un grado suficiente de homogeneidad, presuponiendo que ésta es la condición indispensable para la conformación de un objeto pasible de esclarecimiento crítico: de hecho, en efecto, hasta las literaturas provenientes de grupos sociales en pugna corresponden a una estructura social que no por estratificada deja de ser única y total. (10–11)

Years later (1981), Cornejo himself would recognize that even if this proposal is valid on a theoretical level, "...ésto no implica... que su realización sea sencilla". In fact, Cornejo refers to the problems still faced by the discipline when trying to apply such a proposal in the following terms:

> No está definido ni remotamente el modo como puede investigarse sobre sistemas literarios profundamente divergentes, que incluyen desde la oposición escritura-oralidad hasta la realización de conceptos antagónicos acerca de lo que es o no es la producción literaria, pues la solución más expeditiva, consistente en el estudio por separado de cada sistema, no parece ser la más correcta. En efecto, ni las dificultuades mencionadas, ni la realidad de la que emergen, borran el hecho de que todos estos sistemas

participan de un proceso histórico común, incluso en los casos extremos en los que las bases sociales de cada uno de ellos corresponden a muy desiguales grados de desarrollo. De hecho, la convergencia en un sólo país de modos de producción capitalistas y no capitalistas... determina profundas disparidades y marcados alejamientos, mas también, condicionan formas de articulación dependiente que ensamblan la totalidad social. (1981b, 120)

Cornejo's project eradicates the idea of unity and seeks to examine plurality, a plurality which he inscribes within a wider category which takes into account the socio-cultural conflict —the category of totality, understood as the "globalización de todos los sistemas por acción de la historia que los preside" (120).[22] Cornejo correctly states that, although the empirical recognition of the plurality of the literary systems produced in Latin American societies calls attention to the illegitimacy of homogenizing those societies, it does little on a theoretical and methodological level for the concrete treatment of the body of Latin American literatures. He points out that the concept of plurality also risks introducing a completely disintegrating vision, which could lead to, "las zonas de confluencia... [y] los movimientos articulatorios que efectivamente se realizan en el curso de la historia" being overlooked. Cornejo finds the solution in a historical approach to literature, which not only enables the understanding of plurality in terms of the "desarrollo desigual de nuestras sociedades...", but also shows, "...un nivel integrador concreto: el que deriva de la inserción de todos los sistemas y subsistemas en un solo curso histórico global" (1982, 47–48).

Cornejo believes that if, on a social level, "...no parece haber mayores dudas acerca de que inclusive en los casos más agudos de disgregación, cuando un solo espacio es compartido por modos de producción precapitalistas y capitalistas, existe un grado variable pero efectivo de articulación que permite comprender la totalidad...", it is also true that, "...hasta los sistemas literarios más alejados entre sí tienen en común el estar situados dentro de un solo proceso histórico" (48). This is the framework within which Cornejo examines *indigenismo* and heterogeneous literatures.

Cornejo's quest constitutes one of the most convincing contributions within criticism at the time to the discussion of unity and diversity in the continental literary process. It is also one of the most ambitious attempts within criticism to escape the pressure of integrating visions which can

---

[22] On the categories of plurality and totality in Cornejo's discourse, see also (1983, 43–46, 47 and 49–50).

only lead to the concealment of divisions, the denial of conflicts and contradictions, and the simplification of the "espesor" (Cornejo's term) of the multiple processes of literary production in Latin American societies.

Cornejo's initial proposal is to undertake this task on the basis of the study of (erudite) literatures in which the socio-cultural heterogeneity is evident in the production process. This work is more urgent in the countries traumatized by conflicts that involve class and ethnic confrontation:

> Una posibilidad de acercamiento a este nuevo espacio problemático... consiste en trabajar sobre objetos literarios que en su propia constitución reflejan, de una parte, el carácter plural y heteróclito de la literatura latinoamericana, pero de otra dan razón de su totalidad conflictiva; ésto es, aquellos movimientos literarios que se instalan en el cruce de dos o más formaciones sociales y de dos o más sistemas de cultura. (121)

Cornejo distinguishes two "systems of literary production" in the Latin American continent: one he labels "homogenous" ("homogéneas"), and defines as the literature of "...una sociedad que se habla a sí misma...", since, "...la movilización de todas las instancias del proceso literario [se produce] dentro de un mismo orden socio-cultural...". He includes urban literatures within this category: those which are written and read by the Latin American middle classes and deal with their own experience. The other system he calls "heterogeneous" ("heterogéneas"), a notion developed from his observation of *indigenismo*, but with the capacity to make possible a re-reading of the general process of Latin American literature since the Conquest. In his early writings, Cornejo characterizes heterogeneous literatures on the basis of, "...la duplicidad o pluralidad de los signos socio-culturales de su proceso productivo: se trata, en síntesis, de un proceso que tiene por lo menos un elemento [referente, instancia de producción o instancia de distribución y consumo] que no coincide con la filiación de los otros y crea, necesariamente una zona de ambigüedad y conflicto" (1978, 11–130).[23] In other words, the insertion of those elements in divergent socio-cultural spaces produces the tension and formal ambiguity which characterize the resulting text.

This conception of heterogeneity is, however, reformulated in much more radical terms in his latest writings; there, heterogeneity does not only affect the relationship between these elements ("instancias"), but also penetrates them, "haciéndolas dispersas, quebradizas, inestables y heteróclitas dentro de sus propios límites"; with this Cornejo attempts a more detailed examination not only of their internal configuration, but also

---

[23] For a detailed description of the various elements of production with regard to the referent of the heterogeneous literatures, especially the *indigenista* novel, see Cornejo Polar (1980, 64–67).

of the transactions carried out in "los bordes de sistemas culturales disonantes [e incluso] incompatibles" in which the Andean literatures function (1994, 16–17). Likewise, the subject matter of late Cornejo is redefined: the application of the notion of heterogeneity is no longer restricted to the sphere of erudite literatures, but is extended to the analysis of Andean "theatrical" traditions [Cornejo's quotes] (16–17).[24]

In Latin America, this system of text production, which is still in practice, was initially introduced by the Chronicles of the Conquest which, according to Cornejo, "...se limitan a reproducir, en los términos que específicamente les corresponden, un hecho histórico insoslayable: la conquista, y a marcar el inicio de lo que Mariátegui llamaba las literaturas no orgánicamente nacionales" (1978, 13–14).[25] The Chronicles also constitute the extreme manifestation of literary heterogeneity, since the productive and receptive elements belong to a reality which is totally alien to the enigmatic referent which they intend to explain. This referent is worked through forms which belong to Western traditions, originating in a society which, in effect, imposes its parameters and culture over that very referent. The resulting text is addressed to a public which is totally unfamiliar with this referent and which is immersed in another reality: "[t]odas las crónicas... llevan implícito un sutil y complejo juego de distancias y aproximaciones: si por una parte producen una red comunicativa donde antes sólo había desconocimiento o ignorancia, por otra parte, pero al mismo tiempo, ponen de relieve los vacíos que separan y desarticulan la relación de las fuerzas que movilizan" (13).[26]

What has been said on form does not imply that the referent passively accepts this imposition, or that the form remains unmodified in the process of dealing with that referent. In fact, the significance of the formal transformations which operate in heterogeneous literatures depends on the degree of distance between the referent and the circuit of production and consumption, as well as on the correlation of forces between them: the productive process may totally drown out the referent, in which circum-

---

[24] See especially his interpretation of Andean "dramatic" representations of the "diálogo de Cajamarca" (1994b, 50–89).

[25] See also (1989b, 79–80). For a radical reading of the chronicles which emphasizes both the presence of the autochtonous voice and a counter-hegemonic account of the historical and cultural experience of the aftermath of the conquest, see Martin Lienhard (1991). This line of research, which emphasizes "intercultural dialogue" (his term) is extended by Lienhard to a wide range of colonial and nineteenth century texts in the annotated anthology that he publishes in Biblioteca Ayacucho (1992).

[26] See also Cornejo Polar (1980b, 33–36).

stance the referent's influence on the form is minimal or even non-existent, as is the case with most of the chronicles; alternatively, the referent may succeed in imposing itself on the form, fundamentally changing it, as occurs with the heterodox chronicles, that of Guamán Poma de Ayala, for example. The range of formal modifications which take place between these two extreme alternatives, illustrated here by the chronicles, can be found, according to Cornejo, at different points in the Latin American literary process, including the literature of emancipation and culminating with its paradigm par excellence, *indigenista* narrative (14–16).

Far from regarding the literary form as a neutral category, Cornejo conceives of it as a "...factor directamente comprometido en el curso y significación de las literaturas heterogéneas" (15). Cornejo stresses the need for criticism to clarify the representations of socio-cultural plurality within Latin American literature, not only in terms of their content but, more importantly, in terms of the literary forms that are produced. Referring to *indigenismo* the Peruvian states that, as important as

> ...lo que el indigenismo puede *decir* acerca de la naturaleza heteróclita y problemática de los paises andinos... [es] esta viva formalización literaria del conflicto, esta ceñida reproducción, en términos estéticos, de la desgarradura interior que define a las sociedades multinacionales...
> (1989b, 80; in italics in the original)

He adds that it is this very dimension of *indigenista* narrative which guarantees its continued relevance, "...proponiendo al lector contemporáneo un espacio de reflexión y polémica acerca de aspectos básicos de la realidad americana y de otras extensas zonas del mundo también se produjeron rupturas históricas como la de la conquista y colonización de América" (80).

This vision of the active part played by form in the cultural processes involved in the production of such texts contributes to a re-reading of the role of the dominated sectors of the population in that production of texts, such as their capacity to articulate counter-hegemonic responses, to modify elements originating from the dominant culture, and even penetrate it with their own cultural forms. This perspective also offers an alternative to the emphasis on the content of the texts and the reductionist view of the nature of literary production to which sociological criticism so frequently limits itself.

Cornejo's interpretation of *indigenismo* as a heterogeneous literature vindicates its very nature and even its premise of heterogeneity, in contrast to that criticism which traditionally judged it in terms of whether or not it had the capacity to produce a vision "desde adentro" of the indigenous world which it attempts to represent. Referring back to Mariátegui again, who never believed that one could demand *indigenista* literature to be indigenous literature, Cornejo stresses the fact that *indigenismo* is necessarily defined by the exterior nature of all the elements involved in its production. *Indigenismo* is the work of a middle class which took on the task of representing, via Western cultural norms, the conflicts of sectors belonging to a different socio-cultural referent: the confrontations between a peasantry to a greater or lesser degree indigenous, and "gamonalismo". "Este difícil diálogo intersocial e intercultural [Cornejo reminds us] constituye el cimiento más profundo del indigenismo". This is why he reiterates that, without seeking "...una homogeneidad que le está vedada por definición, el indigenismo realiza una pauta contraria, de heterogeneidad, y en ella encuentra sus mejores posibilidades ideológicas y literarias..." (1978, 16–20).[27] And he concludes that,

> ...el indigenismo, el mejor indigenismo, no sólo asume los intereses del campesinado indígena; *asimila también, en grado diverso, tímida o audazmente, ciertas formas literarias que pertenecen orgánicamente al referente*. Se comprende que esta doble asimilación de intereses sociales y de formas estéticas, constituye el correlato dialéctico de la imposición que sufre el universo indígena del sistema productor del indigenismo: es por así decirlo su respuesta. [my emphasis] (21)

For Cornejo, *indigenismo* not only reproduces the fracture of Andean culture and society, it also incarnates the capacity for resistance of the dominated cultures, "...el vigor de los pueblos que la conquista no pudo liquidar" (21).[28] In his work on Alegría, published in 1978, Cornejo stresses that the process of "impregnación" of a genre of Western origin, such as the *indigenista* novel, by forms originating in the indigenous culture, such as "..las formas míticas, épicas o del relato folklórico...", transcends the dimension of the "purely formal", to reach an ideological level. Cornejo believes that, "...el grado de permeabilidad de la estructura novelesca parece estar en relación directa con la adhesión del narrador a los valores e intereses del pueblo indio". He finds a progression throughout the historical development of the *indigenista* novel, which is a correlative of "...la creciente integración de la zona andina en el sistema de la sociedad nacional...". This progression is expressed in terms of a greater degree of heterogeneity in the early stages ("primeras sequencias"), leading into "...una cada vez más audaz asimilación de formas generadas por el referente..." in more recent works. This is the case with the *neoindigenista*

---

[27] See also (23–24).
[28] See also (1989b, 54–56).

novels, but this does not in any way imply "...la cancelación de la heterogeneidad de base" (1989b, 56–57).[29] In his study, "Sobre el 'neoindigenismo' y las novelas de Manuel Scorza" (1984), Cornejo emphasizes that "...la disgregación sociocultural del mundo andino no ha desaparecido aunque... se ha reformulado en los últimos decenios y... por consiguiente, la literatura que trata de revelar ese carácter sigue conservando su razón de ser" (1989b, 216). We cannot overstate that, in Cornejo's opinion, the very premise of the existence of *indigenismo* arises from the fact that its enunciation is part of a universe alien to that of the referent and that it would cease to be *indigenismo*, "...si su producción no vinculara conflictivamente a ese mundo con el otro sistema socio-cultural que convive con él dentro de las fronteras del país" (1982, 90).

That essential heterogeneity is evident even in the most recent *neoindigenista* work: the cycle of novels entitled *La guerra silenciosa*, published by Manuel Scorza throughout the 1970s which is inspired by the peasant movements of the 1950s and 1960s. In this work Scorza, seeks to articulate certain aesthetic proposals of the "nueva novela" (i.e. "magical realism", through which he appropriates and reworks, literarily, Quechua mythical rationality), with the *indigenista* tradition (social novel), and to introduce the latter into the internationalized literary circuit. Thus, Cornejo comments on the heterogeneous nature of Scorza's narrative and its significance within the *indigenista* tradition:

> ...el ciclo de Scorza reproduce, dentro de una tradición que comienza con las viejas crónicas de América, la constitución actual de la heterogeneidad andina. En otras palabras: si se inserta en la modernidad más puntual y si se refiere al arcaismo de la sociedad indígena, es porque esa modernidad y ese arcaismo siguen coexistiendo, contradictoriamente, dentro de un mismo espacio nacional. No es poco mérito de *La Guerra Silenciosa* haber puesto el problema sobre el eje de la contemporaneidad. (1989b, 211–16)

Furthermore, although for Cornejo the author's external position with regard to the referent defines the essence of *indigenismo*, this by no means suggests, as the Italian Latin Americanist Roberto Paoli would wish, the idea supposedly implied by the category of heterogeneity that it is impossible for the *indigenista* writer to know the indigenous world (1980, 257-58). For Cornejo, the indigenous universe is simply "other", different from that of the writer; this does not, however, necessarily make it "impenetrable" (Paoli's term) or unknowable. Through his concept of heterogeneity, Cor-

---

[29] See also (1980b, 25–26).

nejo seeks, on the one hand to question and even eradicate the traditional concern of criticism when evaluating *indigenismo*; that is, the extent to which the writer does or does not express the indigenous world "desde adentro". As we have already stated, from Cornejo's point of view, the writer's vision is always exterior. On the other hand, with his concept of heterogeneity, Cornejo seeks to account for the very literature whose writers and readers are alien to the referent: "...mediante...[dicha noción] se trata de definir una producción literaria compleja cuyo carácter básico está dado por la convergencia, inclusive dentro de un solo espacio textual, de dos sistemas culturales diversos" (1980a, 88).

In order to understand the relevance of the role that Cornejo assigns to the category of heterogeneity in his reading of *indigenista* narrative, it is worthwhile reproducing this lengthy quote in which he holds that said category should,

> ...comprenderse...como un ejercicio cultural que se sitúa en la conflictiva intersección de dos sistemas socioculturales, intentando un diálogo que muchas veces es polémico, y expresando, en el nivel que le corresponde, uno de los problemas medulares de la nacionalidad: su desmembrada y conflictiva constitución. La novela indigenista no es sólo un testimonio literario más o menos certero, más o menos "interno", del mundo indígena; más que eso, aunque obviamente también siéndolo de algún modo, la novela indigenista no tanto enuncia su problemática cuanto — con mayor profundidad — la plasma en su forma, en su estructura general, en su significado. Es un caso excepcionalmente claro para comprender de qué manera la literatura no sólo explicita verbalmemte los conflictos y tensiones de una sociedad, sino que los encarna y reproduce en su propia constitución. (1980b, 88–89)

Evidently, Cornejo's proposal is not exhausted in the treatment of literary forms in the context of ethnic conflicts; on the contrary, his proposal offers very stimulating ways of dealing with the intertextual operations that take place between popular and elite cultures in other Latin American societies in which the fragmentations have not continued with the same intensity or depth as in the Andean societies, the main subject of his reflections. Equally, if we transcend the literary field and enter into the realm of general debate on Latin American culture, we should acknowledge the parallel insights that Cornejo's critical discourse may offer to the new approaches to the functioning of globalization and mass communication processes, and their interaction with popular culture, approaches which begin to gather momentum in the continent in the 1980s.[30]

---

[30] For a synthesis of the current Latin American debate on communication and culture,

The possibility of applying the category of heterogeneity to other literary and cultural phenomena, even outside Latin America, is nevertheless criticized by Roberto Paoli, who denies the epistemological legitimacy of the notion, and considers its versatility to be an indication of its operative ineffectiveness:

> La ajenidad, en rigor, es un riesgo y, al mismo tiempo, un límite cognoscitivo que afecta a demasiadas corrientes de la literatura y puede anidar hasta en las regiones más familiares de la experiencia. En otras palabras, se trata de un concepto cuya validez es tan susceptible de extensión que resulta operativamente ineficaz. (258)

Cornejo sees absolutely no validity in Paoli's criticism. On the contrary, although he agrees with the Italian's description of the notion of heterogeneity as having "generic" value, the Peruvian correctly stresses that this category must be applied in conjunction with a historical perspective. In his opinion, it is this very perspective which accounts for the different types of heterogeneity and the diversity of resulting literary projects. In effect, this leads to another objection from Paoli: he sees heterogeneity as an imprecise notion which, "...no permite [siquiera] distinguir variantes al interior del indigenismo..." (1980a, 87–88). In this connection, Cornejo makes the legitimate clarification that,

> ...heterogeneidad es un concepto teórico general que esclarece el carácter básico de un grupo más o menos extenso de literaturas, pero la gama concreta de sus manifestaciones, su tipología y proceso, sólo pueden ser reconocidos a través del conocimiento histórico. Después de todo, la diferencia entre la heterogeneidad de lo gauchesco y la heterogeneidad del indigenismo no es un problema teórico sino histórico. (89)

It is through a historical approach of the "modo de producción heterogéneo" of *indigenista* narrative and through an examination of the resulting concrete forms, that Cornejo proposes to elucidate the variants within the movement. To tackle this problem he puts forward at least two parameters: on the one hand, to determine "...el grado de asimilación de los intereses sociales auténticos del pueblo indígena...", or conversely, *indigenismo*'s incapacity to appropriate them, or, even, the extent to which they are "...tergiversados o negados...". On the other hand, as has been suggested, when reconstructing Cornejo's reading of the Chronicles of the Conquest, "...la eficiencia con que se asumen ciertas estructuras temático-formales indígenas y se las inscribe productivamente en el discurso literario indigenista...", or instead, "...la manera como este discurso repele

---

see Martín Barbero (1987 and n.d.) and García Canclini (1990).

tales estructuras y se encierra dentro de la normatividad occidental" (89).

But the category of heterogeneity in Cornejo's work is not offered solely as an interpretive tool for *indigenista* narrative, for the discourse of the colonial chronicles, or for indigenous theatrical practices. It also acts as the nucleus for a demythifying approach towards those discourses that homogenize Latin American socio-cultural experience, an approach which seeks to illustrate the plural and broken configurations of societies that have been corroded through inequality and injustice (1994b, 22–23).

"New Latin American Narrative" in Antonio Cornejo Polar's Discourse

Although Cornejo's fundamental contribution to Latin American criticism comes from his research into *indigenismo* and his theoretical and methodological proposal for the treatment of heterogeneous literatures, an overall appraisal of his work demands a consideration of his writings on "new Latin American narrative". Cornejo dedicated some studies to the main representatives of this narrative, concentrating mainly, but not exclusively, on Peru. In these articles, which alternate with those dedicated to the central theme of his research, he proposes some general hypotheses on the question of the "new novel" and its international dimension.[31] While one cannot compare the density of these studies with those which constitute the core of his discourse, to give a complete picture of Cornejo's views on Latin American and Peruvian literatures, his vision of that other system of literary production which he calls "homogéneo" merits a brief reconstruction here. As has already been noted, this literature is primarily confined to the urban middle classes and, especially after the 1960s, would largely be articulated to the internationalized circuit of culture.

These studies do not constitute the central concern of this book, since they do not represent Cornejo's most important contribution to the quest for independence within Latin American criticism or to its need to give account of the specificity of the continent's literary and cultural process. Nor do these studies fundamentally resolve the methodological difficulties faced by the majority of nationalist critical projects of the Latin American left during the last few decades in their attempt to account for the literatures articulated to international culture. In any case, these writings should be read with a view to determining to what extent Cornejo sets the "new novel" as a literary project, in opposition to that of *indigenismo*, as well as the significance he confers on the latter within Peruvian letters.

---

[31] See Cornejo Polar (1975 and 1982, 231–56).

In Cornejo Polar's writings, *indigenismo*, as literary system, cultural manifestation and expression of a social project, is set against the Peruvian version of the "new Latin American novel", taking the work of Mario Vargas Llosa, its most prestigious representative, as a paradigm. The *indigenista* movement, "...se vincula a los procesos de reestructuración social..." caused by modernization, while the "new novel" would be articulated to that very process of modernization which would, in fact, constitute the reverse of the social circumstances of *indigenismo*. For Cornejo, Vargas Llosa completes the modernizing project which the "generación del 50" had proposed for Peruvian narrative, but had been unable to achieve. Vargas Llosa's success would be due to his incorporation into the international publishing circuit. Literary modernization in Peru would thus be the correlative of economic modernization of Peruvian society (1989b, 269–70).

Cornejo is concerned with the treatment of history within some of the most important sectors of "new Latin American narrative", as well as being interested in the inclination of the latter for virtuosity, technical and formal autonomy, and the erasing of its own production process and immediate surroundings. This removes any critical relationship between the reader and the work, as Cornejo makes clear, principally in his articles on Vargas Llosa. The Chilean José Donoso, as we shall see, also plays a paradigmatic role within that narrative, exhibiting some of the problems which Cornejo considers to be intrinsic to the movement, in terms of its destruction of history and the principle of identity (1975, 215–16).

For Cornejo, Vargas Llosa's *La guerra del fin del mundo* represents the culmination of a process which began in his early narrative and continued throughout his writing career (1989b, 271). The process involves a disintegration of the sense of history in his novels and aims for maximum autonomy, ultimately seeking, through the perfection of their construction, "...la trasmutación del caos (referencial, significativo) en orden (formal) y [entregarse] al lector como objeto plenamente hecho y acabado, perfecto, borrando así las quiebras y conflictos de los que surge" (1981b, 241–42). Cornejo believes that Vargas Llosa thereby distances himself from a modern tradition which sets up a "...diálogo...desmitificador con el lector...", as is the case, for example, with *El zorro de arriba y el zorro de abajo*, or *Yo el supremo*, and his work is articulated to a, "...sistema literario que tiene como regla la presentación del texto como realidad precisa e inmodificable, hecha de una vez y para siempre, que pueda admitir ciertos niveles de diálogo y cuestionamiento salvo en lo que toca a su propia existencia" (242). According to Cornejo, this tendency among certain Latin American writers, including Vargas Llosa, can be explained in terms of the modernization and internationalization of the publishing industry which pressurizes the writers to convert their work into, "...objeto de comercio... que reproduzca, como tal, los caracteres generales de la mercancía, comenzando por la ruptura del vínculo entre ese objeto, que tiene que ser perfecto en su aparencia, y su siempre conflictivo proceso de producción, lo que es visible, hasta su exceso en algunos casos, en un vasto sector de la nueva narrativa hispanoamericana" (242).

Cornejo reads the trajectory of Donoso's work as a continual search for aesthetic break-up and reformulation in relation to traditional narrative. This is accentuated in *El lugar sin límites* and culminates in his novel *El obsceno pájaro de la noche*. The latter takes to the extreme elements already evident in his first novel: primarily the theme of destruction, as the core of the narration and the key to its composition and form, and which Cornejo describes as "...una obra apocalíptica..." (216–20). In his words: "...el lenguaje de *El obsceno pájaro de la noche* es un cruel simulacro que parece crear cuando en realidad detruye" (224). Another manifestation of the break-up pointed out by the Peruvian critic is the universalization of the meaning of the novel from *El lugar sin límites* onwards, since, in the preceding novels, Donoso referred to a more or less specific socio-historical context (220). In *El obsceno pájaro de la noche*, this context is erased and the group's fate of deterioration and disintegration, which is the basis of the narration, acquires universal scope which, for Cornejo, constitutes de-historicization: "La destrucción de una clase y del orden social que la explica se transforma en la destrucción de todo orden posible y del universo en su conjunto..." This is explained in terms of a shifting of perspectives: "El hablante básico de la novela aparece visceralmente integrado en el orden destruido y es incapaz de reconocer otras posibilidades de existencia. Si *su* mundo desaparece quiere decir que *el* mundo está aniquilado" (224–25; emphasis in the original). This concealment of the social tendency of the meaning of the novel is, in the Peruvian critic's opinion, "...resultado de un proceso ideológico" (225).

This process is common to a significant sector of the "new Latin American narrative", which, with its loss of the historical dimension, would also lose its critical scope with regard to the societies in which it is produced, and, more importantly, its capacity to prefigure social alternatives:

> El proceso de la narrativa de José Donoso deviene representativo de un amplio sector de la nueva narrativa hispanoamericana. En ella es frecuente observar desarrollos ideológicos similares, vale decir, la extensión a términos universales, con intención ontológica, de determinadas formas de conciencia social que ciertamente no tienen esa amplitud y

profundidad. En algunos de estos casos el sentido proveniente del texto implica una saludable remosión de hábitos y valores sociales, un cuestionamiento profundo del orden establecido, cuya liquidación se anuncia, pero sólo excepcionalmente se descubre la visión dialéctica que permite descubrir en la destrucción de un sistema la construcción de otro distinto y mejor. Es claro que la nueva narrativa hispanoamericana no accederá a esta visión dinámica de nuestra realidad mientras no recupere para sí el sentido y la experiencia de la historia. (225)

For Cornejo, the chief task of this narrative should be the retrieval of history.

From Cornejo's succinct reflections on the process of modernization and internationalization of Latin American literature, it is evident that his rejection of some of its proposals is above all due to his position on literary production which we have examined in this study: the fact that, for him, in Latin America, literature takes on an unavoidable commitment to social reality and that literature's avoidance or minimalization of the historical perspective acts in detriment to its social function, in other words, its task of revealing the referent and the forging of alternative projects for Latin American societies. Furthermore, Cornejo's option for literature, which is openly politically committed and testimonial to the exclusion of other conceptions of literature, is not an isolated position within the discipline. As we have seen in the chapters dedicated to Rama and Losada, this was a generalized position within Latin American criticism of the left at the time. Although it was rearticulated by the cultural discourse of the Cuban Revolution, this position has links with earlier tendencies within the literary and cultural process in Latin America. The debate provoked by this conception of the function of literature is far from over. In this connection, we must emphasize the importance of Mariátegui and Beatriz Sarlo's contributions to criticism in terms of their approach both to the relationships and mediations between the spheres of literature, politics and ideology, and to the plurality of the literary production of the region.

Finally, Cornejo adopts a critical, although somewhat unclear, attitude regarding the routes followed by literary modernization and the effects of its forced articulation to the international publishing circuits in economically dependent societies such as those of Latin America. This is an analytical perspective which is treated as a marginal issue in Cornejo's work, and it remains open to discussion within criticism today.

CHAPTER 5
BEATRIZ SARLO: TOWARDS A READING OF PLURALITY

This chapter offers a selective reading which cannot possibly do justice to the richness of Beatriz Sarlo's works. Rather than attempting an exhaustive reconstruction of her critical writings, the purpose here is to explore the proposals within them which directly or indirectly are articulated to the debate opened by Latin American autonomous criticism in the 1970s, in order to point towards solutions to the problematic aspects which have already been discussed. While this is obviously not the exclusive focus of Sarlo's work, it does occupy a dominant position in her writings immediately following the fall of the military dictatorship. Even if also fascinating, Sarlo's recent work will not be considered here as it is not of direct relevance to the central concerns of this study. Both in her articles published in *Punto de Vista* since 1990 and in her book *Escenas de la vida posmoderna* (1994), Sarlo has, throughout the decade, been writing about the expansion of mass media industry and its role in the transformation of the political and cultural sphere of *fin de siècle* Argentina. Sarlo challenges populist celebrations of the supposedly democratizing and emancipating effect on culture which this industry's domination of it is said to be having. She is similarly concerned with the increasing process of marginalization to which the "classic" intellectual and his/her critical role within society are being subjected by the expansion of mass media culture.[1]

The ideological reductionism of the city and its cultural production is a position extensively shared by 1970s left-wing critics in Latin America. It is evident to varying degrees, as has been noted in the discourse of Antonio Cornejo Polar, Angel Rama and Alejandro Losada. The work of Beatriz Sarlo, however, may offer alternatives. Her objective is, to a certain extent synthesized in her comments at Campinas (1983) on the need for Latin American criticism to account for the density of interweaving processes within the various literary manifestations in the continent:

> ...¿cómo podemos hacer para llegar al sistema literario complejo? En una sociedad están funcionando al mismo tiempo elementos que son pertene-

---

[1] Amongst these articles it is particularly worth seeing: Sarlo (1990, 1991, 1992, 1993a, 1994a and 1995). To place Sarlo's critical discourse in relation to the British tradition of "Cultural Studies", see Sarlo (1997).

> cientes al sistema popular, al sistema culto, elementos que vienen de sistemas anteriores, elementos que anuncian los posteriores, elementos residuales. Además yo creo que están en comunicación. Por ejemplo yo me planteo el problema de la inflexión criollista que tiene la vanguardia argentina, inflexión que es contemoránea al criollismo urbano que plantea el tango. Yo diría que hay ideologemas de la poesía de Borges en la década del veinte y hasta el treinta y cinco que son ideologemas correspondientes a los del tango. Es un sistema que habla de la circulación social de los discursos... aunque la musicalizada en el proyecto; lo que a mí me preocupa es cómo pueden quedar representados de algún modo, cómo el espesor del funcionamiento de la literatura en una sociedad puede quedar representado. (Pizarro 1985, 19–20)

It must be emphasized that Sarlo's critical proposal has the benefit of the perspective made possible by the changes taking place in the Latin American intellectual field throughout the 1980s. The project towards a Latin American criticism which had gained momentum in the preceding decade, however, had arisen in the context of the political polarization experienced by Latin American societies after the 1960s, the military dictatorships of the southern cone and the upsurge of North American intervention, as well as the rise of a generalized attitude of commitment to anti-imperialist and revolutionary struggles among left-wing intelligentsia. The hegemony of Dependency Theory within the social sciences is another important feature of the intellectual atmosphere of the 1960s and 1970s. As has already been noted, the uncritical transposition of such a framework to the sphere of cultural studies would have a legacy of theoretical and methodological problems for Latin American criticism. Among these are the difficulties the latter encounters when tackling processes of cultural production in their specificity, and its resorting to Manichaean schemes for the interpretation of the history of Latin American literature and culture.

Beatriz Sarlo's work explores these questions within Argentinean criticism and stands as a crucial point of reference for Latin American criticism. It is particularly useful to examine some of the theoretical and ideological premises and some of the key themes which form the basis of her critical project, as well as the historical circumstances in which it is written. Her discourse should be read in the broader context of its contribution to the endeavor of Argentinean left-wing intelligentsia from the early 1980s to produce an "autobiografía colectiva" (as she often calls it).[2] Amongst the objectives of this "autobiografía" are a questioning of

---

[2] For further reading of Sarlo's questioning of the role and responsibilities of the left-wing intellectual, see her articles published in *Punto de Vista* after 1983, especially: (1983b, 1984c, 1985, 1985b, and 1986).

some of the principles guiding the political activity of the left in the previous two decades, a re-evaluation of its own degree of responsibility for the defeat of 1976, and an exploration of alternatives for the future.

Although this process takes place within the Argentinean intellectual sphere, despite differences in traditions and circumstances, many of the problems Sarlo deals with in relation to Argentina have clear correlatives with issues pertaining to other areas within the Latin American intellectual and political field. We are more specifically referring to her critique of a particular reading of Argentinean culture, a reading dominated by perspectives stemming from populist nationalism and Dependency Theory which had led to the elision of the divisions between intellectual and political discourse. The 1960s and 1970s left ideological legacies for the intelligentsia in general, and for the critic in particular; *Una modernidad periférica* (1988) can largely be read as an attempt to find solutions to the problems created by these legacies.

Sarlo's point of departure is the questioning of the place, identity and function of the left-wing intellectual in relation to the political and cultural fields, as established throughout the 1960s and 1970s in Argentina. According to Sarlo, during those years the discourse of the intellectual had been subordinated —she would say "cannibalized"— to that of politics, and the tensions between these spheres had undergone a process of erasure leading to a loss of the critical dimension:

> El discurso de los intelectuales pasó de ser diferente al de la política, aunque se emitiera en función política o para intervenir en su debate, a ser la duplicación, muchas veces degradada (porque violaba sus propias leyes) del discurso y la práctica política. De la etapa crítica...habíamos pasado del servilismo, sea cual fuere el amo (partido, líder carismático, representación de lo popular o de lo obrero) que nos convertía en siervos. De la etapa crítica pasamos a la etapa racionalizadora. (1985a, 2)

The borders between the two spheres must be recognized and confronted if the intellectual is to have his/her identity and critical function restored. Sarlo does acknowledge the distinction between these spheres, countering a perspective which attempts to homogenize the heterogeneous and erase ruptures and conflicts. Thus, she proposes,

> ...repensar las relaciones entre cultura, ideología y política, como relaciones gobernadas por una tensión ineliminable que es la clave de la dinámica cultural, en la medida en que cultura y política son instancias disimétricas y, por regla general, no homológicas. Se trataría, entonces, de pensar, al intelectual como sujeto atravesado por esta tensión y no como subordinado a las legalidades de una u otra instancia, listo para sacrificar en una de ellas lo que defendería en la otra. (6)

Sarlo is not interested in a marginalization of politics with regard to the work of the intellectual, but in a redefinition of the relations between them, of the very concept of politics and of the place of political discourse within the public sphere. She is interested in the search for a new space for the discourse of the intellectual, and particularly for his/her critical discourse in which neither political responsibility nor his/her specific identity as an intellectual are dispensed with.[3]

For Sarlo, the deep-rooted persistence of nationalist perspectives in Argentinean criticism is a prime example of the breakdown of divisions between political ideology and cultural thought, and is responsible for numerous reductionist versions of literary processes. The most important works in Sarlo's criticism in the period under consideration here examine the relationship between nationalism and culture in the Argentinean intellectual sphere following the Generation of "Centenario". These works rest on the premise that the debate on the national question accompanies the process of Argentina's cultural formation. Without attempting to provide a definitive explanation of this peculiarity of Argentinean cultural history, Sarlo sets out to display the various projects of national culture formulated by Argentinean literature and to explain them either in terms of their hegemonic character within the intellectual sphere, or, in terms of the conflictive co-existence of their various endeavors which are at times counter-hegemonic and at other times simply intended to gain a space within the cultural field (Sarlo & Altamirano 1980, Sarlo 1982 and 1988). One of Sarlo's most interesting contributions is her lucid critical distance with regard to the different nationalist formulations which constitute the subject of her discourse. This distance enables her to carry out a very fruitful and necessary dismantling of the mythical content of categories and paradigms central to these nationalist discourses which have produced extremely reductionist interpretations of literary processes. Furthermore, Sarlo questions the legitimacy of these categories and paradigms. We are referring to dubious notions such as "cosmopolitan" or "non-national" and, even, "anti-national" literature which are set up in opposition to "national literature" not only within Argentinean criticism, but also within Latin American criticism in general. Another equally dubious concept is that which holds that only rural popular cultures can be bearers of "lo nacional", while urban cultures have been "denationalized" by the cosmopolitanism of the surroundings (1984c, 24–25). Sarlo offers an alternative interpretive framework for the reading of these strategies of

---

[3] For her conception of the political attitude of the artist and critic, see Sarlo (1985b).

(mythical) construction of lineages and traditions, as will be seen in the discussion of *Una modernidad periférica*; in fact, this book offers a more fruitful perspective on the dynamic of cultural processes than that based on a bi-polar conception of the history of Latin American culture.

The tenacious presence of nationalist discourses is not exclusive to Argentina. It is a constant feature within the continent's thought since the setting up of the independent Republics in the nineteenth century. As we have already stated, it functions as an axis of the most important Latin American contemporary critical discourses. Rama, Losada and Cornejo, in contrast to Sarlo, are not only concerned with understanding the persistence of confrontations between the diverse nationalist projects within literary and cultural production. Their discourse is, in fact, articulated to these debates as nationalist projects themselves. Sarlo's critique of the populist nationalism of the Argentinean left in the last two decades provides new elements for the examination of the nationalist dimension underlying the Latin American critical project. Although we have mainly concentrated on an analysis of Rama's nationalism, we hope that such an analysis will also throw some light on the nationalist dimension of Cornejo and Losada's writings.

It must be emphasized that our intention is neither to assimilate Rama into Argentinean cultural history nor to overlook the context in which Sarlo's discourse is formulated, that is to say, the beginning of the 1980s, from within the left-wing of an intellectual sphere which undertakes the re-evaluation of its participation in the revolutionary struggle of the preceding decade and its tragic defeat. Sarlo's position regarding the relationship between nationalism and culture is not independent from her questioning of the populist nationalism of the Argentinean left. Her distance rests on this critique. It is also necessary to point out that Sarlo never projects her critique onto the Latin American intellectual field. Nevertheless, it is difficult to ignore its relevance both to the interpretation of the project towards a Latin American criticism in the 1970s, and to the search for solutions to some of the theoretical and methodological problems of the latter.

Rama's discourse is produced under circumstances very different to those prevailing at the time of Sarlo's writing. Rama's work on transculturation in Latin America is written during the second half of the 1970s, in a context which has not experienced the brutality of the Argentinean left's defeat and which still lacks the perspective that comes only with the passing of time, and the process of self-criticism undergone by the Argentinean left upon which Sarlo will build her discourse. We have already stated that Rama's discourse and its nationalism are articulated to the anti-imperialist, Third-Worldist and Latin Americanist dimensions of Cuban revolutionary discourse. Sarlo not only sheds light on such an articulation, but also provides solutions to some of the problematic areas within Latin American criticism which have so much to do with the mythifying nature of categories inherited from this nationalist perspective.

Sarlo questions the legitimacy of a national identity defined by contrast with a Buenos Aires conceived as, "...sede de intelectuales más sensibles a las novedades europeas que a la cultura del pueblo, [como] Babilonia que, en el goce de una cultura sofisticada y cosmopolita pierde de vista los valores de las culturas regionales y populares" (25). For Sarlo, a critical project constructed on the basis of a national-populist discourse denies the possibility of accounting for the real density of the cultural fabric of Argentinean society:

> Me resisto a pensar la cultura argentina como una empresa de homogenización realizada en nombre de la identidad nacional, de la clase obrera o del pueblo (según sean las perspectivas políticas que la izquierda adopte sobre el asunto). Tampoco me parece fiel a los hechos pensar la historia de esta cultura como una batalla interminable en la que se enfrentan contingentes nacionales y antinacionales, como fue inexacto pensar este proceso en tanto contraposición simple de una línea "progresiva" y otra reaccionaria. Finalmente, la tentación que acecha a la izquierda es también la de un paternalismo misional, que la impulsa a salvar a los sectores populares, de los peligros de la cultura "alta" y cosmopolita y, en nombre del respeto debido a las culturas regionales, campesinas a celebrar panglosianamente lo que pueda haber sido resultado de la desigualdad, la injusticia y la privación. (25)

Certain elements of this critique are relevant to an interpretation of Rama's position on national identity which, at times, undermines his discourse of transculturation. We are referring in particular to those elements dealing with, on the one hand, his ideological condemnation of urban intellectual production for its cosmopolitanism and his Manichaean opposition between the latter and regional cultures, and, on the other, to his notion of unification of Latin American culture on the basis of a definition of "lo nacional" which plays down the plurality of the cultural projects which, in fact, make up the continent's culture. The Uruguayan critic's interest in Latin American regional cultures takes place, however, within a very different context from that of Sarlo. It is crucial to remember that his work on narrative transculturation in Latin America focuses on societies where modernization has penetrated more slowly and unevenly than in the southern cone region, and where, consequently, enormous peasant —and in the case of Peru indigenous— sectors have survived together with traditional cultural systems in conflictive coexistence with expanding modern urban centers. Furthermore, his retrieval of these traditions does not seek to cut them off from the cultural dynamics of society in general, and certainly not from "erudite" culture. On the contrary, he seeks to highlight their links with modernity and Western traditions and, above all, to bring their counter-proposals to light. In calling into question the problematic aspects of his nationalist vision, our intention is not by any means to invalidate his crucial contribution to Latin American cultural criticism.

In *Una modernidad periférica,* Sarlo explores the movements which seek to restructure the Argentinean cultural field, in their interrelation with the processes of social transformation which take place in the 1920s and 1930s. The modernization of Argentina and in particular Buenos Aires, serves as the premise of her interpretation. Modernization functions as the central axis articulating the heterogeneous cultural and aesthetic responses with change, and it is this that Sarlo sets out to clarify. She is interested in showing the specificities of Argentinean modernity in the 1920s and 1930s, without resorting to the reductionist paradigms used by nationalist critical models. Her proposal constitutes an attempt to offer an alternative interpretation which nevertheless accounts for the specific features of Argentinean culture. Thus, her definition of Argentinean culture rests on a basic hypothesis which characterizes it as a "cultura de mezcla". A blend of ideologies, discourses and cultural practices is Argentinean culture's way of operating par excellence, and it is this formula which Sarlo extends to the rest of Latin America:

> En efecto, una hipótesis que intentaré demostrar se refiere a la cultura argentina como una cultura de mezcla, donde coexisten elementos defensivos y residuales junto a los programas renovadores; rasgos culturales de la formulación criolla al mismo tiempo que un proceso descomunal de importación de bienes, discursos y prácticas simbólicas... La mezcla es uno de los rasgos menos transitorios de la cultura argentina: su forma ya "clasica" de respuesta y reacondicionamientos... (1988, 28)

For Sarlo, what is specific to Latin America, and in particular Argentina, is not the supposed preservation of traditions untouched by foreign influences and, therefore, bearers of "lo nacional". On the contrary, Sarlo starts from the premise that the modern Argentinean intellectual field (in its entirety and not just "una élite extranjerizante") is, in fact, articulated to the international intellectual field, and that this inevitably involves contact with imported practices and discourses. Sarlo is interested in exploring the various ways in which these practices and discourses are appropriated and reformulated to adapt to the needs of the Argentinean cultural sphere; the specificity of its production rests on this very process.

The great social transformations undergone by Argentina already from the end of the nineteenth century, and which would be intensified in the early 1920s, take place at a vertiginous speed, in contrast to the much more gradual process of change experienced in the metropoli. This involves the articulation, rather than the simple co-existence, of a modern space —importing aesthetic discourses and projects from metropolitan modernity— with a traditional space, or at least a sphere in which traditional elements survive. The specificity of Latin American culture is to be found in the light of these intersections, the conditions which they create and the particular pressures which they effect on the producers of culture.

This is undoubtedly one of the most useful contributions to Latin American criticism. Here, Sarlo breaks with an interpretation which understands Latin American literary production as mere mimetic acts. Instead, she is interested in demonstrating how the writers of the period experience the urbanization process in Buenos Aires from a heterogeneous cultural space which combines tradition and modernity and, of course, how they produce aesthetic projects distinct from those of the metropoli. This perspective entails a much more dynamic and historical notion of cultural processes as it discards the idea of imitation, which, in any case, implies an attitude of passive reception and mechanical reproduction which leaves no place for creativity. Another advantage of Sarlo's approach is the productivity which she derives from that which an interpretation based on the notion of imitation would simply perceive as "distortions" or faults in the "quality" of the copy. She looks to these "deviations" in order to understand the processes of refunctionalization of the "model" which are taking place. Incidentally, Sarlo also abandons the opposition between the "original" model and the "reproduction" in her critical proposal. This is not an attempt to ignore the peripheral condition of the Latin American countries, nor to overlook the fact that this condition determines, among other things, an intertextual relationship with the metropolitan intellectual spheres which is always *asymetrical* (Sarlo's term). She aims to reinterpret its functioning on the basis of recognizing that this intertextuality does not occur in a socio-cultural vacuum. The imported discourses enter into an intellectual field which is already well established, with its own tensions and debates, to which they must respond if they are to be effective. But Sarlo's position must also be understood in relation to the nationalist critical models grounded in Cultural Dependency Theory, since they are built on both a notion of art as reflection and on a concept of appropriation of metropolitan discourses whose only function would be to "denationalize" culture (1983a, 87).

Through this approach, Sarlo distances herself from the old inferiority complex which Latin American criticism has suffered from with regard to metropolitan cultures, and which virtually forces it into juggling acts in its attempt to guarantee the literature of the continent a respectable international position. Sarlo is not interested in proving that the "copies" are not so bad after all, or in resorting to mythical demonstrations of the "originality" of the literary works. Neither does she wish to deny Latin American culture's articulation with the international intellectual field. Sarlo breaks with a hierarchical vision of cultural processes, chiefly between metropolis and periphery, but also between "erudite" production and popular production, as exemplified by her readings of Borges and Arlt respectively.

For Sarlo, one of the most thought-provoking aspects of Borges is the notion of the "margins" ["orillas"] of Buenos Aires —that creole suburb where pampas and city fuse. Through this invention, Borges intervenes in at least two debates: the national identity debate, in which the Argentinean cultural system at the time is engaged, and the debate surrounding the articulation of that system to the international intellectual field. Borges' Buenos Aires "margins" are also, "...las orillas de la literatura universal, [que es] pensada como espacio propio y no como territorio a adquirir" (1988, 50). Borges proposes a formula of universality for Argentinean literature which grows out of its creole margins, and, simultaneously, "...acriolla la tradición universal..." (181). The peculiarly Argentinean universality which Borges affords his literature is produced by its placing itself, "...con astucia, en los márgenes, en los repliegues, en las zonas oscuras, de las historias centrales. La única universalidad posible para un rioplatense" (49). Certainly, Sarlo's discourse incorporates and applies this Borgesian solution; we do not have to look far to confirm this: the very title of the book is an ironic reference to the "periphery" label, divesting it of its hierarchical connotation. Sarlo's re-reading of Argentinean modernity is also an attempt to re-evaluate and resemanticize "peripheral" cultural production.

In Sarlo's opinion, Arlt's writing is constructed on the basis of its own limitations which have a socio-cultural origin; from "...el resentimiento causado por la privación cultural de origen...", Arlt throws down his "challenge" to the "instituciones estético-ideológicas" (50) and engages in an almost "savage" process of appropriation of the prestigious knowledge ("saberes prestigiosos") which has been denied him, and of the marginal knowledge ("saberes marginales") to which he has access from his marginal condition. But this process of "canibalización... deformación... perfeccionamiento... y parodia" (52), also becomes a strategy for his writing. He responds with sarcasm to the unequal distribution of culture at the same time as affirming it: "Exhibición de cultura y exhibición de incultura: el discurso doble de la ironía niega y afirma, al mismo tiempo, la necesidad y la futilidad de la cultura" (52). *Power,* in all its forms and relations and its fundamental association with *knowledge,* is the hegemonic theme in Arlt's work. His "assault" on power is effected through his conquest of knowledge and this is done from the alternative circuits of marginal knowledge, which, for the popular sectors, "...suplen la ausencia o la debilidad de los circuitos formales". From this alternative space which "...está en los márgenes de las instituciones, [alejado] de las zonas prestigiosas que autorizan la voz..." (56), Arlt produces his discourse and justifies a place for himself within the modern Argentinean intellectual field, in spite of and in opposition to his exclusion from the circuits of institutional knowledge.

It is worth noting that Sarlo's critical thought is not something imposed upon the corpus she is examining, but rather arises out of that very examination. Her interpretation of Borges and Arlt are just two examples, although they are especially interesting in that they shed light on one of the most stimulating aspects of her discourse, that is to say, her re-evaluation of a cultural production realized from the "periphery" —the term is used with some irony— of the system of modern societies. Like Arlt, Sarlo's disourse exploits the limitations imposed by the "marginality" of the "periphery", breaking down the hierarchies of the central discourses, discrediting the perspectives which deny Latin American modernity as well as those which can only find "desfases" and poor "reproducciones" in the literature of the continent as a result of its material "backwardness" and cultural restrictions. Sarlo's work offers the possibility of a *positive* reading of what, until now, has always been read negatively by criticism: the marginality of modern Argentinean culture and the asymmetry of its relations with the central intellectual fields resulting from its peripheral condition. What Sarlo suggests is the extent to which Argentinean —and, we would argue, Latin American— writers can turn the disadvantages of their marginal position into productive conditions. Sarlo argues that it is the very marginality of this situation that makes possible their strategies of "descentramiento" and "desbordamiento", as well as of irreverent exaggeration of the "models" originating in the metropolitan intellectual sphere. In fact, these are procedures used within her own critical discourse; the peripheral situation of the Argentinean intellectual in relation to the central traditions —as Borges himself proposes in his article "El escritor argentino y la tradición" (1961, 151–62)— confers upon his/her writing the distance which opens the way to a critical radicalism and innovation of which the work of Borges himself is one of the most prominent examples.[4]

Although Sarlo does not engage in an open debate with the Latin American sphere, her critical project also entails a questioning of those models which reduce the multiplicity of the continent's literary production to two opposing paradigms, one "cosmopolitan" and the other "local". Sarlo proposes an alternative to the old, recalcitrant and Manichaean reading which conceives of Latin American literary production as a confrontation between "national" literatures and "denationalized" literatures. All these terms and their correlative mythologies are eradicated from her critical discourse. The inadequacy of these notions is demonstrated in the picture of the Argentinean intellectual field of the 1920s and 30s outlined by Sarlo:

> La búsqueda de nuevas formas de nacionalismo es uno de los signos del período...He trabajado con la hipótesis de que este clima ... no afectaba sólo a la fracción de derecha del campo intelectual. Más bien, la situación de desconcierto frente a un mundo donde se estaban viviendo grandes transformaciones que incluían procesos políticos o económicos y la redefinición de los lugares del intelectual y de la cultura respecto del estado, concernía, en términos globales, a las élites de escritores y artistas, que se consagran a la elucidación de los rasgos nacionales a partir de un análisis del presente o de una relectura de la historia. (1988, 243–44)

On the one hand, the concern for Argentinean national identity embraces the whole political spectrum of the intellectual field which is undergoing a process of restructuring. This preoccupation runs through all the literary projects of the time, including those which are supposedly "self-referential" and which are stigmatized by nationalist criticism as

---

[4] For an alternative reading of the notion of "imitation", which together with that of Sarlo offers a new perspective on the examination of the relationship between discourses produced in the periphery and discourses originating in the central zones, see Schwartz (1992). In contrast to Sarlo, Schwartz does not discard the notion of imitation but instead reformulates it. The Brazilian critic insists that imitation is inevitable in dominated societies and that the philosophical disqualifying of the notion does not solve a practical problem linked to a concrete organization of power (82). For him, what is imperative is to challenge a conception of imitation which, "...counterposes national and foreign, original and imitative... [because they] ...are unreal oppositions which do not allow us to see the share of the foreign in the nationally specific, of the imitative in the original and the original in the imitative... [and he concludes that to copy] ...is not a false problem, so long as we treat it pragmatically, from an aesthetic and political point of view freed from the mythical requirement of creation *ex-nihilo*" (16–17).

"cosmopolitan" and ignorant of the national question. Borges' work, for example, cannot be understood in all its dimensions if it is reduced to the *ultraista* formula and if his avant-garde *criollista* program —a truly national identity formula— is ignored. Borges' "margins", the definition of the "true" Argentina, have more to do with the invention of a *criollo* world and tradition than with the new "cosmopolitan" society from which he writes.[5] In fact, the "argentinidad" proposed by Borges totally excludes immigrants and should be read as a response —amongst the many other responses with which he competes— to the profound changes which modernization is causing in Argentinean society in general and in the intellectual field in particular. By showing that the whole intellectual field is concerned with the debate on national identity, Sarlo defies the longstanding belief that the political is an exclusive monopoly of the left's literary production. On the other hand, Sarlo writes, the whole of the intellectual field is also importing discourses; the difference lies only in the various interpretive systems which each group appropriates and legitimizes. Clearly, from this point of view the notions of the "national" and the "cosmopolitan" dissolve and lose any applicability. As well as demolishing these schemes stemming from Dependency Theory and nationalist positions, Sarlo discredits the reductionist and homogenizing tendency of bi-polar interpretations of Latin American literary production. She does this through approaching the intellectual field in a manner that takes its complexity and plurality of responses to modernization into account, showing the heterogeneity of its composition and production, without overlooking either the existence of contradictions or of ideological and aesthetic interplay. Her critical vision values the quest itself over and above closed formulas and finished models. Her reading is open to the constant reformulation and active character of culture and, as such, offers an important alternative to the crisis of global models.

Sarlo's work, as good modernist writing itself, is presented as a proposal of open interpretation which is being constantly reformulated; she does not propose the construction of a model, or of a paradigm for Latin American criticism. Her focus is upon the intellectual field of Argentina, or even Buenos Aires. Furthermore, her discourse completely lacks the Latin Americanist dimension of the Spanish-American critical projects formulated in the 1970s. Nevertheless, despite her reticence to debate with them, Sarlo administers a hard blow to the Latin American left's populist nationalism and their Manichaean interpretations of culture. Her views on

---

[5] This approach to Borges's work is further developed by Sarlo in her book *Jorge Luis Borges. A writer on the Edge* (1993b).

the relationship between culture and politics, between metropolitan and peripheral cultural production, between literary and national discourse, between popular culture and "erudite" culture, and between the reading of the texts and the production of the cultural sphere are all capable of incorporation into Latin American criticism. Although she never sets out to resolve the methodological problems within Latin American criticism, Sarlo succeeds in opening new avenues for the cultural debate in the region.

CHAPTER 6

FIN DE SIÈCLE: ASSESSMENT AND PERSPECTIVES

The discourses examined in this study share, above all, a preoccupation with articulations between socio-cultural and literary processes. Each affirms, in some way, a need for the critic to turn to history as a dimension of his/her analysis, a dimension which becomes indispensable when seeking to establish the specific character of literature produced in societies which, since their origins, have been dominated by, and bound to, external centers of power. The Conquest of the Latin American continent inaugurates a conflictive relationship between the cultural formations inherited from the victors of the sixteenth century and those inherited from the indigenous and Afro-American peoples, which neither the liberal nor the neoliberal eras have resolved.

The complexity of this relationship, and the ways in which it has been dealt with in Latin American literature, has engaged the attention of the most important critics of the continent. A list has been proposed here —by no means exhaustive— of key moments in Latin American cultural criticism. Mariátegui's work is put forward as one of the initial mainstays of this criticism, and certainly remains relevant to current developments. Next there is the group of intellectuals involved in the movement towards Latin American criticism in the 1970s, the central figures of which are Rama, Losada and Cornejo. Finally, there is the re-reading undertaken by Beatriz Sarlo, in the 1980s, of Argentine modernity and of the cultural nationalism of her country's criticism. We trust to have made evident the relevance of these critics' theories to current debates concerning the region's culture.

It is worth noting, parenthetically, that the thirty or forty years which separate the formulations made by Mariátegui on nation and culture in Peru and Rama's concern with the absence of a cultural dimension within criticism, are dominated by immanentist approaches to literature primarily associated with Stylistics. Later on, structuralist methods are articulated to the Stylistic tradition, thereby giving further validity to already well-established immanentist perspectives. As has already been shown elsewhere, one of the effects of the predominance of such critical perspectives is the exclusion of a significant part of the Latin American literary corpus, namely, that part which makes a prominent feature of its social content. Clearly, then, it is in reaction to this critical climate that Rama, Losada and Cornejo set themselves against the reading of texts in an absolute historical vacuum, instead restoring a viewpoint which would enable the discipline to re-establish articulations between a literary work and the socio-cultural conditions of its production, as the minimum prerequisite for the task of giving Latin American literature its own identity.

Among the principal objectives of this study has been the tracing of the trajectory of three of the most fertile contributions to the project of forging an autonomous criticism, reconstructing their methodological proposals, discussing the applicability of their main categories, and establishing both the progressive steps which they have afforded the discipline and the problematic aspects which they may have introduced at a certain point. Amongst the advances are their surpassing of the national models of literary history and their questioning of the criteria of periodization that governed them, as well as the reappraisal of the innovative role that literatures articulated to traditional cultures played in the wider context of Latin American literature. Thus was challenged a criticism modeled on the modernization path followed by the misleadingly named *nueva narrativa*, which was unable to recognize in any other literary paradigms —especially if they drew on regional or autochtonous traditions— an ability to interact with modernity, let lone any ability to call modernity itself into question. Rama, Losada and Cornejo contribute in equal measure to the expansion and de-elitization of the corpus of Latin American literature. They contribute also to the recovery of rural popular cultures, as well as highlighting their vitality and their creative and contestatory potential. Amongst the problematic aspects isolated are a number of perspectives common, to a greater or lesser degree, to the autonomist discourses. One such is the tendency to dilute the specificity of the aesthetic sphere and subject it to the logic of politics and ideology, a tendency patent, for example, in the approach to the processes of intertextuality between the metropoli and Latin America on the basis of the questionable notion of "cultural dependency". Another is the reduction of the plurality of projects that form the Latin American literary corpus (a plurality that, paradoxically, constitutes one of the key directions of their critical proposals) to bipolar readings of the corpus, recognizing those literatures articulated to traditional rural cultures as the exclusive standard-bearers of nationhood.

We hope to have succeeded in proposing some useful suggestions for the addressing of these problems through the use of the writings of Mariátegui and Sarlo, which, in effect, offer theoretico-methodological corrections, at the level of their subtle handling of the relationships between aesthetics, politics and ideology, for example, or the balance reached by both as regards the treatment of form, which does not succumb to the overemphasis on content which autonomist criticism inherited from sociology. In addition —and perhaps this constitutes one of their most useful lessons— each of these authors, in their own way, demonstrates that "lo nacional", without having to be abandoned, can be redefined and understood in a more complex way, allowing truly pluralist readings of the construction of the cultural modernity of their respective countries. In the final analysis, these readings continue to emphasize the particular traits of the region's processes.

Although the cultural context of *fin de siècle* —with its globalization processes— demands that questions should be reformulated, that methodologies should be rethought and that maps should be re-drawn (García Canclini 1990), there is no erasing of the preoccupations with "lo nacional", with the production and refashioning of local identities, with the role that popular culture may play (Martín Barbero 1987, 45), with the capacity for resistance which the region can put up against "una homogenización inexorable... una uniformización aculturada" (Achugar 1996, 847). Perhaps the persistence of these preoccupations is inevitable: ultimately, the inequalities at the very heart of Latin American societies have not been overcome,[1] nor have the inequalities between those societies and the metropolitan centers of power. To echo Hugo Achugar's words, cultural criticism has the task of keeping this agenda at the forefront of its analysis of the new juncture (Achugar 1996, 855).

---

[1] Jorge Castañeda reminds us that the old social agenda of the nationalist Left remains open, since the majorities, descendants of the peoples vanquished five hundred years ago, are still excluded from the nation. Thus, the Left has no alternative but to keep up the fight, albeit after redefining the terms of its nationalism and rethinking its strategies in order to include as part of the nation those majorities who have never had a nation to call their own (1994, chapters 9 and 10).

BIBLIOGRAPHY OF WORKS CITED AND CONSULTED

GENERAL

Achugar, Hugo. "Notas para un debate sobre la crítica literaria latinoamericana." *Revista Casa de las Américas* 110 (1978): 3–18.

Althusser, Louis. "Ideology and Ideological State Apparatuses." *Lenin and Philosophy*. London: New Left Books, 1971.

Anderson, Danny J. "Cultural Studies and Hispanisms." *Siglo XX/20TH Century* 14: 1–2 (1996): 5–13.

Anderson, Perry. "Modernization and Revolution." *New Left Review* 144 (1984): 96–113.

Aricó, José., ed. *Marx y la América Latina*. Lima: Ediciones CEDEP, 1980.

———, "La producción de un marxismo americano." *Punto de Vista* 25 (1985): 7–12.

Arguedas, José María. *Formación de una cultura nacional indoamericana*. México: Siglo XXI, 1975.

Bennet, Tony. *Formalism and Marxism*. London & New York: Methuen, 1979.

Beverley, John with Diana, G. & Lecuna, V. "A Little Azúcar. Una conversación sobre estudios culturales." *Siglo XX/20TH Century* 14: 1–2 (1996): 15–35.

Bolívar, Simón. *Doctrina del Libertador*. Caracas: Biblioteca Ayacucho, 1976.

Borges, Jorge Luis. "El escritor argentino y la tradición." *Discusión*. Buenos Aires: Emecé Editores, 1961. 151–62.

Bourdieu, Pierre. *Problemas del estructuralismo*. México: Siglo XXI, 1967.

Bueno Chávez, Raúl. "Sentido y requerimientos de una teoría de las literaturas latinoamericanas." *Revista de Crítica Literaria Latinoamericana* 29 (1989): 295–307.

Candido, Antonio. "Literatura y subdesarrollo." *América Latina en su literatura*. Ed. Carlos Fernández Moreno. México: UNESCO/Siglo XXI, 1972.

———, *Formação da Literatura Brasileira: Momentos Decisivos*. São Paulo: Itaiaia, 1975.

———, "Para una crítica latinoamericana." *Punto de Vista* 8 (1980): 5–9.

Castañeda, Jorge. *Utopia Unarmed: The Left After the Cold War*. New York: Vintage Books, 1994.
Castro, Fidel. "Palabras a los intelectuales'." *La Revolución cubana*. México: Ed. ERA, 1972.
Cueva, Agustín. "Para una interpretación sociológica de *Cien Años de soledad*." *Revista Mexicana de Sociología* XXXVI:1 (1974): 59–76.
De La Campa, Román. "Latinoamérica y sus nuevos cartógrafos: discurso poscolonial, diásporas y enunciación fronteriza." *Revista Iberoamericana* LXII: 176–177 (1996): 697–717.
Eagleton, Terry. *Criticism and Ideology*. London: New Left Books, 1976.
Fernández Moreno, Carlos., ed. *América Latina en su literatura*. México: UNESCO/Siglo XXI, 1972.
Fernández Retamar, Roberto. "Conversación sobre el arte y la literatura." *Revista Casa de las Américas* 22–23 (1964): 130–38.
———, *Ensayo de otro mundo* La Habana: Instituto del Libro, 1967.
———, "Diez años de revolución: el intelectual y la sociedad." *Revista Casa de las Américas* 56 (1969): 7–52.
———, *Para una teoría de la literatura hispanoamericana y otras aproximaciones*. La Habana: Casa de las Américas, 1975.
———, "La contribución de las literaturas de la América Latina a la literatura universal en el Siglo XX." *Revista de Crítica Literaria Latinoamericana* 5 (1976): 17–29.
———, "Algunas anotaciones sobre la cultura en la Cuba revolucionaria." *Hispamérica* 19 (1978): 43–50.
———, *Calibán y otros ensayos*. La Habana: Casa de las Américas, 1979.
———, *Para el perfil definitivo del hombre*. La Habana: Editorial Letras Cubanas, 1981.
———, "Calibán revisitado." *Revista de Crítica Literaria Latinoamericana* 24 (1986): 245–55.
———, "José Martí en los orígenes del antiimperialismo latinoamericano."*Revista de Casa de las Américas* 151 (1985): 3–11.
Flores Galindo, Alberto. *Buscando un inca*. La Habana: Casa de las Américas, 1986.
Foucault, Michel. *La arqueología del saber*. México: Siglo XXI, 1970.
Franco, Jean. "The Crisis of the Liberal Imagination." *Ideologies and Literature* 1:1 (1976–1977): 5–24.
———, "From Modernization to Resistance: Latin American Literature 1959–1976." *Latin American Perspectives* V:1 (1978): 77–97.
———, "Angel Rama y la transculturación narrativa en América Latina." *Sin Nombre* 3 (1984): 68–73.
———, "Border Patrol'." *Travesía. Journal of Latin American Cultural*

Studies 1: 2 (1992): 134–42.
García Canclini, Néstor. "De qué estamos hablando cuando hablamos de lo popular?" *Punto de Vista* 20 (1984): 26–31.
———, "Cultura y política." *Nueva Sociedad* 92 (1987): 116–30.
———, ed. *Políticas culturales en América Latina. Cultura y sociedad.* México: Grijalbo, 1987.
———, *Culturas híbridas: estrategias para entrar y salir de la modernidad.* México: Grijalbo, 1990.
———, "Los estudios culturales de los ochenta a los noventa." *Punto de Vista* 40 (1991): 41–48.
Goldmann, Lucien. *Le dieu caché.* Paris: Gallimard, 1956.
———, *Pour une sociologie du roman.* Paris: Gallimard, 1964.
———, *Marxisme et sciences humaines.* Paris: Gallimard, 1970.
Gramsci, Antonio, *Cuadernos de la cárcel: literatura y vida nacional.* México: Juan Pablos Editor, 1976.
The Modern Prince and other Writings. New York: International Publishers, 1980.
Halperin Donghi, Tulio. *Historia contemporánea de América Latina.* Madrid: Alianza Editorial, 1969.
———, "Nueva narrativa y ciencias sociales hispanoamericanas en la década del sesenta." *Hispamérica*, 27 (1980): 3–18.
Henríquez Ureña, Pedro. "Seis ensayos en busca de nuestra expresión." *Obra crítica.* México: Fondo de Cultura Económica, 1960. 241–330.
Humphrey, Richard. *Georges Sorel. Prophet without Honour: A Study in Anti-Intelectualism.* New York: Octagon Books, 1971.
Jennings, J.R. *Georges Sorel. The Character and Development of his Thought.* London: The Macmillan Press, 1985.
Jitrik, Noé. "Blanco, negro, ¿mulato? Lectura de *El reino de este mundo* de Alejo Carpentier." *Araisa* (1975).
Kaliman, Ricardo. "Documentos de trabajo: Jornadas andinas de literatura latinoamericana (JALLA) Workshops, 1995." *Dispositio* XVIII: 44 (1993): 251–66.
Leenhardt, Jacques. "Uma Figura-chave da Crítica Latino-americana." *Literatura e Historia na América Latina*, Sâo Paolo: Edusp, 1993.
Lienhard, Martín. *Cultura popular andina y forma novelesca. Zorros y danzantes en la última novela de Arguedas.* Lima: Latinoamericana Editores, 1981.
———, "La tarea crítica en América Latina." *Cuadernos de Marcha* 25 (1984).
———, *La voz y su huella: Escritura y conflicto étnico-social en América Latina 1492-1988.* Hanover: Ediciones del Norte, 1991.

———, *Testimonios, cartas y manifiestos indígenas (desde la Conquista hasta comienzos del siglo XIX)*. Caracas: Biblioteca Ayacucho, 1992.

Losada, Alejandro. "La contribución de Angel Rama a la historia social de la literatura latinoamericana." *Revista Casa de Las Américas* 150 (1985): 44–57.

Lukács, Georges. *El alma y las formas*. Barcelona: Grijalbo, 1970.

———, *La teoría de la novela*. Barcelona: Grijalbo, 1970.

———, *Materiales sobre el realismo. Obras completas*. Vol 8. Barcelona: Grijalbo, 1977.

Macherey, Pierre. *Pour une théorie de la production littéraire* . Paris: Gallimard, 1966.

Mariaca Iturri, Guillermo. *El poder de la palabra*. La Habana: Casa de Las Américas, 1992.

Martí, José. *Cuba, Nuestra América, Los Estados Unidos*. México: Siglo XXI, 1973.

Martín Barbero, Jesús. *De los medios a las mediaciones*. México: Gustavo Gili, 1987.

———, *Procesos de comunicación y matrices de cultura: Itinerario para salir de la razón dualista*. México: Gustavo Gili, n.d.

Martínez, José Luis. *Unidad y diversidad en la literatura latinoamericana*. México: Joaquín Mortiz, 1972.

Maturo, Graciela. *Hacia una crítica literaria latinoamericana*. Buenos Aires: Fernando García Gambeiro, 1976.

Mignolo, Walter. "Teorizar a través de fronteras culturales." *Revista de Crítica Literaria Latinoamericana* 33 (1991): 103–112.

———, "Posoccidentalismo: las epistemologías fronterizas y el dilema de los estudios (latinoamericanos) de área." *Revista Iberoamericana* LXII: 176–177 (1996): 679–96.

Morandé, Pedro. *Cultura y modernización en América Latina*. Madrid: Ediciones Encuentro, 1987.

Moraña, Mabel. *Literatura y cultura nacional en Hispanoamérica (1919-1940)*. Minneapolis: University of Minnesota, 1984.

Navarro, Desiderio. "Eurocentrismo y antieurocentrismo en la teoría literaria de América Latina y Europa." *Revista de Crítica Literaria Latinoamericana* 16 (1982): 7–26.

———, "Otras reflexiones sobre eurocentrismo y antieurocentrismo en la teoría literaria de la América Latina y Europa." *Revista Casa de las Américas* 150 (1985): 68–78.

Osorio T. Nelson. "La nueva narrativa y los problemas de la crítica en Hispanoamérica actual." *Actas del Simposio Internacional de Estudios Hispánicos*, 1976.

———, "Situación actual de una nueva conciencia crítico-literaria." *Revista de Crítica Literaria Latinoamericana* 29 (1989): 285–94.
Paz, Octavio. *El laberinto de la soledad*. México: Siglo XXI, 1950.
———, *Posdata*. México: Siglo XXI, 1970.
Perus, Françoise. "La crítica latinoamericanista hoy." *Revista de Crítica Literaria Latinoamericana* 33 (1991): 89–94.
Pizarro, Ana. "Sobre las direcciones del comparatismo en la América Latina." *Revista Casa de las Américas* 135 (1982): 40–49.
———, coord. *La literatura latinoamericana como proceso*. Buenos Aires: Centro Editor de América Latina, 1985.
———, *Hacia una historia de la literatura latinoamericana*. México/Caracas: El Colegio de México/Universidad Simón Bolívar, 1987.
———, "Angel Rama: A Lição Intelectual Latino-americana."*Literatura e Historia na América Latina*, Ed. Ligia Chiappini & Flávio Wolf de Aguiar. São Paulo: Edusp, 1993. 243–53.
Portuondo, José Antonio. "Literatura y sociedad." *América Latina en su literatura*. Ed. Carlos Fernández Moreno. México: UNESCO/Siglo XXI, 1972. 392–405.
———, "Crítica marxista de la estética burguesa contemporánea." *Revista Casa de las Américas* 71 (1972): 5–13.
———, *La emancipación literaria de Hispanoamérica*. La Habana: Casa de las Américas, 1975.
Rincón, Carlos. "Sobre crítica e historia de la literatura hoy en Hispanoamérica." *Revista Casa de las Américas* 80 (1973): 143–57.
———, *El cambio en la noción de literatura y otros estudios de teoría y crítica latinoamericana* Bogotá: Instituto Colombiano de Cultura, 1978.
Roa Bastos, Augusto. "Una utopía concreta: la unidad iberoamericana." *Revista Casa de las Américas* 172–173 (1989): 98–106.
Rowe, William. Rulfo. *El llano en llamas*. London: Grant & Cutler/Támesis Books, 1987.
———, "Liberalismo y autoridad: una lectura política de Vargas Llosa." *Nuevo Texto Crítico* 8, (1991): 91–100.
———, *Memory and Modernity: Popular Culture in Latin America*, London: Verso, 1992.
———, *Ensayos de hermenéutica cultural*. Rosario-Lima: Beatriz Viterbo Editora / Mosca Azul Editores, 1996a.
———, *Ensayos arguedianos*. Lima: Universidad Mayor de San Marcos / Sur, 1996b.
Santiago, Silviano. *Vale quanto pesa (Ensaios sobre questões político-*

culturais). Rio de Janeiro: Editora Paz e Terra, 1982.
Schwartz, Roberto. "Brazilian Culture: Nationalism by Elimination." *Misplaced Ideas. Essays on Brazilian Culture.* London: Verso, 1992. 1-18.
Sheridan, Alan. *Michel Foucault: The Will to Truth.* London: Tavistock, 1980.
Soler, Ricaurte. *Idea y cuestión nacional latinoamericanas.* México: Siglo XXI, 1980.
Sorel, Georges. *Reflections on Violence.* London: George Allen & Unwin Ltd., 1925.
Sosnowski, Saúl. "Sobre la crítica de la literatura hispanoamericana: Balance y Perspectivas." *Cuadernos Hispanoamericanos,* 443 (1987): 143-59.
Stubbs, Jean. *Cuba: The Test of Time.* London: Latin America Bureau, 1989.
Terán, Oscar. "Latinoamérica: naciones y marxismos." *Socialismo y Participación,* 11 (1980): 169-90.
———, "Aníbal Ponce: El marxismo sin nación?" *Cuadernos de Pasado y Presente,* 18 (1983): 7-49.
Vidal, Hernán. "Teoría de la dependencia y crítica literaria." *Ideologies and Literature* II: 13 (1980): 116-22.
———, "Para una redefinición culturalista de la crítica literaria latinoamericana." *Ideologies and Literature* IV: 16 (1983): 121-32.
Viñas, David. *Indios, ejército y frontera.* México: Siglo XXI, 1982.
Williams, Raymond. *Marxism and Literature.* Oxford: OUP, 1977.
Yurkievich, Saul., coord. *Identidad cultural de Iberoamérica en su literatura.* Barcelona: Editorial Alhambra, 1986.

ANTONIO CORNEJO POLAR

Achugar, Hugo. "Repensando la heterogeneidad latinoamericana (a propósito de lugares, paisajes y territorio)." *Revista Iberoamericana* LXII: 176-177 (1996): 845-61.
Cornejo Polar, Antonio. *Los universos narrativos de José María Arguedas.* Buenos Aires: Ed. Losada, 1973.
———, "José Donoso y los problemas de la nueva narrativa latinoamericana." *Acta Litteraria Academiae Scientiarum Hungaricae* 17:1-2 (1975): 215-26. Also in *Sobre literatura y crítica latinoamericana.* Caracas: Universidad Central de Venezuela, 1982. 109-22.
———, "Para una interpretación de la novela indigenista." *Revista Casa de las Américas* 100 (1977a).
———, "El indigenismo y las literaturas heterogéneas: su doble estatuto

socio-cultural." *Revista de Crítica Literaria Latinoamericana* 7 (1978): 7–21. Also in *Sobre literatura y crítica latinoamericana*. Caracas: Universidad Central de Venezuela, 1982. 67–86.

———, "Sobre el concepto de heterogeneidad. Respuesta a Roberto Paoli." *Revista de Crítica Literaria Latinoamericana* 12 (1980a): 264–67.

———, *Literatura y sociedad en el Perú: la novela indigenista*. Lima: Lasontay, 1980b.

———, *Cultura nacional: problema y posibilidad*. Lima: Lluvia, 1981a.

———, "El problema nacional en la literatura peruana." *Sobre literatura y crítica latinoamericana*. Caracas: Universidad Central de Venezuela, 1982. 19–31.

———, "Para una agenda problemática de la crítica literaria latinoamericana: diseño preliminar." *Revista Casa de las Américas* 126 (1981b): 117–22. Also in *Sobre literatura y crítica latinoamericana*. Caracas: Universidad Central de Venezuela, 1982. 33–42.

———, *Sobre literatura y crítica latinoamericana*. Caracas: Universidad Central de Venezuela, 1982.

———, "Literatura peruana: totalidad contradictoria." *Revista de Crítica Literaria Latinoamericana* 18 (1983): 39–50. Also appendix in *La formación literaria del Perú*. Lima: Centro de Estudios y Publicaciones (CEP), 1989c.

———, "Inmediatez y perennidad: la doble audiencia de la literatura de la fundación de la república." *Revista de Crítica Literaria Latinoamericana*. 20 (1984): 45–54.

———, "Novela nacional, regional o latinoamericana." *Ejercicio Crítico* 1 (1985): 55–59.

———, "Literatura peruana y tradición indígena." *Literaturas Andinas* 1 (1988a).

———, "Sistemas y sujetos en la historia literaria latinoamericana." *Revista Casa de las Américas* 171 (1988b): 67–71.

———, "Los sistemas literarios como categorías históricas. Elementos para una discusión latinoamericana." *Revista de Crítica Literaria Latinoamericana* 29 (1989a): 19–24.

———, *La novela peruana: siete estudios*. Lima: Ed. Horizonte, 1989b, second expanded edition. (First edition 1977)

———, *La formación de la tradición literaria en el Perú*. Lima: Centro de Estudios y Publicaciones (CEP), 1989c.

———, *Clorinda Matto de Turner, novelista*. Lima: Lluvia, 1992.

———, "Prólogo." G. Mariaca Iturri. *El poder de la palabra*. La Habana: Casa de Las Américas, 1992.

———, "El discurso de la armonía imposible." *Revista de Crítica Literaria*

Latinoamericana 38 (1993): 73–80.

———, "Mestizaje, transculturación, heterogeneidad." *Revista de Crítica Literaria latinoamericana* 40 (1994a): 368–371.

———, *Escribir en el aire. Ensayo sobre la heterogeneidad socio-cultural de las literaturas andinas.* Lima: Editorial Horizonte, 1994b.

———, "Condición migrante e intertextualidad multicultural: el caso de Arguedas." *Revista de Crítica Literaria Latinoamericana*, 42 (1995): 101–109.

———, "Una heterogeneidad no dialéctica: sujeto y discurso migrantes en el Perú moderno." *Revista Iberoamericana* LXI: 176–177 (1996): 837–44.

Núñez, Charo. "*Escribir en el aire.* Ensayo sobre la heterogeneidad socio-cultural de las literaturas andinas." *Hispamérica* 69 (1994): 109–12.

Moraña, Mabel. "*Escribir en el aire,* 'heterogeneidad' y estudios culturales." *Revista Iberoamericana* LXI: 170–71 (1995): 279–86.

Paoli, Roberto. "Sobre el concepto de la heterogeneidad: A Propósito del indigenismo literario." *Revista de Crítica Literaria Latinoamericana* 12 (1980): 257–63.

ALEJANDRO LOSADA

Borel, Jean. "Alrededor de la historia de AELSAL." *La literatura en la sociedad de América Latina.* Munich: Wilhelm Fink Verlag, 1987. 200–208.

Cornejo Polar, Antonio. "Losada, Alejandro: *Creación y praxis. La producción literaria como praxis social en Hispanoamérica y el Perú.*" *Revista de Crítica Literaria Latinoamericana.* 5 (1977b): 130–32.

Lienhard, Martín et al. "Alejandro Losada." *Revista Iberoamericana* LII: 135–36 (1986): 631–44.

Losada, Alejandro. "La obra de José María Arguedas y la sociedad andina." *Eco* 162 (1974): 592–20.

———, "Problemas y tareas de la crítica literaria contemporánea. Discursos críticos y proyectos sociales en Hispanoamérica." *Acta Litteraria Academiae Scientiarum Hungaricae* 17 (1975a): 275–84.

———, "Los sistemas literarios como instituciones sociales en América Latina." *Revista de Crítica Literaria Latinoamericana* 1 (1975b): 39–61.

———, "Discursos críticos y proyectos sociales en América Hispánica." *Acta Litteraria* 17 (1975c): 275–80.

———, "Ciro Alegría como fundador de la realidad hispanoamericana." *Acta Litteraria* 17 (1975d): 71–92.

———, *Creación y praxis. La producción literaria como praxis social en Hispanoamérica y el Perú*. Lima: Universidad Mayor de San Marcos, 1976a.

———, "Estructura social y producción cultural en América Latina. Las literaturas dependientes (1780–1920)." *Actas del Simposio Internacional de Estudios Hispánicos*. Budapest: Hungarian Academy of Sciences, 1976b. 93–109.

———, "Rasgos específicos de la producción cultural ilustrada en América Latina. Los modos de producción cultural de los estratos medios urbanos en América Latina. Las culturas dependientes (1780–1920) y las culturas autónomas (1880–1970)." *Revista de Crítica Literaria Latinoamericana* 6 (1977a): 7–36.

———, "La literatura urbana como praxis social en América Latina." *Lateinamerika Studien* 3 (1977b): 1–41. Also in *Ideologies and Literature* 4 (1977c): 33–62.

———, "Bases para una estrategia de investigación del cambio cultural en América Latina." *Eco* XXXII: 196 (1978): 337–74.

———, "Rasgos específicos del realismo social en América hispánica." *Revista Iberoamericana* XLV: 108–109 (1979a): 413–42.

———, "El desarrollo de las culturas autónomas en América Latina. Ensayo de comprensión de los horizontes culturales de los intelectuales de América Latina como praxis social de distintos grupos sociales." *Bildung und Ausbildung in der Romania*. Ed. R. Kloepfer. Munich: Wilhelm Fink Verlag, 1979b. 318–36.

———, "Creación y praxis social en América Latina. La nueva narrativa como práctica de la marginalidad." *Iberomania* 11 (1980a): 113–32.

———, "Cultura nacional o literatura revolucionaria? La producción de los intelectuales autónomos en las sociedades periféricas." *Nova Americana* 3 (1980b): 287–330.

———, *La literatura en la sociedad de la América Latina: Los modos de producción entre 1780 –1980. Estrategias de investigación*. Berlin: Freien Universität, 1980c.

———, "Bases para un proyecto de historia social de la literatura en América Latina." *Revista Iberoamericana* XLVII: 114–15 (1981b): 167–88.

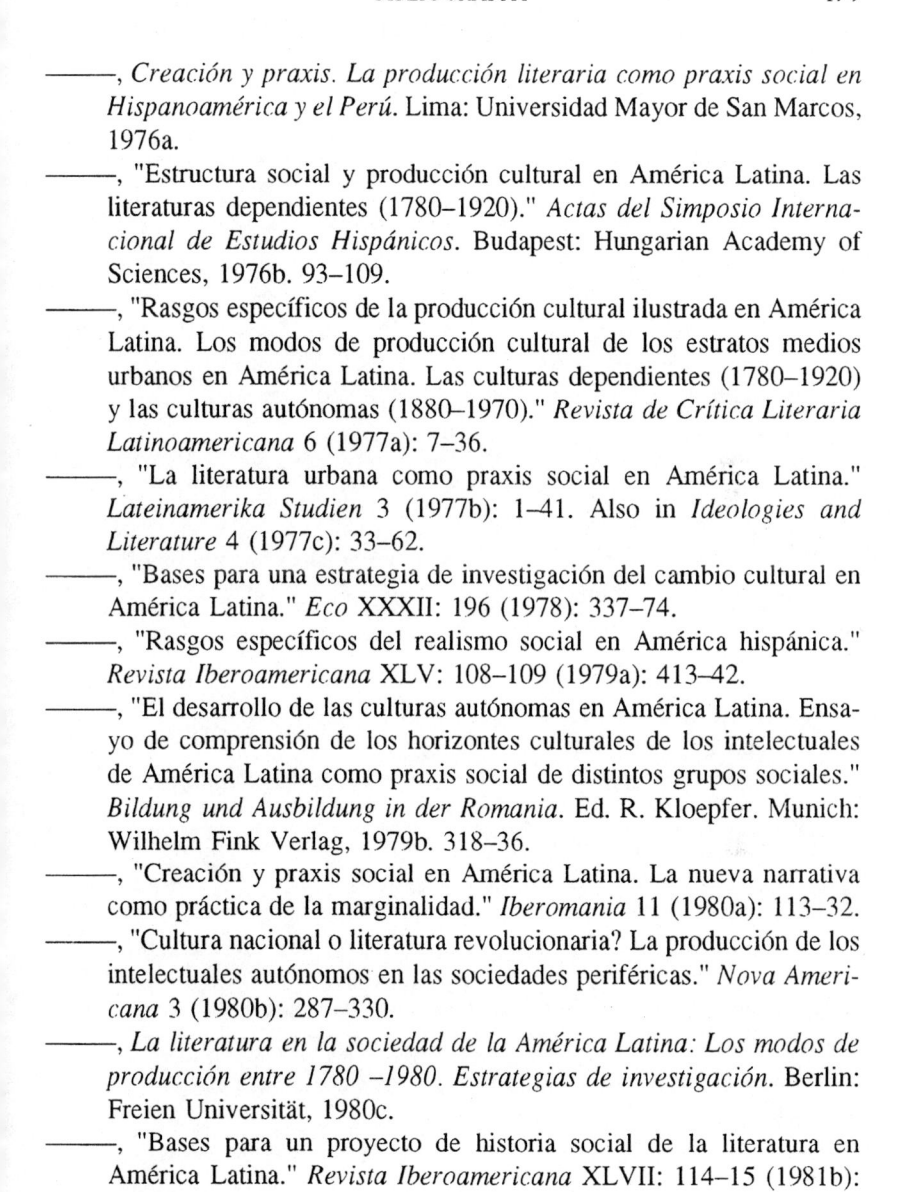

———, *La Literatura en la sociedad de América Latina. Perú y el Río de la Plata, 1837–1880* Frankfurt: Verlag Klaus, 1983a.

———, "Articulación, periodización y diferenciación de los procesos literarios en América Latina." *Revista de Crítica Literaria Latinoamericana* 17 (1983b): 7–38. Also in *La literatura latinoamericana en el Caribe*. Ed. Alejandro Losada. Berlin: Lateinamerika-Institut, 1983c.

1–48.

———, "La internacionalización de la literatura del Caribe en las metrópolis complejas." *La literatura latinoamericana en el Caribe.* Ed. Alejandro Losada. Berlin: Latinamerika-Institut, 1983c. 266–351. Also in *La literatura en la sociedad de América Latina.* Munich: Wilhelm Fink Verlag, 1987. 61–91.

———, "La internacionalización de la literatura latinoamericana." *Caravelle* 42 (1984a): 15–40.

———, "La literatura marginal en el Río de la Plata, 1900–1960. Informe de investigación." *Hispamérica* 39 (1984b): 19–28.

———, "La historia social de la literatura latinoamericana." *Revista de Crítica Literaria Latinoamericana* 24 (1986): 21–29.

———, *La literatura en la sociedad de América Latina.* Munich: Wilhelm Fink Verlag, 1987.

Ventura, Roberto. "Sistemas literarios y estructuras sociales en América Latina, in memoriam." A. Losada. *La literatura en la sociedad de América Latina.* Munich: Wilhelm Fink Verlag, 1987. VII–XXVII.

JOSE CARLOS MARIATEGUI

Abril, Xavier et al. *Mariátegui y la literatura.* Lima: Empresa Editora Amauta, 1980.

Aricó, José., ed. *Mariátegui y los orígenes del marxismo latinoamericano.* México: Siglo XXI, 1978.

———, "Mariátegui y la formación del partido socialista del Perú." *Socialismo y Participación* 11 (1980): 139–68.

Cornejo Polar, Antonio. "Apuntes sobre literatura nacional en el pensamiento crítico de Mariátegui." Xavier Abril et al. *Mariátegui y la literatura.* Lima: Empresa Editora Amauta, 1980c.

Dessau, Adalbert. "Literatura y sociedad en las obras de José Carlos Mariátegui." *Tres estudios.* Lima: Biblioteca Amauta, 1971. 51–109.

Flores Galindo, Alberto. *La agonía de Mariátegui. La polémica con la Komintern.* Lima: Desco, 1980a.

———, "Los intelectuales y el problema nacional." *Buelna* 4–5 (1980b): 48–59.

Franco, Carlos. "Sobre la idea de nación en Mariátegui." *Socialismo y Participación* 11 (1980): 191–208.

Garrels, Elizabeth. "Mariátegui, la edad de piedra y el nacionalismo literario." *Escritura* 1 (1976): 115–28.

———, *Mariátegui y la Argentina. Un caso de lentes ajenas.* Gaithersburgh: Ediciones Hispamérica, 1982.

Larsen, Neil. "Indigenismo y lo 'poscolonial': Mariátegui frente a la actual coyuntura teórica." *Revista Iberoamericana* LXII: 176–177 (1996): 863–73.

Mariátegui, José Carlos. *El artista y la época*. Lima: Biblioteca Amauta, 1959.

———, *Temas de nuestra América*. Lima: Biblioteca Amauta, 1960.

———, *Historia de la crisis mundial*. Lima: Biblioteca Amauta, 1964a, 2nd ed. (first ed.: 1959).

———, *La escena contemporánea*. Lima: Biblioteca Amauta, 1964b, 3rd ed. (first ed.: 1925).

———, *Defensa del marxismo*. Lima: Biblioteca Amauta, 1969a, 4th ed. (first ed.: 1959).

———, *Cartas de Italia*. Lima: Biblioteca Amauta, 1969b.

———, *Peruanicemos al Perú*. Lima: Biblioteca Amauta, 1970a (first published: 1928).

———, *El alma matinal y otras estaciones de hoy*. Lima: Biblioteca Amauta, 1970b, 4th ed. (first ed.: 1950).

———, *Signos y obras*. Lima: Biblioteca Amauta, 1970c (first ed.: 1959).

———, *Figuras y aspectos de la vida mundial*. Vols. I–III. Lima: Biblioteca Amauta, 1970d.

———, *Ideología y política*. Lima: Biblioteca Amauta, 1980, 2nd. ed. (first ed.: 1969).

———, *Siete ensayos de interpretación de la realidad peruana*. Lima: Biblioteca Amauta, 1985, 47th ed. (first ed.: 1928).

Melis, Antonio. "Mariátegui: Primer marxista de América." *Tres estudios*. Lima: Biblioteca Amauta, 1971. 11–41.

———, "Estética, crítica literaria y política cultural en la obra de José Carlos Mariátegui, apuntes." *Textual* 6 (1973): 66–69.

———, "El debate sobre Mariátegui: resultados y problemas." *Revista de Crítica Literaria Latinoamericana* 4 (1976): 123–32.

———, "La lucha en el frente cultural." *Mariátegui en Italia*. Ed. B. Podestà. Lima: Empresa Editora Amauta, 1981. 127–42.

———, "Medio siglo de vida de José Carlos Mariátegui." Xavier Abril et al. *Mariátegui y la literatura*. Lima: Empresa Editora Amauta, 1980. 125–34.

Moraña, Mabel. *Literatura y cultura nacional en Hispanoamérica (1919–1940)*. Minneapolis: University of Minnesota, 1984.

Moretic, Yerko. *José Carlos Mariátegui*. Santiago de Chile: Ediciones de la Universidad Técnica del Estado, 1970.

Paris, Robert. "Para una lectura de los Siete ensayos." *Textual* 5–6 (1972).

———, "El marxismo de Mariátegui." *Mariátegui y los orígenes del marxismo latinoamericano*. Ed. José Aricó. México: Siglo XXI,

1978. 119–44.

———, "Mariátegui, un 'sorelismo' ambiguo." *Mariátegui y los orígenes del marxismo latinoamericano.* Ed. José Aricó. México: Siglo XXI, 1978. 155–61.

———, *La formación ideológica de José Carlos Mariátegui.* México: Siglo XXI, 1981.

———, "La formación ideológica de Mariátegui." *Mariátegui en Italia.* Ed. B. Podestà. Lima: Emopresa Editora Amauta, 1981.

Podestà, Bruno, ed. *Mariátegui en Italia.* Lima: Biblioteca Amauta, 1981.

Posada, Francisco. *Los orígenes del pensamiento marxista en Latinoamérica: Política y cultura en José Carlos Mariátegui.* Madrid: Ciencia Nueva, Madrid, 1968.

———, "Estética y marxismo en José Carlos Mariátegui." *Textual* 5–6 (1972): 24–31.(Also in *Buelna* 4–5 (1980): 73–86

Rouillon, Guillermo. *Bío-bibliografía de José Carlos Mariátegui.* Lima: Universidad Mayor de San Marcos, 1963.

Rowe, William. "José Carlos Mariátegui: 1994." *Travesia: Journal of Latin American Cultural Studies* 3:1–2 (1994): 290–98.

Sylvers, Malcolm. "La formación de un revolucionario." *Mariátegui in Italia.* Ed. B. Podestà. Lima: Empresa Editorial Amauta, 1980. 19–77.

Terán, Oscar. "Los escritos juveniles de Mariátegui." *Buelna* 4–5 (1980a): 18–24.

———, "Latinoamérica: Naciones y marxismos." *Socialismo y Participación* 11 (1980b): 69–90.

———, *Discutir Mariátegui.* México: Universidad Autónoma de Puebla, 1985.

Vanden, Harry E. *Mariátegui: Influencias en su formación ideológica.* Lima: Biblioteca Amauta, 1976.

ANGEL RAMA

Barrenechea et al. "Rama y la cultura hispanoamericana." *Texto Crítico* 31–32 (1985): 309–17.

Blixen, Carina & Barros-Lemes, Alvaro. *Cronología y bibliografía de Angel Rama.* Montevideo: Fundación Internacional Angel Rama, 1986.

Candido, Antonio. "Uma Visão Latino-americana." *Literatura e História na América Latina.* Eds. Ligia Chiappini & Flávio Wolf de Aguiar. São Paulo: Edusp, 1993. 263–69.

De La Campa, Román. "Hibridez posmoderna y transculturación: política de montaje en torno a Latinoamérica." *Hispamérica* 69 (1994): 3–22.

Franco, Jean. "Angel Rama y la transculturación narrativa en América Latina." *Sin Nombre* 3 (1984): 68–73.
Leenhardt, Jacques. "Uma Figura-chave da Crítica Latino-americana." *Literatura e História na América Latina*. Eds. Ligia Chiappini & Flávio Wolf de Aguiar. São Paolo: Edusp, 1993. 253–62.
Losada, Alejandro. "La contribución de Angel Rama a la historia social de la literatura latinoamericana." *Revista Casa de las Américas* 150 (1985): 44–57.
Martínez A., Agustín. "Angel Rama: la tradición culturalista en la crítica literaria latinoamericana." *ECO* 265, (1983): 1–11.
Martínez, Tomás Eloy. "Angel Rama o el placer de la crítica." Angel Rama. *La crítica de la cultura en América Latina*. Caracas: Biblioteca Ayacucho, 1985. xxv–xli.
Moraña, Mabel (ed.), 1997. *Angel Rama y los estudios latinoamericanos* (Pittsburgh: Instituto Internacional de Literatura Iberoamericana).
Pizarro, Ana. "A Lição Intelectual Latino-americana." *Literatura e História na América Latina*. Eds. Ligia Chiappini & Flávio Wolf de Aguiar. São Paolo: Edusp, 1993. 243–52.
Osorio, Nelson. "Angel Rama y el estudio comprensivo de la literatura latinoamericana." *Revista Casa de las Américas*. 143 (1985): 153–62.
Prego, Omar. "Angel Rama: la crítica como iluminación." *Cuadernos de Marcha*, 25 (1984).
Prieto, Adolfo. "Encuentros con Angel Rama." *Texto Crítico* 31–32 (1985): 33–36.
Rama, Angel. "Sentido y estructura de una aportación original de una comarca del tercer mundo: Latinoamérica." México: Universidad Nacional Autónoma de México, n.d. (Talk given in Genoa, 1965).
Rama, Angel with Washington Buño and Rafael Laguardia. "Una política cultural autónoma'." *Hacia una producción cultural autónoma para América Latina*. Montevideo: Universidad de la República, 1968. 41–50.
Rama, Angel. "Una nueva política cultural en Cuba." *Cuadernos de Marcha* 49 (1971): 47–68.
———, *Diez problemas para el narrador latinoamericano*. Caracas: Síntesis Dosmil, 1972a.
———, *La generación crítica (1939–1969)*. Montevideo: Arca, 1972b.
———, "Mezzo secolo di narrativa latinoamericana." *Latinoamerica, 75 narratori*. Vol 1. Ed. Franco Mogni. Florence: Vellechi, 1973. 3–72.
———, "El área cultural andina (Hispanismo, mesticismo, indigenismo)." *Cuadernos Americanos* 6 (1974a): 136–73.
———, "Un proceso autonómico: de las literaturas nacionales a la literatura

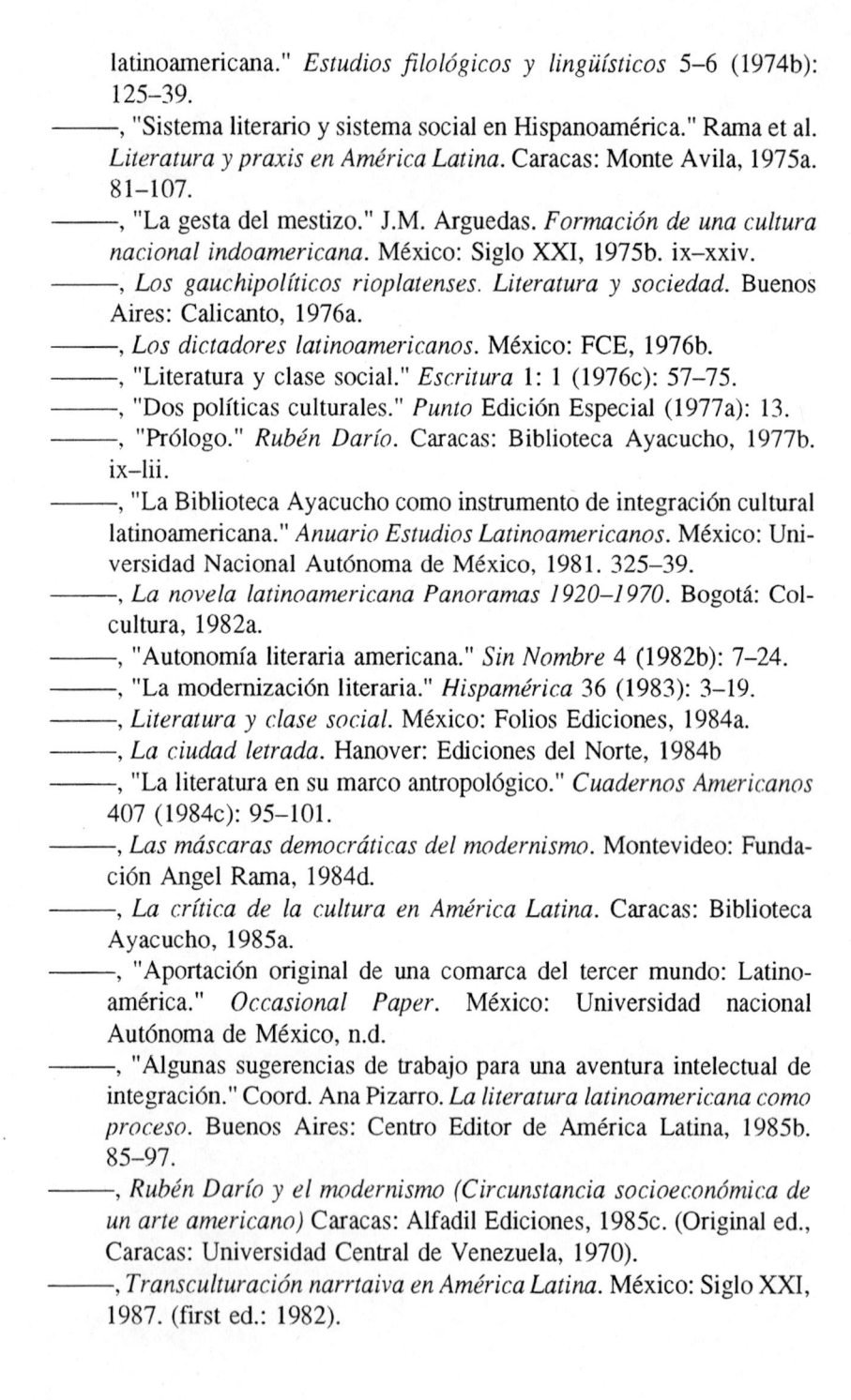

latinoamericana." *Estudios filológicos y lingüísticos* 5–6 (1974b): 125–39.

———, "Sistema literario y sistema social en Hispanoamérica." Rama et al. *Literatura y praxis en América Latina*. Caracas: Monte Avila, 1975a. 81–107.

———, "La gesta del mestizo." J.M. Arguedas. *Formación de una cultura nacional indoamericana*. México: Siglo XXI, 1975b. ix–xxiv.

———, *Los gauchipolíticos rioplatenses. Literatura y sociedad*. Buenos Aires: Calicanto, 1976a.

———, *Los dictadores latinoamericanos*. México: FCE, 1976b.

———, "Literatura y clase social." *Escritura* 1: 1 (1976c): 57–75.

———, "Dos políticas culturales." *Punto* Edición Especial (1977a): 13.

———, "Prólogo." *Rubén Darío*. Caracas: Biblioteca Ayacucho, 1977b. ix–lii.

———, "La Biblioteca Ayacucho como instrumento de integración cultural latinoamericana." *Anuario Estudios Latinoamericanos*. México: Universidad Nacional Autónoma de México, 1981. 325–39.

———, *La novela latinoamericana Panoramas 1920–1970*. Bogotá: Colcultura, 1982a.

———, "Autonomía literaria americana." *Sin Nombre* 4 (1982b): 7–24.

———, "La modernización literaria." *Hispamérica* 36 (1983): 3–19.

———, *Literatura y clase social*. México: Folios Ediciones, 1984a.

———, *La ciudad letrada*. Hanover: Ediciones del Norte, 1984b

———, "La literatura en su marco antropológico." *Cuadernos Americanos* 407 (1984c): 95–101.

———, *Las máscaras democráticas del modernismo*. Montevideo: Fundación Angel Rama, 1984d.

———, *La crítica de la cultura en América Latina*. Caracas: Biblioteca Ayacucho, 1985a.

———, "Aportación original de una comarca del tercer mundo: Latinoamérica." *Occasional Paper*. México: Universidad nacional Autónoma de México, n.d.

———, "Algunas sugerencias de trabajo para una aventura intelectual de integración." Coord. Ana Pizarro. *La literatura latinoamericana como proceso*. Buenos Aires: Centro Editor de América Latina, 1985b. 85–97.

———, *Rubén Darío y el modernismo (Circunstancia socioeconómica de un arte americano)* Caracas: Alfadil Ediciones, 1985c. (Original ed., Caracas: Universidad Central de Venezuela, 1970).

———, *Transculturación narrtaiva en América Latina*. México: Siglo XXI, 1987. (first ed.: 1982).

Revista Casa de Las Américas 26 (1964): 2 and 41 (1967): 2–4.
Ruffinelli, Jorge. "Angel Rama: la carrera del crítico de fondo."*Escritura* 15 (1983): 123–131.
Sosnowski, Saúl. "Angel Rama: Un sendero en un bosque de palabras." Angel Rama. *La crítica de la cultura en América Latina.* Caracas: Biblioteca Ayacucho, 1985. IX–XXIII.
Vogt, Carlos. "Entrevista a Angel Rama." *Escritura* 27 (1989): 9–29.

BEATRIZ SARLO

Sarlo, Beatriz & Altamirano, Carlos. "La Argentina del Centenario: campo intelectual, vida literaria y temas ideológicos." *Hispamérica* 25–26 (1980a): 33–59.
Sarlo, Beatriz. "La literatura de América Latina, unidad y conflicto." *Punto de Vista* 8 (1980a): 3–14.
———, "Angel Rama y Antonio Cornejo Polar: Tradición y ruptura en América Latina." *Punto de Vista* 8 (1980b): 10–14.
———, "Sobre la vanguardia, Borges y el criollismo." *Punto de Vista* 11 (1981): 3–8.
———, "Vanguardia y criollismo." *Revista de Crítica Literaria Latinoamericana*, 15 (1982): 39–69.
———, *Literatura/ Sociedad.* Buenos Aires: Hachette, 1983a.
———, "La perseverancia de un debate." *Punto de Vista* 18 (1983b): 3–5.
———, "Literatura y política." *Punto de Vista* 19 (1983c): 8–11.
Sarlo, Beatriz & Altamirano, Carlos. *Ensayos argentinos.* Buenos Aires: Centro Editor de América Latina, 1983b.
Sarlo, Beatriz. "Una alucinación dispersa en agonía." *Punto de Vista* 21 (1984a): 1–4.
———, "La cultura después de la dictadura." *Nueva Sociedad* 73 (1984b): 78–84.
———, "La izquierda ante la cultura: del dogmatismo al populismo." *Punto de Vista* 20 (1984c): 22–25.
———, "Intelectuales: escisión o mímesis." *Punto de Vista* 25 (1985a): 1–6.
———, "Una mirada política: Defensa del partidismo en el arte." *Punto de Vista* 27 (1985b): 1–4.
———, "Clío revisitada." *Punto de Vista* 28 (1986): 23–26.
———, *Una modernidad periférica: Buenos Aires 1920 y 1930.* Buenos Aires: Ediciones Nueva Visión, 1988.
———, "Lo popular en la historia de la cultura." *Punto de Vista* 35 (1989a): 19–24.
———, "Borges y la literatura argentina." *Punto de Vista* 34 (1989b):

6–10.

———, "Basuras culturales, simulacros políticos." *Punto de Vista* 37 (1990): 14–17.

———, "El audiovisual político." *Punto de Vista* (1991): 21–28.

———, "La teoría como chatarra: Tesis de Oscar Landi sobre la televisión." *Punto de Vista* 44 (1992): 12–18.

———, "Arcaicos o marginales? Situación de los intelectuales en el fin de siglo." *Punto de Vista* 47 (1993a): 1–5.

———, *Jorge Luis Borges. A Writer on the Edge*. London: Verso, 1993b.

———, "El relativismo absoluto o cómo el mercado y la sociología reflexionan sobre estética." *Punto de Vista* 48 (1994a): 27–31.

———, *Escenas de la vida posmoderna*, Buenos Aires: Ariel, 1994b.

———, "La democracia mediática y sus límites." *Punto de Vista* 52 (1995): 11–16.

———, "Cultural Studies Questionnaire." *Travesia. Journal of Latin American Cultural Studies* 6: 1 (1997): 85–92.

INDEX

Achugar, Hugo, 169
Adán, Martín, 17, 22, 27, 39, 109
 "Gira", 39
Alegría, Ciro, 128, 129–131, 132, 145
Altamirano, Carlos, vii, 156
Amado, Jorge, 81
Amauta, 17, 19, 34, 39
Andrade, Mario de, 99
Arguedas, José María, 52, 60, 65–67, 81, 86, 99, 107, 117, 135
 —*ríos profundos, Los*, 66
 —*zorro de arriba y el zorro de abajo, El*, 150
Aricó, José, 29
Arlt, Roberto, 162
Assis, Machado de, vii
Asturias, Miguel Angel, 81, 97, 100, 114
Barbusse, Henri, 19
Barnet, Miguel, 81
Barrios, Domitila, 81
Biblioteca Ayacucho, 50, 65
Bolívar, Simón, 11, 55
Borges, Jorge Luis, vii, 95, 97, 99, 101, 102, 109, 117, 162
 —"escritor argentino y la tradición, El", 162
Bryce Echenique, Alfredo, 107
Bueno, Raúl, 4
Cabrera Infante, Pedro, 81
Candido, Antonio, 107
Carpentier, Alejo, 97, 100, 139
Castañeda, Jorge, 11, 62, 73
Césaire, Aimé, 99
Chronicles of the Conquest, 143

Clarté, 19
Colonidista, 28
Cornejo Polar, Antonio, vii, x, 3, 4, 5, 11, 12, 16, 43–45, 47–48, 53, 66, 73, 86, 94, 96, 123–152, 153, 157, 167, 168
 —*Escribir en el aire: ensayo sobre la heterogeneidad socio-cultural en las literaturas andinas*, 124, 129, 137
 —"estructura del acontecimiento de *Los perros hambrientos*, La", 128
 —"imagen del mundo en *la serpiente de oro*, La", 130
 —"Literatura peruana: totalidad contradictoria", 137
 —*Literatura y sociedad en el Perú: la novela indigenista*, 129
 —"Migrant, 124
 —*novela peruana: siete estudios, La*, 128, 133
 —"problema nacional en la literatura peruana, El", 137
 —"Problemas de la crítica hoy", 133
 —"Problemas y perspectivas de la crítica literaria latinoamericana", 127, 131
 —"Sobre el 'neoindigenismo' y las novelas de Manuel Scorza", 146
Cortázar, 81, 109
Cosmopolitanism, 41–42, 46, 48, 57, 73, 93, 94, 100, 101, 104, 156, 158

Criollismo, 137, 154
Cueva, Agustín, 139
Darío, Rubén, 68-69, 71
Deleuze, Gilles & Félix Guattari,
—*What is Philosophy*, viii
Dependency Theory, 11, 71, 95, 135, 154, 155, 160, 164, 168
Di Prisco, Rafael, 50
Donoso, José, 81, 151–152
—*lugar sin límites, El*, 151
—*Obseno pájaro de la noche, El*, 151
Eguren, José María, 109
Escritura, 50
Fernández, Macedonio, 95
Fernández Retamar, Roberto, 4, 9
—*Para una teoría de la literatura hispanoamericana y otras aproximaciones*, 9
Flores Galindo, Alberto, 16, 27, 29
García Canclini, Néstor, 123, 132, 133, 169
García Márquez, Gabriel, 52, 60, 114, 117, 139
Goldmann, Lucien, 83, 110
Gramsci, Antonio, 31–33, 37, 126
—"Modern Prince, The", 31–33
Güiraldes, Ricardo, 102
Hauser, Arnold, 83, 110
Henríquez Ureña, Pedro, 55
Heterogeneity, x, 4, 12, 44, 45, 94, 125, 133, 138–149
Hibridization, 123
Hispanicism, 43, 45
Humphrey, Richard, 31
Indigenismo, 12, 15, 27, 33, 34, 37, 39–48, 81, 83, 95, 96, 114, 116, 128–132, 133, 134, 135, 137, 138, 141, 142, 144–149, 150
Jitrik, Noé, 139

Lienhard, Martín, 86, 90–91, 106, 107, 110
Lezama Lima, José, 81, 109
Losada, Alejandro, ix, x, 5, 10, 11, 12, 53, 56–58, 65, 73, 77–121, 123, 152, 153, 157, 162, 168
—Aesthetic/cultural paradigm, 91, 117–118
—*Autoproducción social*, 89
—"Bases para un proyecto de una historia social de la literatura en América Latina", 95
—"historia social de la literatura latinoamericana, La", 119
—Horizon of existence, 116
—*Creación y praxis*, 81, 84, 85, 87, 91, 94, 111
—Literary system, 80, 81, 84, 107–110
—Mode of literary / cultural / social production, 79–80, 111–115
—Autonomous literatures, 91, 92, 118
—Dependent literatures, 80, 91, 92, 113
—Marginal literatures, 80, 92, 94, 95, 103, 104, 113
—Social-revolutionary literatures, 80, 92, 96, 97, 103, 104, 113
—Periodization 93–94, 118–120
—"Rasgos específicos de la producción ilustrada en América Latina", 112
—Social praxis, 84, 105–107
—*Sujeto Productor*, 79, 89–90, 92, 99, 110–111, 116, 117, 120
Lukács, George, 83, 84, 85, 87, 89, 116

Macherey, Pierre, 112
Machiavelli, Niccolo,
—*Prince, The*, 31, 32, 33
Marcha, 49
Mariaca Iturri, Guillermo, 4
Mariátegui, José Carlos, vii, ix, 4, 5, 7, 12, 15–48, 96, 117, 123, 126, 144, 152, 166, 168
—"Aspectos viejos y nuevos del futurismo", 19
—"Defensa del disparate puro", 39
—*Disparate*, 21, 22, 26, 39
—"emoción de nuestro tiempo. Dos concepciones de la vida, La", 24
—"hombre y el mito, El", 37
—"intervención de Italia en la guerra, La", 37
—"lucha final, La", 35, 37
—"Nacionalismo y vanguardia en la literatura y en el arte", 40, 41
—"nacional y lo exótico, Lo", 40
—"proceso de la literatura, El", 4, 7, 15, 37, 42, 43, 45, 46, 47
—"realidad y la ficción, La", 27
—*Siete ensayos de interpretación de la realidad peruana*, 16
Martí, José, 11, 117
Martín Barbero, Jesús, 169
Melis, Antonio, 16, 24–28, 31
Mestizaje, 43, 109, 110, 124
Modernismo, 51, 67, 68–70, 83, 101, 108, 113, 137
Modernity, x, 52, 57, 80, 94, 96, 99,100, 101, 102, 115, 129, 159, 160, 162, 168, 169

Modernization, 40, 53, 54, 56–58, 61–63, 68–71, 74, 75, 92, 95, 101, 102, 117, 133–135, 149–152, 159–162, 168
Morales Saravia, José, 106
Morandé, Pedro, 56–57, 64
Myth, 18, 22, 25, 26, 27, 28, 30–38, 47
Nation / national identity / national literature / nationalism, ix, 6, 7, 8, 10–13, 16–19, 27, 32–48, 50, 54, 56, 58–76, 79, 89, 91, 94, 95, 101, 102, 104–105, 111, 113, 115, 118, 120, 126, 138–140, 155–165, 167–169
Neo-indigenismo, 145, 146
Neruda, Pablo, 117
New Latin American literature / narrative / novel, 96–97, 99, 130, 149–152, 168
novela "del lenguaje" La , 81, 136
Núñez, Estuardo, 28
Onetti, Juan Carlos, 97
Ortiz, Fernando, 49
Osorio, Nelson, 54–55
Paoli, Roberto, 146–148
Paz, Octavio, 99, 101, 117
Pizarro, Ana, 10
Pre-modernismo, 137
Post-modernismo, 137
Poma de Ayala, Guamán, 143
Popular culture, viii, 6, 12, 36–38, 42, 47, 51, 52, 61, 66, 71, 75, 94, 101, 103–105, 107, 126, 136, 147, 156, 165, 169
Popular-national, 18, 33, 126
Portuondo, José Antonio, 4
Punto de Vista, 153
Rama, Angel, ix, 4, 5, 8, 11, 12, 49–76, 86, 94, 105, 123, 139, 152, 153, 157–158, 162, 168

—*ciudad letrada, La,* 52, 74
—"Diez problemas para el novelista latinoamericano", 64
—"Literatura y clase social", 51
—*máscaras democráticas del modernismo, Las,* 68
—"Medio siglo de narrativa hispanoamericana", 60
—New regionalism, 57, 64
—*Rubén Darío y el modernismo,* 67–70
—"Sistema literario y sistema social en Hispanoamérica", 8, 51
—*Transculturación narrativa en América Latina,* 66, 75
Regional culture, 53, 58–60, 63, 71, 158, 161, 168
Revista Casa de Las Américas, 64
Ribeyro, Julio Ramón, 107, 134
Rincón, Carlos, 4
Riva Agüero, José de la, 43, 45
Roa Bastos, Augusto, 52, 56, 99
—*Yo el supremo,* 150
Romanticism, 108, 109, 117
Rosa, João Guimarães, 52
Rulfo, Juan, 52, 99, 114
Rowe, William, 5, 29, 86
Sánchez, Luis Alberto, 43
Sarduy, Severo, 81
Sarlo, Beatriz, vii, ix, 5, 13, 53, 95, 152, 153–165, 166, 168
—*modernidad periférica: Buenos Aires 1920 y 1930, Una,* 157

—*Escenas de la vida posmoderna,* 153
Sarmiento, Domingo Faustino, 71, 130, 135
Scorza, Manuel, 107, 135, 146
—*Guerra silenciosa, La,* 146
Social realism, 97
Sorel, Georges, 28, 30–31, 32, 33
Sosnowski, Saúl, 4
Spengler, Oswald,
—*Decadencia de occidente, La,* 27
Sylvers, Malcolm, 31, 37
Terán, Oscar, 28, 29
Tradition, ix, 17, 57, 94, 98, 99, 103 104, 160, 162, 168
Transculturation, 4, 12, 49, 51–53, 57–62, 64–67, 70, 71, 73–76, 94, 123, 139, 157, 158, 161
Universalist / universality / universalism / universalization, viii, ix, 5–9, 18, 51, 61, 64, 70, 71, 72, 82, 125, 130, 133, 136, 138, 139, 151
Valcárcel, Luis Eduardo,
—*Tempestad en los Andes,* 27
Vallejo, César, 109
Vargas Llosa, Mario, 107, 130, 150
—*guerra del fin del mundo, La,* 150
Ventura, Roberto, 96, 106, 109, 110

In the same series

An Analysis of the Short Stories of Juan Carlos Onetti: Fictions of Desire
Mark I Millington

Contemporary Women Writing in Latin America (Volume One)

Contemporary Women Writing in the Caribbean (Volume Two)

Contemporary Women Writing in Canada and Quebec (Volume Three)
edited by Georgiana M M Colvile

*Inequality and Difference in Hispanic and Latin American Cultures:
Critical Theoretical Approaches*
edited by Bernard McGuirk and Mark I Millington

Machado de Assis and Feminism: Rereading the Heart of the Companion
Maria Manuel Babao Lisboa

The Poetry and Poetics of Cesar Vallejo: The Fourth Angle of the Circle
Adam Sharman